ISBN 978-1-330-28746-0
PIBN 10014299

1 MONTH OF
FREE
READING

at

www.ForgottenBooks.com

By purchasing this book you are eligible for one month membership to ForgottenBooks.com, giving you unlimited access to our entire collection of over 1,000,000 titles via our web site and mobile apps.

To claim your free month visit:

www.forgottenbooks.com/free14299

English
Français
Deutsche
Italiano
Español
Português

www.forgottenbooks.com

Mythology Photography **Fiction**
Fishing Christianity **Art** Cooking
Essays Buddhism Freemasonry
Medicine **Biology** Music **Ancient
Egypt** Evolution Carpentry Physics
Dance Geology **Mathematics** Fitness
Shakespeare **Folklore** Yoga Marketing
Confidence Immortality Biographies
Poetry **Psychology** Witchcraft
Electronics Chemistry History **Law**
Accounting **Philosophy** Anthropology
Alchemy Drama Quantum Mechanics
Atheism Sexual Health **Ancient History**
Entrepreneurship Languages Sport
Paleontology Needlework Islam
Metaphysics Investment Archaeology
Parenting Statistics Criminology
Motivational

PROGRESSIVE DEMOCRACY

BY

HERBERT CROLY

AUTHOR OF "THE PROMISE OF AMERICAN LIFE"

New York

THE MACMILLAN COMPANY

1915

Norwood Press
J. S. Cushing Co. — Berwick & Smith Co.
Norwood, Mass., U.S.A.

To
L. E. C.

TABLE OF CONTENTS

PROGRESSIVE DEMOCRACY

INTRODUCTION

No matter whether they do or do not approve of what is going on, candid commentators on American politics will presumably agree that the political development of the country has recently entered upon a novel and critical phase. Until 1912 the group of political and economic traditions and ideas which came to a head during and immediately after the Civil War, and which was associated with the Republican party, continued on the whole to prevail. Since 1912 another group of political and economic ideas and methods has clearly become of preponderant importance. No doubt, previous to 1912 the prestige of the traditional system had been steadily waning. The opposition to it had for a number of years been rapidly becoming bolder and more radical. No doubt also this traditional system has not been as completely superseded as its enemies sometimes fondly imagine. Its roots lie deeper than is often suspected and they are more intimately entangled with that which is permanently valuable in the American tradition. Still, while fully admitting that the transition may not be as abrupt as it seems, we have apparently been witnessing during the past year or two the end of one epoch and the beginning of another. A movement of public opinion, which believes itself to be and calls itself essentially pro-

B   1

gressive, has become the dominant formative influence in American political life.

The best evidence of the power of progressivism is the effect which its advent has had upon the prestige and the fortunes of political leaders of both parties. For the first time attractions and repulsions born of the progressive idea, are determining lines of political association. Until recently a man who wished actively and effectively to participate in political life had to be either a Democrat or a Republican; but now, although Republicanism and Democracy are still powerful political forces, the standing of a politician is determined quite as much by his relation to the progressive movement. The line of cleavage between progressives and non-progressives is fully as important as that between Democrats and Republicans. Political leaders, who have deserved well of their own party but who have offended the progressives, are retiring or are being retired from public life. Precisely what the outcome will be, no one can predict with any confidence; but one result seems tolerably certain. If the classification of the great majority of American voters into Democrats and Republicans is to endure, the significance of both Democracy and Republicanism is bound to be profoundly modified by the new loyalties and the new enmities created by the aggressive progressive intruder.

The extent to which the acid of progressivism has succeeded in disintegrating American political traditions and classifications is the more remarkable because it has made such rapid headway against such apparently powerful resistance. When Mark Hanna died, early in 1904, the traditional political system appeared to be unassailable in the fortified strength of its position. It had every advantage of custom, prestige, resources, training, experience, competence and success. Strenuous but futile efforts had been made to arouse against it the public conscience and the public intelligence. Mr. Hanna himself had recently been reëlected Senator by a huge majority after a campaign in which he had been aggressively attacked as the living incarnation of the hide-bound traditional Republicanism. He had not been afraid to run on a frankly and crassly conservative platform, and had just coined the phrase "stand-pat" as a sufficient description of his own policy and that of his party. Political leaders could afford to boast of their conservatism on the stump, because conservatism had not come to mean reaction, while even a moderate radicalism was considered revolutionary. Anybody who squinted in the direction of economic and social reform was stigmatized as a Bryanite or at worst a Socialist, and was thereafter supposed to be excluded from the universe of polite political discourse. The remnant, who associated political with economic reorganization, were comprehensively condemned as "Populists." Once that sentence had been passed on a man, he was considered as much beyond the pale as a heretic would have been to the mediæval church. In the minds of men like William Barnes, Jr., Populism is still associated with a kind of damnable moral and intellectual perversity.

During the intervening ten years the complexion, and to a

certain extent even the features, of the American political countenance have profoundly altered. Political leaders still pride themselves upon their conservatism, but candid conservatives, in case they come from any other part of the country but the South, often pay for their candor by their early retirement. Conservatism has come to imply reaction. Its substantial utility is almost as much under-valued as that of radicalism formerly was. The whole group of prevailing political values has changed. Proposals for the regulation of public utility companies, which would then have been condemned as examples of administrative autocracy, are now accepted without serious public con-troversy. Plans of social legislation, which formerly would have been considered culpably "paternal," and, if passed at the solicitation of the labor unions, would have been declared unconstitutional by the courts, are now con-sidered to be a normal and necessary exercise of the police power. Proposed alterations in our political mechanism, which would then have been appraised as utterly extrava-gant and extremely dangerous, are now being placed on the headlines of political programs and are being incorporated in state constitutions. In certain important respects the radicals of 1904 do not differ in their practical proposals from the conservatives of 1914. A political leader who in 1904 would have dared to go as far in economic regulation, social reform and political reorganization as Nicholas Murray Butler and Elihu Root are now prepared to go, would have been considered by Mark Hanna as a very dangerous man.

The rapidity and the extent of this alteration in American political physiognomy has palpably been the result of the gross excesses committed by the beneficiaries of the old order. If the responsible managers of large industries of the country and their political allies lost public confidence, it was because of their own flagrant misdeeds. They were caught "with the goods on." The ill-will of public opinion could be stirred up against them, because they had unscrupulously violated the laws, and abused their opportunities. An era of political and business "muck-raking" ensued, the object of which was not a clear-headed patient diagnosis of the country's political and business malady, but an arousing of the American conscience against malefaction in high places. The agitation was a complete success. The better public opinion of the country became convinced of the existence of flagrant abuses in connection with its political and economic management. It began dimly to understand that these abuses had been rendered possible as the result of an alliance between an overgrown business system and a superannuated political system. But during this "muck-raking" period the time was not ripe either for a searching diagnosis or for effective remedial measures. Its dominant characteristic was that of resentment against individuals.

The fierceness of this attack soon revealed the weakness which was concealed behind the frowning fortifications of the old order. Its strength was more apparent than real, and its successes up to 1904 had been due less to its own ability than to the deficiencies of its opponents. The

attacks which had been made upon it during the last decade
of the nineteenth century had been sincere, and they had
been aimed at real and flagrant evils; but they had been
unintelligently planned, insufficiently informed and inad-
equately organized. Its assailants consisted of groups of
local malcontents, who were prompted to protest by superficial economic grievances, but who were incapable of giving
a genuinely national impulse either to their complaints or to
their remedies. The Bryanism of that period might have
been useful as a protest — in case it had not gained enough
temporary popularity to be dangerous as an alternative.
The government of a great country cannot be confided to a
band of ignorant economic agitators, no matter how sincere
their aspirations nor real their grievances. Under the circumstances the American people may be excused for placing the Republicans in power, and in waiting until a safer
substitute could be provided for the old order.

The very completeness of the Republican triumph, however, was destined to be fatal to the Republican system.
Instead of making its beneficiaries more circumspect and
more responsible, it encouraged them to push their advantages to the limit and to render themselves liable to irre-
trievable exposure. They laid themselves bare to the
" muck-rakers " and had only themselves to blame should
the resulting exposure prove abhorrent to right-minded
men. Thus they succeeded far better than their enemies
could have done in making public opinion understand the
gravity of the existing evils and abuses. By permitting
conservatism to become associated with political and

economic graft, they stimulated inquisitive people to ask how deep the association lay. Thus they gave their own case away. When the wave of attack broke over them, they could offer no effective resistance. As proof after proof accumulated of the reality of the abuses, and of the alliance between political and business misbehavior, the defenders of the system retorted by only declaring that the assaults were compromising the safety of the admirable and beneficent American political and social system. They called the protecting deities of traditional Americanism to their assistance, and by so doing succeeded not in purifying themselves, but in defiling their celestial shelter. What kind of gods were these which could even plausibly be called upon to protect a system of business exploitation and political trickery?

Thus by almost imperceptible degrees reform became insurgent and insurgency progressive. For the first time in four generations American conservatism was confronted by a pervasive progressivism, which began by being dangerously indignant and ended by being far more dangerously inquisitive. Just resentment is useful and indispensable while it lasts; but it cannot last long. If it is to persist, it must be transformed into a thoroughgoing curiosity which will not rest until it has discovered what the abuses mean, how they best can be remedied, and how intimately they are associated with temples and shrines of the traditional political creed. The conservatives themselves have provoked this curiosity, and they must abide by its results.

Just here lies the difference between modern progressivism and the old reform. The former is coming to be remorselessly inquisitive and unscrupulously thorough. The latter never knew any need of being either inquisitive or thorough. The early political reformers confined their attention to local or to special abuses. Civil service reform furnishes a good example of their methods and their purposes. The spoils system was a very grave evil, which was a fair object of assault; but it could not be successfully attacked and really uprooted merely by placing subordinate public officials under the protection of civil service laws and boards. Such laws and boards might do something to prevent politicians from appropriating the minor offices; but as long as the major offices were the gifts of the political machines, and as long as no attempt was made to perfect expert administrative organization as a necessary instrument of democracy, the agitation for civil service reform remained fundamentally sterile. It was sterile, because it was negative and timid, and because its supporters were content with their early successes and did not grow with the growing needs of their own agitation. In an analogous way the movement towards municipal reform attained a sufficient following in certain places to be embarrassing to local political bosses; but as long as it was a non-partisan movement for "good government" its successes were fugitive and sterile. It did not become really effective until it became frankly partisan, and associated good municipal government with all sorts of changes in economic and

political organization which might well be obnoxious
to many excellent citizens. In these and other cases the
early political reformers were not sufficiently thorough.
They failed to carry their analysis of the prevailing
evils far or deep enough, and in their choice of remedies they never got beyond the illusions that moral exhortation, legal prohibitions and independent voting
constituted a sufficient cure for American political abuses.

The best illustration of the superficiality of the early
political reformers is offered by their easy acceptance of
economic abuses. The Mugwumps did not suspect for
one moment that there was anything radically wrong
with the American economic system, or that many grave
political evils must be regarded as incidental to an inhuman economic organization. They were usually tariff
reformers; but beyond that they did not go. The abolition of protectionism constituted in their opinion a sufficient
remedy at once for the element of unjust discrimination
in the American national economy, for the undesirable
dependence of the political machines upon the business
interests, and for the dangers of industrial combinations. The tariff was the root of all evil. The grievances
of wage-earners or farmers either failed to interest them
or were usually attributed to protectionism. They looked
upon the economic radicals of the period with the same
unfriendly eyes as did the ordinary machine politician
or the self-preoccupied business man. A forerunner, like
Henry Demarest Lloyd, they classified as at best an
amiable crank and at worst a troublesome demagog.

The Mugwumps themselves belonged for the most part to the upper ranks of business and professional life in the large eastern cities, and being entirely satisfied with the prevailing Manchester economics, they were intellectually and morally contemptuous of labor-unionism, Grangerism and Populism. Every ebullition of political and economic discontent was appraised and condemned from the standpoint of a fixed and finished economic and political creed.

All this disconnected political and economic agitation had, however, a value of which the agitators themselves were not wholly conscious. Not only was the attitude of national self-satisfaction being broken down in spots, but the ineffectiveness of these local, spasmodic and restricted agitations had its effect on public opinion and prepared the way for a synthesis of the various phases of reform. When the wave of political "muck-raking" broke over the country, it provided a common bond, which tied reformers together. This bond consisted at first of the indignation which was aroused by the process of exposure; but it did not remain for long merely a feeling. As soon as public opinion began to realize that business exploitation had been allied with political corruption, and that the reformers were confronted, not by disconnected abuses, but by a perverted system, the inevitable and salutary inference began to be drawn. Just as business exploitation was allied with political corruption, so business reorganization must be allied with political reorganization. The old system must be confronted and superseded by a new system — the result of an alert social intelligence as well as an aroused individual conscience.

More than any other single leader, Theodore Roosevelt contributed decisively to the combination of political with social reform and to the building up of a body of national public opinion behind the combination. Under his leadership as President, reform began to assume the characteristics, if not the name, of progressivism. He was peculiarly qualified to bring about the transition. His own early political career had been associated with the movements towards civil service and municipal reform, but he had never been an ordinary Mugwump. Instead of representing a limited class in the eastern cities, he had mixed with all sorts of Americans in many different parts of the country. Neither did he allow his power of effective political association with others to die of non-partisanship. His human sympathies were lively and varied enough to prevent him from becoming a "doctrinaire," or from staking, as did the Mugwumps, his own personal future and the supposed welfare of the country on a rigid political and economic creed. Thus he remained flexible and open-minded. He was able, as was no other political leader, to collect under his own leadership a large proportion of the old reformers and a large measure of the new and more liberal progressivism. He was the hero of the first moral revulsion against the abuses of the established order — a revulsion which for the time being united a substantial majority of the good citizens of the country.

This first union of effective progressive sentiment could not last. Under Mr. Roosevelt's leadership there had been tied together many discordant factions. The bond of union was partly derived from the leader's own personal popularity. It was partly partisan, because he continued to control the machinery of the Republican party. It was partly moral, because of the indignation which had been aroused by the exposures. Finally, it was beginning to be partly ideal and formative, in that many progressives began to discern the need of the substitution of a new and better order for the old. After the term of Mr. Roosevelt's official leadership ceased, the latent discord among these elements soon rose to the surface. The hollowness of the conversion of official Republicanism to progressivism almost immediately developed and resulted in an outbreak of insurgency on the part of the genuine progressives in that party. At the same time the tide of moral indignation began to subside, and progressives began to search much more frankly and unscrupulously for some positive political and economic principle and method which would constitute a sufficient basis for agitation and a sufficient bond of union. In the pursuance of this search they necessarily became more than ever curious. They began to inquire whether the domination of partisan machines was a normal result of the American system of government or an unwholesome eruption on its comely countenance. They went on to ask whether any relation could be traced between an autocratic economic organization or an individualistic legal system and the reign of political bosses. And in considering these questions they were pushed more and more towards the supposition that the United States never had been a genuine political democracy, and that if it were to become one, effective measures must be taken to make of it an economic and social democracy.

Just in proportion, however, as progressivism began to be radically inquisitive and to seek the bond of a positive political and social principle, it began to alienate many of its earlier supporters and to gain a more enthusiastic following of a different kind. The earlier reforming agitations had been conceived essentially as attempts to remove excrescences from the traditional system and to restore it to a suppositious condition of pristine purity. They could be defended as a kind of higher conservatism, which proposed to get rid of all the diseased tissue by means of a surgical operation, and then to leave the political and economic body to its own powers of recuperation. They needed to take no risk as to the safety of the patient and to incur no responsibility as to his subsequent behavior. The reformers, who were tied to such a conception of the meaning of the movement, did not relish the transition to progressivism. Certain of them, consisting chiefly of former Republicans and Independents, refused to become progressives, and began to look upon those who did as dangerous and frivolous political empirics. Progressivism, as it developed, began to differ from reform both in its friends and in its enemies.

The result of these new lines of attraction and repulsion has been the bestowal of different values both on progressivism and on conservatism. They both have tended to become more self-conscious than formerly, more definitely formulated and more antagonistic. The progressives found themselves obliged to carry their inquisition to its logical conclusion — to challenge the old system, root and branch, and to derive their own medium and power of united action from a new conception of the purpose and methods of democracy. The conservatives, on their side, could claim without hypocrisy or exaggeration that essential parts of the traditional system were being threatened, and they could ask prudent men to rally to its defence. A sharp issue was created between radical progressivism and its opponents, which could not be evaded or compromised.

It should, however, be added that the issue so created has not been universally accepted as the dividing line between all men of progressive and all men of conservative tendencies. The majority of thoroughgoing progressives are Republican insurgents, whose progressivism has been sharply defined as a result of warfare with their former partisan associates. No similar change has as yet taken place within the Democratic party, which still presents the spectacle of avowed progressives and avowed conservatives lying without apparent discomfiture in the same political bed. The controversies between the two factions of the former Republican party are to a large extent ignored by the Democrats, who have been seeking to convince public opinion that progressivism consists

chiefly in the advocacy of certain specific economic reforms, which were not sufficiently emphasized by either
of the former Republican factions.

The divergent economic interpretations which have been
attached to progressivism as a result of this situation
can, perhaps, best be made explicit by considering the
differences, as developed during the presidential campaign of 1912, between the progressives who supported
Mr. Wilson and those who supported Mr. Roosevelt.
Roosevelt progressivism can fairly be charged with many
ambiguities, but in one essential respect its meaning is
unmistakable. Its advocates are committed to a drastic
reorganization of the American political and economic
system, to the substitution of a frank social policy for the
individualism of the past, and to the realization of this
policy, if necessary, by the use of efficient governmental
instruments. The progressivism of President Wilson,
on the other hand, is ambiguous in-precisely this essential
respect. The slightest question need not be raised as to
his sincerity, but his deliberate purpose seems to have been
to keep progressivism vague — with a vagueness that is
elusive and secretive rather than merely flexible. His
tendency is to emphasize those aspects of progressivism
which can be interpreted as the emancipation of an essentially excellent system from corrupting and perverting
parasites. His version of progressivism, notwithstanding
its immediately forward impulse, is scrupulously careful
not to be too progressive, and, like the superseded reform
movements, poses as a higher conservatism.

This aspect of Wilson progressivism receives its least equivocal expression in the doctrine of the "New Freedom." The purpose of the "New Freedom" is much clearer than its meaning. It is to serve as a kind of an intellectual antidote to such heresies as "New Nationalism" and the "New Democracy." It seems to be based upon the principle, enunciated by Mr. Wilson during the campaign, that the history of human liberty is the history of the restriction of governmental functions. The most important policies in which it is embodied are tariff reform and the ruthless eradication of any monopolistic control over business transactions. By reducing the tariff, not only is commerce liberated and the competitive system freed from its shackles, but necessarily unjust privileges are abolished. By eradicating any trace of monopoly, or any possibility of organized control over business, and by comprehensively identifying restraint of trade with restraint of competition, the wholesome action of automatic economic forces is further encouraged. Such is the "New Freedom" on its economic side, and its difference from the old freedom is plainly one of method rather than of purpose. Not a word that President Wilson uttered during or since the campaign indicated any tendency on his part to substitute for an automatic competitive economic régime one in which a conscious social purpose, equipped with an adequate technical method, was to play a decisive part. The "New Freedom" looks in general like a revival of Jeffersonian individualism. It proposes to contribute to human amelioration chiefly by the negative policy of doing away with discrimination, by expressly disparaging expert contribution to the business of government, by opposing the extension of national responsibility, and by intrusting the future of democracy to the results of coöperation between an individualistic legal system and a fundamentally competitive economic system.

I am aware that the foregoing interpretation of Wilson progressivism may not be entirely just. Any attempt to define the "New Freedom" incurs the danger of attaching too precise a meaning to a doctrine which has been left so essentially and apparently so deliberately vague. Be it recognized that Mr. Wilson's version of progressivism, whatever its underlying tendency and meaning, is a high and serious doctrine, which is the outcome of real elevation of purpose and feeling, and which up to date has had on the whole a beneficial effect on public opinion. Be it recognized also that in Mr. Wilson's situation a certain amount of ambiguity has a manifest practical value. He is a Democrat as well as a progressive. Harmony within his party has been essential to the successful passage of legislation to which he and his party were committed. The Democrats were undoubtedly the only organized political agency to which could be intrusted the work of passing a sufficiently drastic revision of the tariff; and drastic revision of the tariff may well be considered of so much importance to the welfare of the country that a leader would be justified in purchasing its accomplishment by a very considerable tribute to party unity. He would have good reason, consequently, for emphasizing any possible analogies between progressivism and the historic tradition of his own party. But there is no necessary finality about an emphasis. He is, I think, by way of being a realist in politics rather than a doctrinaire. He can understand the authority of human opinions and social needs which do not fit into antecedent theories. If at some future time the practical importance of interpreting progressivism along the lines of traditional Democracy should be diminished, and the need of a different method of handling economic and social problems should become more imposing, the progressive principle might receive at his hands a very different emphasis.

But while sound reasons may exist for the elusive and secretive nature of Mr. Wilson's progressivism, derived both from his own temperament and from his practical necessities, it is surely a fair matter for criticism. Just because progressivism is a high and serious affair, just because it seeks and needs to win converts as well as accomplish results, just because it can advance towards its goal only by entering into the souls of men and taking possession, it requires candor and integrity of spirit as well as flexibility. Wilson progressivism is, on the one hand, either too vague and equivocal to inspire sufficient energy of conviction, or else it is progressivism with its eyes fastened more on the past than on the future. It obscures the fundamental issue. What we need above all to know is the effect of progressivism upon the old order and the spiritual opportunities afforded by it for the establishment of a new order. "We are witnessing," says President Wilson in the "New Freedom," "we are witnessing a renaissance of public spirit, a reawakening of sober public opinion, a revival of the power of the people, the beginning of an age of thoughtful reconstruction, that makes our thought hark back to the great age in which democracy was set up in America." Remark how every phrase of this version of a doctrine which is called progressive confronts the past and turns its back upon the future. Progressivism is not a new birth of public spirit; it is a rebirth. It is not an awakening of public opinion to something novel; it is a reawakening. It is not aiming at an unprecedented vitalizing of democracy, but at its revival along traditional lines. A "thoughtful reconstruction" is promised; but the "thought" which prompts the revision "harks back to the great age" of primitive American democracy. The projected reconstruction is only a restoration. Small wonder that a progressivism of this kind finds a large part of its support among conservatives.

Yet if there is one aspect of progressivism about which American public opinion needs to be fully and clearly informed it is the relation between progressivism and conservatism. Are they supplementary ideas, as President Wilson seems to imply in the foregoing quotation, in such wise that the most thoroughgoing progressive reconstruction will merely restore us to a condition analogous to that of the primitive American democracy? Or

does a real antagonism exist between the old order and
the new order which some progressives are trying to substitute for it? By promoting progressive sentiment, is
Mr. Wilson bestowing increasing authority and popularity
upon a state of mind which in its ultimate results will
prove inimical to institutions and ideas cherished by a
large part of his followers? Will the increase of progressivism inevitably involve responsibilities and incur dangers to which prudent people should not be committed
without full warning? In short, are conservatives, like
Senator Root, justified in being alarmed at the innovations
which contemporary radicalism is proposing? Or will it
be possible to accomplish all the reforms demanded by
the progressive principle without doing harm to any essential ingredient of the traditional American political
and economic order?

In this connection I do not want to raise any question
as to the relation between conservatism and progressivism
in their essential aspects. An opportunist realistic conservatism may well exist, which is supplementary rather
than inimical to progressivism. But such is not the character of contemporary American conservatism. The particular expression of the conservative spirit to which
progressivism finds itself opposed is essentially, and, as
it seems, necessarily doctrinaire and dogmatic. It is
based upon an unqualified affirmation of the necessity of
the traditional constitutional system to the political salvation of the American democracy. That system is not
being appraised by its friends primarily as a serviceable

political and legal instrument, wrought under the stress of historical vicissitudes, for the satisfaction of comparatively permanent but possibly changing social needs. It has been and is being acclaimed rather as a consummate system of law and government, framed under the guidance of a final political philosophy, to satisfy the essential conditions of individual liberty and wholesome political association. "The fact is," says one of its defenders on its behalf, "that in the history of mankind some things after long toil and tribulation are settled once for all. They neither invite nor permit amendment or improvement." Another of its apologists declares in relation to the quoted approval of an essential part of the system, "These are sentiments not for a particular epoch, but for all time. To assume that society can ever be constructed on any other principle is like assuming that we may get beyond the influence of the law of gravitation." Or, again, according to Chief Justice Miller, the Constitution declares "those natural and fundamental rights of individuals for the security and common enjoyment of which governments are established." Thus the peculiar justification of our traditional constitutional government does not consist in its past and present serviceability or in its nice adaptation to our special political needs and customs, but rather in its quality of embodying the permanent principles of righteous and reasonable political action.

The foregoing quotations have been derived either from contemporary or almost contemporary defenders of the traditional system; but as every one familiar with American political literature knows, they could be duplicated by similar quotations from publicists, dating from every period of American history and belonging to every important American partisan organization. Ever since the Constitution was established, a systematic and insidious attempt has been made to possess American public opinion with a feeling of its peculiarly sacred character. All commentators do not declare in so many words that it embodies ultimate political truth; but no matter whether they verbally disparage the superstitious worship of the Constitution or participate in it, the practical effect of their interpretation remains much the same. They consider the preservation of the existing constitutional system in its fundamental characteristics as essential to the political safety of the American democracy as Joseph de Maistre considered the preservation of legitimacy essential to the safety of European nations.

Such being the merits of the traditional system in the eyes of its friends, they not unnaturally feel licensed to scold its adversaries. The paramount duty of every patriotic citizen must be the defence of this priceless political heritage. In the performance of such a sacred duty words should be used as weapons rather than counters. Progressives who propose to eradicate or seriously to alter a system which does not admit of essential improvement must be exposed rather than merely refuted. They are accused of being neurotic perverts or unscrupulous demagogs. Those who manifestly cannot be grouped in either of these classes are required to make up for a sound nervous system and an apparent public spirit by grave deficiencies of knowledge and intelligence. They are charged with hopeless superficiality and utter ignorance of the recorded history of government and human society. They become a conspicuous illustration of the vital truth that the failure or unpopularity of such an admirable system can result only from the inability of American citizens to live up to the high intellectual and moral responsibilities imposed upon them by its successful operation.

Conservatives always take a grave risk when they flourish such portentous claims on behalf of a group of time-honored political institutions. A position becomes vulnerable in proportion as it is exposed, and once the critical and inquisitive spirit is aroused, no position could be more exposed than that assumed at present by American conservatism. As I shall point out in a later discussion, it was obliged in candor to occupy this aggressive and advanced strategic situation; and progressives may well rejoice in such a sharp definition of the issue and such an opportunity for an open fight. They have more to fear from a furtive than from a frank enemy.

But before they engage in any attack a careful study needs to be made of the coveted citadel. The position which American conservatism has elected to defend, exposed as it is, may still be defensible. It assuredly does arouse on the part of its defenders an admirable loyalty of conviction. Many abuses have flourished under the protection of the traditional constitutional system; but it has none the less a long and honorable career, and it has contributed enormously to American political safety and prosperity. It has given stability, order and security to a political experiment, undertaken in a new country under peculiarly hazardous and trying conditions. Whether or not it actually makes for permanent political health and individual and social welfare, it has apparently been doing so, and its friends ardently believe that it is as useful as ever. Some such conviction bestowed a semblance of respectability and even of dignity upon the opposition within the Republican party to the nomination of Mr. Roosevelt in the spring of 1912 — an opposition which in the absence of genuine conviction would scarcely have dared to defy the plainly declared will of a majority of Republicans. Conservatism of this kind, much as it likes to abuse its progressive opponents, cannot be vanquished by the imputation of selfish motives or by the free use of derogatory epithets. Progressivism will not be able to overthrow it without the support of a very good cause, very large battalions, great tenacity of purpose and very thorough preparation and organization.

Many sincere conservatives are profoundly suspicious of progressivism, because they fail to discover in the new doctrine any trustworthy substitute for the existing system — a system which with all its deficiencies has probably enabled a larger proportion of its beneficiaries to live bravely than any other political and economic system. The providing of such a substitute is the peculiar, the indispensable need of progressivism. It would be mere nihilism for progressives to attack the exposed citadel of conservatism, unless they were equipped permanently to occupy at least an equally advanced and exposed position. If progressivism is to be constructive rather than merely restorative, it must be prepared to replace the old order with a new social bond, which will be no less secure than its predecessor, but which will serve still more effectually as an impulse, an inspiration and a leaven. The new system must provide, that is, not merely a new method, important as a new method may be, but a new faith, upon the rock of which may be built a better structure of individual and social life.

In the following pages the question will be considered whether any substitute is needed for the traditional system, and whether progressivism offers any prospect of living up to the manifest requirements of the part. Both of these questions will be answered in the affirmative, but the value of the book, so far as it has any, will consist not so much in the attainment of definite conclusions as in the spirit which characterizes the attempt to reach them. Whatever may be the outcome of the prevailing ferment in American public opinion, it unquestionably imposes a specific and a novel patriotic duty upon the loyal American citizen. Whether conservatives like it or not, the foundations of the traditional system are being tested both by the strain of new social and economic condition and by a flood of suspicion and criticism. If it is going to survive, not only must its adaptability to new exigencies be proved, but also its power to survive the severest possible inquisition. Public opinion can no longer be hypnotized and scared into accepting the traditional constitutionalism as the final word in politics. If it is successfully to defend its position, conservatism must itself become critical, aggressive, inquisitive and contemporary. The issue has been declared. A momentous discussion has been started. Whether the results of that discussion are beneficial or the reverse will depend chiefly upon the enterprise, the patience, the good humor and the insight with which it is carried on.

The one demand made by critics of the traditional system upon its directors and beneficiaries, which the latter should recognize as being unequivocally helpful, is the demand for publicity. Any part either of the creed or the mechanism of the system which shuns the light is necessarily a suspect. A democracy, consisting as it does of many sovereigns rather than one, must publish its important affairs or cease to be a democracy. Obscurity is as dangerous to its welfare as is bad faith. But publicity in its final meaning does not consist in the knowledge and communication of facts. It consists in abundant self-knowledge and in candid and ardent self-expression. Democracies in the fulfilment of their own essential nature are bound to be curious, communicative, and intellectually frank and fearless. In the past the American democracy has been none of these things. It has been intellectually timid and torpid, because it was preoccupied with the frontier of its own life. It accepted without inspection, misgiving or curiosity the inherited array of ideas and institutions. Any attempt to arouse Americans to the necessity of paying more attention to the ideal hinterland is always fought strenuously by people who have some immediate special results of importance to accomplish or some particularly powerful enemy to overcome; and these people are at present quite as likely to call themselves progressives as conservatives. Nevertheless, the really salutary aspect of the present situation is the awakening of American public opinion to the necessity of scrutinizing the national ideal and of working over the guiding principles of its associated life. The American democracy is becoming aroused to take a searching look at its own meaning and responsibilities.

In the case neither of a nation nor of an individual does the contemplation of its responsibilities result necessarily in an effort to redeem them. A democracy must be tempered first of all by and for action. Yet if it cannot combine thought with action, discussion with decision, criticism with resolution, a searching inquisitiveness with a tenacious faith, it cannot avoid going seriously astray. Democracy must risk its success on the integrity of human nature. If among the citizens of a democratic state the intelligence should prove to be the enemy of the will, if individually and collectively they must purchase enlightenment at the expense of momentum, democracy is doomed to failure. A democratic nation must know all about its own doings, and again be it said, knowledge means a search of values as well as a mastery of facts. The American nation seems to have made up its mind to pursue meanings as well as results. If so, it is certainly by way of attaining a new freedom. Its will is being emancipated from the bondage to immediate practical achievement; and its intelligence is being released from the fascination exercised by a rigid and authoritative traditional creed.

Let us, then, temporarily replace the old American acquisitiveness both for money and for results with a new inquisitiveness. Let us prove that we are good American citizens by asking and trying to answer a lot of questions. What is this progressivism, about which all the fuss is being made? How far can it be definitely formulated? What may be the results of its formulation? What is its relation to the traditional American economic and political system? In what respects does it merely carry on ideas which have always been present in that system? In what respects does it introduce new ideas? How far can the new ideas be reconciled with the old? To what extent will the new ideas demand new instruments? Above all, how will progressive democracy act and react upon the character, the discipline and the ideals of the American people? What benefits may it bestow? What burdens may it impose? What risks must it incur? What chances has it of success? How far is it really worth while? Final answers cannot be returned to all of these questions, but tentative answers, in so far as they are the result of candid consideration of the actual facts, should have some use; and since we cannot understand any group of human institutions without some knowledge of its history, any fruitful discussion of the American system must begin with an examination of its origin.

CHAPTER I

The People and the Law

As in the case of every great political edifice, the materials composing the American system are derived from many different sources, and are characterized by unequal values, both as to endurance and as to latent possibilities. The appearance of definiteness and finality which it derives from its embodiment in specific constitutional documents and other authoritative words is to a large extent illusory. Its real origin and meaning are very much more doubtful and complex than these words intimate. Historians are no more agreed as to the former than political theorists are to the latter. An inquirer who is seeking some light as to its meaning by way of an examination of its origin, is obliged in both cases to push into disputed territory; but if he can obtain any foothold in one part of the field, he is much more likely to hold his own in another part.

Both historically and theoretically the American system is based upon an affirmation of popular political authority. When the colonists proclaimed their independence of the British Crown and Parliament, the repudiated sovereign had to be replaced with a capable substitute; and this substitute could consist under the circumstances only of the supposed makers of the Revolution — the American people as a whole. After the Declaration of Independence, the people, whoever they were and however their power was to be organized and expressed, became the only source of righteous political authority in the emancipated nation.

Not unnaturally the new sovereign encountered many difficulties in finding proper instruments for the effective and beneficial exercise of his authority. He had assumed the throne during the distractions and commotions of a Revolutionary War. In organizing his government he had either hastily to improvise the immediately necessary mechanism, or else seize already existing instruments, however poorly they served his needs. He could not even affirm the reality of his own sovereign power. Its effective exercise was divided among thirteen separate governments, so independent of one another that thirteen partial sovereigns instead of one whole sovereign had been created. In almost all of these states the new sovereigns were delegating instead of exercising their own authority. The executive power having fallen into disrepute because of its association with the English Crown, the only effective instrument of government consisted of a representative assembly, which assumed control of practically the entire machinery of the state. Popular sovereignty became in its actual exercise the granting of technical omnipotence to a group of petty parliaments.

Such a system was as ill suited to the imperative political and social needs of the American people as it was to their political traditions and theories. They had been accustomed to a government separated into specific powers, no one of which had been entirely trusted. Their representative assemblies had naturally been trusted more than had an alien executive; but even these assemblies had neither won nor enjoyed a good chance of winning their whole confidence. The evidence and technical source of political authority had consisted in royal charters, which defined and secured the rights of citizens and organized the several branches of the government. Political bodies which had become habituated to the assurance, the precision and the guidance of written and comparatively permanent instruments of government, began to be uneasy as soon as its future welfare was placed largely at the mercy of a legislative assembly. To be sure, state constitutions had usually superseded the old charters, but these constitutions were made by the legislatures and could be unmade and remade by them. . What the people naturally craved was a type of state constitution which should affirm the reality of popular sovereignty, limit the power of the separate departments of government, and give both to the individual citizen and to society effective guarantees of stability and security.

Even before independence had been established, this demand was successfully asserted in two of the states of New England. Towards the end of the war, Massachusetts and New Hampshire having been emancipated for some years from the actual presence of the enemy on their soil, their citizens began to consider seriously the problem of permanent political organization. As in other states, proposals were made which looked in the direction of intrusting the framing of the constitutions to the existing assemblies or some similarly elected body; but the people of these states rejected the plan of bestowing constituent powers on their legislatures. The towns stubbornly insisted that, considering the real source of righteous political authority, the new law would be no law unless it were framed by a convention expressly elected for that purpose and unless the proposed constitution were expressly approved by a popular vote. They carried their point. Their new constitutions conformed to the conditions imposed by popular opinion, and contained the assertion that the "people alone have an incontestable, inalienable and indefeasible right to institute government, and to reform, alter or totally change the same when their protection, safety, prosperity and happiness require it." The example proved to be contagious. The great majority of the states followed in the footsteps of these democratic pioneers, whose innovation became decisive in the development of American constitutional practice.

The importance of this assertion by the people of New England of the reality of ultimate popular political responsibility can scarcely be overestimated. Thereafter democracy obtained a new meaning and a new dignity. Here on American soil, for the first time since the birth of representative institutions, and among a people who had been accustomed to representative government, the custom of merely consulting public opinion about political essentials was converted into direct popular control. Law was being made, not only by trusted popular agents for the benefit of the people and with their consent, but in one essential respect by the people themselves. They were to elect representatives to initiate the work, but the representatives had to be expressly chosen for the purpose and their work had to be expressly approved. The most radical and convinced democrat could not ask for any more definite and unqualified recognition of the right and ability of the people to determine their own political organization, behavior and destiny. Neither is the meaning and importance of this assertion of democracy diminished by the fact that the electorate which insisted on having these constitutions authorized by direct popular action was not, according to modern standards, a really or sufficiently democratic electorate. Enough that it spoke in the name of the people and that its self-assertion was considered to be a veritable act of popular sovereign authority.

Emphatic, however, as was this assertion of its direct control over its own political institutions by the primitive American democracy, its willingness to restrict its own effective political power was no less definite and insistent. It did not show the slightest disposition to translate this supposedly effective popular control over the institutes of government into active popular control over governmental behavior. The democracy abdicated the continuing active exercise of effective power in the very act of affirming the reality of its own ultimate legal authority. "The great object of terror and suspicion," says Mr. Henry Adams, "to the people of the thirteen provinces was power, not merely power in the hands of a president or a prince, of one

D

assembly or several, of many citizens or few, but power in the abstract, wherever it existed and under whatever form it was known." This dread of political power was, of course, derived from the spectacle which its unrestrained exercise had presented practically throughout the entire history of mankind. The colonists identified political power with the military power by virtue of which it had made its commands effective. They attached to the active exercise of such power by a democracy the same liability to organized violence which had been exhibited by monarchies and aristocracies. They did not and could not be expected to understand that the growth of democracy would emasculate much of the brute force which the older governments had behind them. To leave political power of any kind legally unchained was from their point of view merely to invite its abuse. The very assertion of express popular control over the fundamental law was associated with the renunciation of its effective exercise in other respects.

This self-denying ordinance of the primitive American democracy was as significant and as unprecedented as was its assertion of its own ultimate popular political responsibility. Modern democrats tend to attribute it to the machinations of the educated propertied classes, who were afraid of their new sovereign and proposed to tie his hands; but that is not the whole story. As Mr. Henry Adams says, all classes of colonists shared this fear of discretionary political power; and associated with this fear was a new ideal, which men were for the first time attempting to make paramount in political organ-

ization. Popular political power, it was believed, must
be virtuously exercised. As Montesquieu had said,
the principle of democracy was virtue. Monarchies and
aristocracies need not be destroyed by the arbitrary and
violent exercise of the sovereign authority, because these
forms of political organization rested on the forcible domination of the many by the few. But an unjust and despotic
democracy was a suicidal contradiction. Such a democracy
would soon be divided against itself into hostile factions.
The conquering faction would necessarily rest its authority
on the effective exercise of military force. It was, consequently, essential to a democracy that its organization
should expressly provide for the subordination of political
power in all its forms to some code of political righteousness.

These early American democratic law-givers had no
misgivings as to their own ability to draw up such a code.
Both the political experience of their own forbears and a
radical analysis of the origin and meaning of society demonstrated the existence of certain individual rights as incontestable, indefeasible and inalienable as the right of the
people to institute and alter their form of government. A
monarchy which refrained from violating these rights would
be contributing to the welfare of its citizens; but a democracy must recognize them or perish. A democracy differs
from other forms of government in that it does not and cannot distinguish the welfare of the state from the welfare of
its individual citizens. Thus the definition and fortification
of a bill of civil rights constituted the core of any stable
and fruitful system of popular government. The sacred

words must be deposited in the ark of the covenant, there to remain inviolate as long as the commonwealth shall endure.

As these bills of rights were formulated in the state constitutions, they combined, however, two very different strains of political tradition and theory. The idea of the paramount authority in nature and reason of certain inalienable individual rights, and of the ability of statesmen to define in advance the essential rules of righteous political behavior was, of course, derived from the prevailing political philosophy. All government had originated in a contract, whereby certain indefeasible liberties had been guaranteed to individuals, and any violation of these liberties emancipated citizens from their allegiance and justified revolution. This general theory had been very serviceable to a people who were practical and successful revolutionists, and who had rebelled against the authority of the British Parliament expressly on the ground, not merely that their traditional rights as British subjects had been violated, but also those fundamental rights deducible from the very nature of just political association. When, however, they came to phrase these indefeasible rights, they were found to be identical with the rights which Englishmen enjoyed under the Common Law and as the result of their rebellions against the abuse of the royal prerogative. The bills of rights did no more in appearance than to forbid the active government from interfering with American citizens in certain specified ways, which need not be enumerated here, but which corresponded to the traditional liberties of an English citizen.

In their new legal and political framework, however, the traditional English liberties came to possess a wholly new emphasis. The constitutions in which they were embodied were considered to be a legal version of the social contract itself; and they acquired from this association a peculiarly sacred and exalted character. In the old country they had been cherished as a priceless political heritage, but they had not for that reason been placed beyond modification or even abrogation by the ordinary law-making authority. In our American states they were transformed into a Higher Law, which derived its authority directly from the people, and over which the active government had no authority. Of course the popular sovereign, which possessed the equally indefeasible right to institute and alter governments, had the legal power to abrogate these individual rights; but at this point the inalienable right of the people to institute governments began to conflict with the equally inalienable liberties of the individual. The people had a right to institute an unrighteous government, but the injured individuals had an equal right to protest and rebel against it. The violation of these individual rights broke the contract upon which society was based and justified revolution. The Higher Law, consequently, was not dependent on the popular will, no matter how deliberately and lawfully expressed, for its sanction. Its ultimate justification was its inherent righteousness, and its effective authority could always be protected by a threatened recourse to the revolutionary alternative.

If these early American law-givers had been sensitive

to theoretical difficulties, they might have been troubled by the contradictions indicated in the preceding paragraph. The indefeasible popular political rights were contradicted by the equally indefeasible popular civil rights. The reasons which made it necessary to subordinate the legislature to a Higher Law made it equally desirable to subordinate the people, as constitution makers, to a Higher Law — which was done so far as possible by placing the Higher Law under the protection of the permanent possibility of revolution. Thus the rational state was based ultimately on an appeal to violence. The arbitrary political or military power which they dreaded and which had been ostentatiously kicked out of the front door, was surreptitiously brought back again by the rear entrance. Neither were these difficulties merely dialectical. The ground was prepared for the violent assertion, which subsequently took place, of individual and local liberties against what was believed to be an unjust exercise of popular political authority. The real problem of rationalizing the exercise of popular political power was evaded rather than faced by the early American law-givers. The way to rationalize political power is not to confine its exercise within the limits defined by certain rules, but frankly to accept the danger of violence and reorganize the state so that popular reasonableness will be developed from within rather than imposed from without.

Nevertheless the early American law-givers, by expressly associating the organization of popular political authority with what was believed to be the reign of justice, made a unique contribution to the democratic government. They headed democracy towards Zion. Somehow and to some extent democracy, in case it is to survive, must combine the two ends which seemed so essential to the framers of the constitution of Massachusetts. Popular political authority must be made effective and it must be made righteous. The degree of success which the American democracy may obtain will depend on its ability to make popular political authority practically effective without any ultimate sacrifice of righteousness, and sufficiently righteous without any sacrifice of ultimate effectiveness. In this sense the American democracy must always derive its vitality from the ideals of the fathers of the Republic — undemocratic in spirit though many of them were.

Our doubts concern, not the validity of the ideal, which did so much to mould constitutions such as that of Massachusetts, but the means which were taken to legalize and organize it. By attempting to define a code of righteous political behavior, which could be enforced as law and which should be morally and legally binding on the people, the constitution makers were by way of depriving the sovereign of his own ultimate and necessary discretionary power. They did not merely associate popular political authority with the ideal law, but they tended to subordinate popular authority to an actual law. It was the Law which bound the popular will under the threat of revolutionary violence, rather than the popular will which was freely to accept and patiently to realize the righteous ideal. The human will in its collective aspect was made subservient to the mechanism of a legal system.

This source of weakness introduced into the foundations of the state had its consequences upon the organization of the government. If the people are to be divided against themselves in order that righteousness may rule, still more must the government be divided against itself. It must be separated into departments each one of which must act independently of the others. "In the government of this commonwealth the legislative department shall never exercise the executive and judicial powers or either of them, the executive shall never exercise the legislative and judicial powers or either of them; the judicial shall never exercise the legislative or executive powers or either of them; to the end that it may be a government of laws and not of, men." The government was prevented from doing harm, but in order that it might not do harm it was deliberately and effectively weakened. The people were protected from the government; but quite as much was the government protected from the people. In dividing the government against itself by such high and rigid barriers, an equally substantial barrier was raised against the exercise by the people of any easy and sufficient control over their government. It was only a very strong and persistent popular majority which could make its will prevail, and if the rule of a majority was discouraged, the rule of a minority was equally encouraged. But the rulers, whether representing a majority or a minority, could not and were not supposed to accomplish much. It was an organization of obstacles and precautions — based at bottom on a profound suspicion of human nature.

Thus was instituted a system of representation by Law. Inasmuch as the ultimate popular political power was trustworthy only in case it were exercised, not merely through the medium of regular forms, but under rigid and effective limitations, the trustworthy agents of that power were not representative men exercising discretionary power, but principles of right which subordinated all officials to definite and binding restrictions. When the sovereign itself has implicitly surrendered its discretion to the Law, the personal agents of the sovereign can scarcely expect to retain theirs. The domination of the Law came to mean in practice a system in which the discretionary discriminating purposive action of the human will in politics, whether collective or individual, was suspect and should be reduced to the lowest practicable terms. The active government was divided, weakened, confined and deprived of integrity and effective responsibility, in order that a preëstablished and authoritative Law might be exalted, confirmed and placed beyond the reach of danger.

While the essential legal and moral aspects of the traditional system were revealed by the constitutions of Massachusetts and New Hampshire, the system only reached its full development in the Federal Constitution and government. The adoption of that Constitution was the first affirmation of the popular political authority of the whole American people — of popular authority in its full national integrity. But just because it sought to organize a complete sovereign power and tended to identify popular with national sovereignty, it was the object of suspicion by the friends of local interests and rights as well as of individual interests and rights. Thus the government established by the new instrument became essentially and unequivocally one of limited powers. In the case of the state constitutions, the law-making power could and did claim to fall heir to a kind of residuary sovereignty, which gave to it large discretionary authority within the limits imposed by the state constitutions — although as soon as this claim began to be admitted it was emasculated in practice by a strengthening of the executive and judicial vetoes. But in the case of Congress, there was far less ground for ambiguity. Nothing but specific powers was granted to the new government; and all powers not granted were reserved to the states or to the people. There were three parties to this constitutional arrangement instead of two. The scruples of the states had to be satisfied as well as the needs of the general government and the demands of the people. The necessity of arranging a balance between popular authority, national authority and state authority strengthened the formal legal element in the system. The control which the people might exercise over the Constitution was diminished and the intricacy of the constitutional mechanism increased, in order that the states might be independent of the general government and the general government independent of the states. The restrictions imposed upon the exercise of popular authority had to be tightened, in order that that popular authority might not be used inimically to the desirable balance of the whole system.

Thus the fundamental Law to which the American people intrusted their ultimate sovereign power unfortunately tended to become more than usually inaccessible. The positively democratic element in the organization of the states consisted in the reality of the popular control over the enactment and amendment of the state constitutions. Even though the actual machinery of amendment was unnecessarily slow and difficult, as it undoubtedly was in the cases of the early state constitutions, still, local popular opinion felt that these governments were the people's governments and their law was the people's law. In the case of the Federal Constitution, on the other hand, the increased elaborateness of the mechanism and the important part played therein by independent local political organizations, impaired the reality and the feeling of popular control. In theory the fundamental Law should have been more completely the people's law than were the state constitutions, because it represented the popular will in its national integrity; but in practice the people have never had much to say about it. It was framed by a convention, the members of which were never expressly elected for the purpose by popular vote. It was ratified, not directly by the electorate, but by conventions which often represented only a small minority even of the legally qualified voters. In seeking to amend it the popular will could not act directly, but must get expressed through Congress and through state legislatures and conventions. Difficult of operation as the machinery of amendment was, it seemed even more difficult and remote because it involved the use of so many intermediate instruments. The whole Federal system was by way of being an able, deliberate, beneficent and finally acceptable imposition on the people rather than an actual popular possession.

I am not raising the question whether **this** imposition can or cannot be justified. If the question should be raised, the answer to it should turn upon the fact that popular opinion came to submit to the situation with so little discomfort. But the consequences were none the less serious. The Federal Constitution even more than the state constitutions was supposed to embody a social contract and a Higher Law — a code of righteous political behavior, any violation of which formed a justification of revolution. It was theoretically subject to popular control, popular control was seldom exercised as it was in the case of the state constitutions. The authority which the Higher Law ought to exercise, according to the political philosophy of the period, was reënforced by the authority which, as a result of its comparative independence, it actually did exercise. The Law in the shape of the Federal Constitution really came to be a monarchy of the Word. It had been imposed upon the popular will, which was the only power capable of disputing its authority; and its friends came more and more to assume that the imposition was wise and beneficent. A systematic attempt was made to justify the supremacy of the Law. The people were warned that, if they rebelled, the just and awful judgment of the Lord would overtake them. Thus the aspirations and the conviction of the early democrats that popular political authority should be righteously expressed hardened into a system, which consecrated one particular machinery of possibly righteous expression. Reverence for law was made to mean reverence for one specific formulation of Law. Reverence for order was made to mean reverence for an established order. All that the American people had to do to insure their political salvation was vigilantly to safeguard the specific formulation of law and order which was found in the sacred writing.

CHAPTER II

THE PIONEER DEMOCRACY AND THE CONSTITUTION

IN the preceding chapter I sketched the origin of the rigid and dogmatic element in the American political system — the element which competes with democracy for the allegiance of the American political conscience and on which contemporary conservatism depends for the grounds of its opposition to democracy. The further question must now be considered of the subsequent history of this authoritative system. How was the Supremacy of the Law consolidated and developed into a satisfactory working organization? How did the American people come to submit to the imposition? As we all know, democratic convictions and ideals, as time went on, exerted more rather than less influence on public opinion. How and why did the American democracy become deeply attached to a political system which tended so stubbornly to escape popular control? If we can succeed in understanding this anachronism, we may reach a point of advantageous observation, from which the existing confusion about the relation between conservatism and progressivism may be reduced to some kind of order.

Radical democratic critics of the Federal Constitution have recently been attributing its acceptance by the

American democracy to a kind of conspiracy. The educated and wealthy classes bulldozed and cajoled the people into submitting to an alien and essentially obnoxious political system. "It is hard," says Professor J. Allen Smith in his book on the "Spirit of American Government," " it is hard to find a satisfactory explanation of the process whereby the worshippers of democracy came to deify an undemocratic Constitution. The desire of the conservative classes to preserve and perpetuate the system by presenting it in the guise of democracy and their influence on the political thought of the people generally must be regarded as the chief factor in bringing about this extraordinary change in public opinion." The change in public opinion to which Professor Smith refers is one which took place between the year 1777 and the years succeeding the ratification of the Constitution. In 1777 the American states were adopting what he believes to be essentially democratic organs of government. Ten years later a far less democratic organ of government had been created, which was first legally ratified, then gradually accepted by public opinion, and finally consecrated as a consummate combination of liberty and democracy. Professor Smith's explanation is that the educated and wealthy classes "put over" the Constitution on the American people, and then hypnotized them into the acceptance of an instrument of class rule as an appropriate system of law and government for a democratic society.

That a comparatively small minority of men, belonging for the most part to a single economic class, did draw the

Constitution up and secure its ratification can scarcely be denied. The recent investigations of Professor Charles Beard indicate that the Constitution was framed chiefly by owners of personal property and their representatives, who lived in and around the larger cities on the Atlantic seaboard. The interests of this class had been adversely affected by the consequences of the Revolution. Public credit was at a low ebb. The state governments, by the free issue of paper money and by laws suspending the payment of debts, had demoralized business and injured private credit. The lack of any effective method of protecting interstate trade against local impediments, or foreign trade against unfair discrimination, was keenly felt. Finally, a large amount of capital had been invested in lands on the frontier, which did not increase in value as fast as its owners anticipated, because no government existed strong enough to protect the frontier from Indian raids. The members of this class, consequently, had every interest to combine and to exert all their influence and energy in establishing a strong central government, which was capable of giving to capitalists the security and the advantages necessary to the production and accumulation of personal property.

They combined and went to work so intelligently and so effectually that, in spite of their comparatively small numbers, they framed an acceptable plan of government and secured its ratification. It is estimated that the friends of the new Constitution did not amount to more than about one-sixth of the possible voters. This small minority was able to impose its will upon the mass of its fellow-countrymen, because its members were energetic, intelligent, resourceful and united. It possessed the prestige of comparative wealth and social position, the habit of leadership, usually a sufficient command of the existing machinery of government, and the determination to succeed at any cost. Its opponents, on the other hand, who belonged to an equally specific economic class, were poor, scattered, disorganized, and unaccustomed to leadership and to united action. They consisted for the most part of small agricultural freeholders. In the older parts of the country the freeholders, having accumulated money, were closely connected with the commercial and professional classes, and were as likely to favor as to combat the proposed Constitution. But the farmers in all the new or comparatively new districts were opposed. If they had been as well organized and as class-conscious as they became a little later, they could have prevented the ratification of the Constitution. Being a debtor class, they had been responsible for much of the legislation which had been objectionable to the owners of personal property. Their interests were local and agrarian; and they were instinctively hostile to a government which would centralize the political power of the country and capitalize its economic resources.

Thus Professor Beard's investigations do indicate that the Constitution was, if you please, "put over" by a small minority of able, vigorous and unscrupulous personal property owners. This class was subsequently organized into the Federalist party, which by its aggressive nationalism

E

finally raised up in its own path an equally energetic and
in the end a better united opposition. The small freeholders in and near the frontier, who had failed to prevent
the ratification of the Constitution, were organized by anti-
Federalist leaders into the Republican party. This class
soon found that they really constituted, both politically
and economically, the dominant element in public opinion.

Such being the situation in general, the question as to
why the American democracy continued to submit to what
was even then considered to be an undemocratic Constitution apparently becomes still more difficult to answer. It
is easy to understand that an able, aggressive, united and
resourceful minority could force the adoption of a political
system against a numerically superior but disorganized
opposition; but within a few years this opposition became
every bit as class-conscious as the Federalists and very much
better organized. As soon as the Republicans assumed
power, why did they not in their own interest undo or modify
the work of the Federalists? Were they prevented from
so doing by the authority which the prestige and intelligence of that formerly dominant class still exercised upon
them? Such seems to be Professor Smith's opinion; but
unfortunately the supposition does not explain the facts.
Doubtless public opinion had been strongly influenced by
the constitutional cult, wherewith the Federalists were
already seeking to sanctify their handiwork; but the local
democracies, which had been organized into the first Republican party, were embittered against the Federalists and
were more likely unreasonably to oppose Federalist initia-

tive than unreasonably to accept it. The failure of Jefferson and his followers, at this particular juncture at least, to attempt the democratization, as they understood democracy, of the Constitution calls for a much more fundamental explanation.

The truth is that the American democracy rallied to an undemocratic Constitution, and have until recently remained loyal to it, because of the nature of their own economic interests. In certain respects the interests of the farmers were opposed to those of the capitalists; but in still more fundamental respects they were capable of adjustment. Both parties were seeking the satisfaction of individual economic purposes. The deification of an undemocratic Constitution was the work of a democracy which wholly failed to understand the proper relation between popular political power and popular economic and social policy. It was the work, that is, of an undemocratic or only a semidemocratic democracy.

In his account of these critical years Professor Smith attaches too much importance, both historically and theoretically, to the fact that soon after the Declaration of Independence the legislatures in many of the states obtained practically complete political authority. He regards this early assertion of legislative omnipotence as the indication of the existence at that moment of genuine democratic conviction. This conviction might have continued to prevail, had not the "conservative classes" been alarmed by the action of the legislative bodies in attacking property. They were provoked to make a strenuous and successful

effort to tie the hands of the people by submitting legislative action to constitutional prohibitions. But legislative
omnipotence, as we shall see later, is far from being an
essentially democratic form of government; and the course
of American constitutional development was not profoundly affected by this little episode of substantially complete legislative authority. That episode was due to the
hasty seizure, in time of revolution and war, of the most
available instrument of effective political power. It could
not last. As soon as the Democrats found time for reflection, they, no less than the Federalists, emphatically repudiated a political system which tended in the direction of
parliamentary government. They had a stubborn and a
reasonable objection to granting to legislatures anything
like constituent power. The significant beginning of American democracy did not consist in the legislative governments which were hastily improvised immediately after
the Declaration of Independence, but in the successful
protest of the towns of Massachusetts and New Hampshire
against the assumption by a mere legislative assembly of
the most essential function of sovereignty. The foundation of the American state was bound to consist, not in a
law of parliament, but in a people's law, framed by delegates expressly elected for the purpose and ratified by direct
popular vote.

To be sure, this people's law was largely preoccupied
with the task of placing limitations upon the effective exercise of popular political power, and resulted in the establishment of anything but a democratic government. But

the inadequacy of the superstructure does not impair the validity of the foundation. Democrats at the end of the eighteenth century lacked the experience, the self-confidence and the social knowledge and ideals, which were necessary for the organizing of a thoroughly democratic political system. Understanding that democracy must make for social righteousness, they used the only means with which they were provided by contemporary social philosophy to secure the social welfare. That philosophy furnished them with the conception of a constitutive social reason which could be embodied in law, but it furnished them with no conception of a positively socialized will. Any free expression of a social will, any functional organization of democracy, looked hostile to the institutes of the social reason. Being obliged to make a choice, democracy elected to side with reason and to subordinate popular government to government by Law.

I do not wish to imply that the democracy was exclusively responsible for the state constitutions. Men who became Federalists were as influential in the framing of the first state constitutions as men were who subsequently became Republicans. The important point is that the political democracy of the period was both asserted and exhausted by the establishment of a people's law, because once having been made it was fundamental and irrevocable. Its full meaning and consequences nobody understood. In devising the details of the system of law and government, both Democrats and Federalists fell back partly on the prevailing political philosophy, but chiefly on the English political tradition. English law and English political precedents constituted the specific material with which both parties really worked. They were not mere political and social theorists. They were building their political structure as much upon traditions as upon ideas.

If the ostensible friends of democracy were imperfect in their friendship, the ostensible enemies of democracy were no less imperfect in their enmity. As political men of affairs the Federalists recognized in part the actual increase of popular political influence which had become effective under the comparatively free economic and social conditions of the new world. The governments, state and Federal, which they did so much to organize, went much further than did any other government of that day in providing for the exercise of popular political power. Moreover, the mere fact that the Federalists were nationalists and were seeking to give integrity to the political system tended to convert them into involuntary democrats. Those ingredients in the national political system which in their development have proved advantageous to democracy, are in point of fact more often of Federalist than of anti-Federalist origin. The ostensible democrats repudiated national sovereignty; and by so doing they repudiated genuine popular sovereignty, which obtains reality and dignity as a result of living integrity of purpose. Statesmen of Federalist tendency put "we, the people" into the Constitution and so made possible a national democracy. In fact, the nationalism of Hamilton, with all its aristocratic leaning, was more democratic, because more constructively social, than the indiscriminate individualism of Jefferson. The early Democrats criticised the Constitution, not because it hampered the effective and responsible expression of the prevailing popular will, but chiefly because it intrusted the central government, as the possible agent of a national policy, with too much power. They accepted without pro- test the least democratic provisions of the Constitution, such as its excessive difficulty of amendment, the indirect election of the Executive, the varying terms of Congress- men, Senator and President. They accepted equally with- out protest the principle of the separation of the powers in its most precise form, and gave in their state constitutions a much more dogmatic expression to that principle than it received in the Federal Constitution. What the local democracies did demand as a condition of accepting the Constitution, was the insertion in the instrument of the bill of rights — a demand which affords the clearest evidence of their idea of an essentially democratic polity. There was undoubtedly some justification for this demand. It seemed fair that a government which constrained the indi- vidual and the states should be constrained in the sup- posed interest of the individual and the states. But whether reasonable or not, the insertion of the bill of rights in the Constitution contributed more than any other fea- ture to convert it into a monarchy of the Law superior in right to the monarchy of the people.

American democrats at the end of the eighteenth century soon found that they had no imperative reason to be dis- satisfied with the Constitution. They would have preferred a weaker government — one more completely divided against itself, and one in which the execution of national policies could be more effectually hindered by local political agencies. But the Constitution was by way of being a democratic instrument, as they understood democracy. If it did not give to the popular will much power and responsibility, neither did it afford much opportunity for the abuse of popular liberty. On the other hand, it did give to the popular will some power and responsibility and it did offer minor opportunities of abuse. It held a sufficiently even balance between the rule of possible majorities and the rule of possible minorities — in such wise that a dominant majority or minority could not get control without exceptional unity of purpose and efficiency of organization. The game of politics was made profitable and exciting without becoming dangerous to society. The stakes were large enough to be very desirable, but not so large as to make politics interfere with business. While the game of politics was being played with a zest which was perhaps more apparent than real, better democrats were playing, in the region temporarily beyond the zone of political interference, the really great game and winning the really valuable prizes.

The really valuable prizes depended on the freedom and the security which had been obtained for the essential business of developing the natural resources of the country and accumulating private property. In this business the democracy, made up as it was of the economic class of agricultural freeholders and pioneers, were as aggressively interested as were the capitalists. The interests of the two classes did not coalesce at this time, but they ran along parallel lines. What a desirable political system meant to a substantial majority of American citizens at the beginning of the nineteenth century was deliverance from interference in the cultivation of their own gardens and protection in the enjoyment of the fruits. Both in its democratic and undemocratic aspects it was the expression of dominant local and individual economic interests.

The peculiar economic conditions which obtained on a rich undeveloped continent enabled the American democracy to accept and employ a legal system which in the old country had been anti-democratic in its origin, its meaning and its effects. The new American system of law and government, constituting as it did a dogmatic embodiment of the English political and legal tradition as that tradition was then understood, was intended above all to strengthen the association between personal liberty and the security of private property. The establishment of that association had been the great political achievement of the English nation. The American law-givers inherited the association and emphasized it. They wrote it into the fundamental Law. The democracy consented, because it expected on the whole to benefit from the association. In Great Britain the association between the rigid protection of the right to property and comparative freedom from legal interference in the task of accumulating it had been and continued to be unfavorable to democracy, in that it resulted in the concentration of wealth in comparatively few hands.

But in the United States the benefit promised to be diffused, because a majority of American citizens could earn a substantial share of the fruits of the country's economic development. American natural resources were so abundant and so accessible that the national economic interest was temporarily promoted by an alliance between the friends of local and individual economic freedom and the friends of a rigid legal protection of property interests.

Thus the difference between the Federalists and the Jeffersonian Democrats, bitter as it was for a while, was never fought to a finish. Their interests were in certain respects divided. The division remained conspicuous in American politics down to the Civil War, and has continued ever since to exercise a considerable, although not a preponderant, influence. The agrarian democracy has always been suspicious of the capitalists who controlled the seaboard states. It has continually harbored the idea that in some way the financial and credit system of the country was being used to its own disadvantage. But deeper than any division between it and the Federalist capitalists lay the common interest of all classes of America in rapid economic development. This work of economic development required a system of law and government which gave complete security to individual rights and social order, and unrestrained freedom to the pursuit of individual and local interests. An essentially individualist democracy had no difficulty in arranging a working compromise with a constitutional nationalism, which, although possessed of a higher sense of collective responsibility, still considered social and political organization chiefly as an instrument for the promotion of individual interests.

The practical fusion of Federalism and Republicanism which occurred soon after the election of Thomas Jefferson to the Presidency, was the inevitable consequence of an alliance between the Constitution and the Democracy. From the point of view of Democrats the alliance seems to have been good practical politics, because they suffered from it less than did their opponents. In a few years the Federalists disappeared as an effective political party. Federalism temporarily ceased to be a progressive political principle, and became almost immediately a revered tradition. If the Republicans had been true to their original convictions and had attempted to tear down the Federalist political structure, Federalists would have continued to be necessary, and Federalism as a positive ideal might have continued to live; but by accepting Federalism the Republicans killed two birds with one stone. They made Federalists unnecessary and Federalism uncontentious; and they did away with differences of principle in American party warfare. The underlying traits of the American Democracy suddenly came to the surface — its lack of positive conviction, its preference for immediate results, its complacency and its disposition to let well enough alone. If the Constitution had been more easily amendable, an effort to amend it might have been made; but when you have possession of the government and your enemies are beaten, why fight for an idea? The American Democracy has never been belligerent except in opposition. It needed to consider itself oppressed; it needed to be threatened in some of its rights; it needed to be worried in some of its interests — in order to be conscious that as a democracy it had anything of much importance to do. As soon as a party attained to power, the grievances of its members. usually disappeared. The political screen was pushed aside and the factory of individual economic interest was uncovered. An abundant material prosperity, derived chiefly from the land and sufficiently divided among good Democrats, satisfied the fundamental need of the party.

The ensuing political situation, which lasted for some twenty-five years, was, however, characterized by certain significant anomalies. A states-rights individualist democracy, which was suspicious of any centralized control, had accepted an authoritative general government and an inaccessible body of public law. It had swallowed an unpalatable political pill because of its saccharine legal and economic coating. Not only did the dose not prove to be as disagreeable as was expected, but the medicine, unlike many other medicines, proved to be a useful and indispensable kind of nourishment for the reluctant patient. The scattered territorial American democracy instinctively dreaded the thing that it most needed. It needed to be pulled and held together by a strong but not an irksome bond. Early in the nineteenth century the necessary cohesiveness was not supplied by any habit of national association or by any conviction of positive national economic purposes and responsibilities. If it was to be quickly acquired, it had to be imposed; and imposed it was. Once connected by the constitutional network, a process of skilful cutting and fitting began, which, while it made the Constitution even more serviceable as a bond, allowed the democracy a large amount of room and diminished its sense of restraint. A certain sense of bondage remained, which produced verbal grumbling rather than an active struggle for release. The American Democracy was becoming united, not in spite of itself, because it consented to the process, but without its own conscious coöperation. It was not purposely contributing to its own increasing cohesion.

Thus the statement that the American nation was made by, if not for, the Constitution is, in a certain sense, true. The service performed by the Constitution in unifying the American people began the work of nationalizing, or, if you prefer, socializing, the American democracy. Probably the democracy, if left to itself, would have reached the same goal by another, although longer, more tortuous and more costly road; but, as things actually fell out, the undemocratic Constitution contributed as much to democratic fulfilment as did any consciously democratic element in the political system. It helped to socialize the American people by preparing them for a higher, more intimate, more diversified and more responsible form of associated life. The Democracy at first submitted, then opened its mind and learned and finally revered — although with its reverence was often mixed some resentment and distrust.

The mixture of some distrust with its reverence had, however, political consequences of the utmost importance. Skilfully as the constitutional government was being fitted

to the American political body, the Democracy felt the need
of more freedom of movement. It gradually began a process of reorganization, which was intended, not to get rid
of the constitutional constraint, but to relax still further
its vigor. It was all very well for the Constitution to mould
the Democracy, but the Democracy as it increased in self-
confidence sought in its turn to mould the Constitution.
The benefits of the system were more than ever recognized,
but so were its dangers. The Democracy needed some
instrument of control; and the attempt to forge and perfect such an instrument dominated the next, the middle,
period of American history.

CHAPTER III

Aggressive and Triumphant Democracy

THE Jeffersonian Democracy was succeeded by the Jacksonian Democracy, which came to the surface as a protest against a revival of aggressive Federalism. The War of 1812 had invigorated national feeling and had exposed many humiliating weaknesses in the national military and financial organization and equipment. A certain part of the Republican party returned to the Hamiltonian principle of an active and responsible governmental policy for the realization of essential national purposes. They recreated the National Bank, reaffirmed the protective principle and proposed a comprehensive plan of internal improvements under Federal supervision. For a while the new group merely called itself the national Republicans; but in the long run a group of Democrats who proposed to accomplish a constructive policy could not but secede from their party associates. As time went on the separation became more and more complete, until finally the national Republicans became the Whigs and the faithful remnant the Democrats.

The Whigs represented in general the same capitalist and money-lending interest as had the original Federalists. This class, having succeeded in getting the Constitution framed and accepted, now sought to build up a national economic system supplementary to it. Owing to the increase in manufactures and domestic commerce, it was sufficiently powerful in the beginning to win some substantial successes; but its boasted national economic system was not based upon a comprehensive balance of sectional economic interests. Its policies of protectionism, internal improvements and a National Bank inured to the benefit of finance, industry and commerce rather than agriculture, and they all tended to a concentrated and centralized rather than a localized economic development. Consequently, as national Republicanism became successful, it was bound to meet with increasing resistance. The local Democracy slowly awoke to the fact that the powers of the Federal government were being used in a manner inimical, or at least indifferent, to its interests. The era of good feeling came to an end. As a result of the awakening, the territorial Democracy became more than ever conscious of its special needs, and more than ever resolved to make them prevail. It began to organize for the benefit of its own political preponderance. As a result of this organization and of its electoral successes, the party passed through a period of most illuminating self-revelation.

The territorial Democracy in this its second phase was in certain respects much more thoroughly nationalized than its predecessor. It had forgotten that the Constitution was imposed upon the nation by a special class and somewhat reluctantly accepted. The pioneer Democrats were, for the most part, children of the Federal system, and they were thoroughly loyal to their political parentage. They would not tolerate for one moment proposals to repudiate the national authority, such as had been made by Jefferson. But if their national allegiance was a matter of positive feeling, they were conscious also that the national system might easily become inimical to their particular kind of democracy. It had an unpleasant way of escaping or even defying local popular control. The Constitution, for instance, as a body of law seemed to possess a peculiar logic and energy of its own, which largely determined its development. The Whigs had been able to accomplish a certain measure of national economic centralization without any sufficient consultation of local public opinion, so that the government as well as the law was exhibiting a disconcerting independence. Slowly the Democrats made up their mind that an increase of popular control was necessary. Although they were more than ever conscious that this constitutional national government was contributing something essential to democracy in its educational aspect, they were also more than ever conscious of the price which democracy, as a mechanism of popular government, was paying for the lesson. Like good tradesmen they wanted to keep the credit, but if possible to buy it at a cheaper price.

No attempt was made to bring about an increase of popular control by the amendment of the Constitution. The Jacksonian Democrats would have dreaded tampering with that sacred instrument almost as much as would the Whigs, because the more the Constitution was amended, the

F

more precarious became the reserved rights of the states. Their great object was to get and to keep the administration of the law and the operation of the government in the hands of good Democrats. Popular control, to their minds, did not mean control by the people as a whole or by any fluctuating majority of the people. Neither did it mean control in the interest of any positive democratic policy. What it did mean was control by men like themselves. They were the people. They needed, not an efficient or sensitive instrument of government, because after they had seized the machine they did not want to accomplish anything of importance with it, but a clumsy and complicated instrument, whose chief value consisted in its mere possession, and which could be completely possessed and operated only by an efficiently organized partisan Democracy. Any kind of government controlled by good Democrats would be democratic. Any kind of government controlled by their opponents would be undemocratic. For democracy, as these pioneers understood it, was a very human and even a very personal matter. It consisted as much as anything else in belonging to a certain social set. Differences of policy, opinion, merit, or, within limits, even integrity were of less importance than differences of personal and class association. Democrats were held together less by common purposes and policies than by common sympathies and antipathies.

Theretofore the Democrats had neglected to be sufficiently careful about their partisan associates. They had a vague idea that they could secure popularized officials by virtue of an ordinary process of election. They were discovering that more important than a choice between candidates was the choice of candidates. Candidates had usually been selected by a caucus of the local or national legislature, and this method of selection by men who had been designated for a wholly different task was one which very largely escaped popular control. What Democracy needed in order to become politically dominant was a method of nominating candidates whose popular sympathies and good faith were unimpeachable. Little by little a pure system of representative democracy was built up for the purpose of nominating desirable candidates. It was based, not on direct popular control over the naming of candidates, but upon mutual confidence within the party, and on the expectation that the whole party would really be represented in the nominating conventions. It proved to be highly successful. Not only did it consolidate the Democracy, organize its leadership, and increase its political power, but it really did give to the party control over its own members and its own candidates. The individual Democrat soon owed so much to his party and became politically so helpless without its support that his partisan allegiance became the dominant fact in his political life. His allegiance to his party, that is, became of more importance than his allegiance to the public or to the specific duties of his office. The foundation was laid for that intensely personal government by parties, with which the American Democracy sought to humanize and control government by Law.

Be it clearly understood that this assertion of Democracy, instead of being accompanied by any disposition to get rid of government by Law, was supplementary thereto. The monarchy of the Law was really threatened more by the positive functional conception of government partly accepted by the Whigs than it was by the negative conception of government accepted by the Democrats. The manner in which the latter revised the state constitutions indicates unmistakably that they believed above all in representation by Law. Only in one respect were they interested in strengthening the human element in the official organization of Democracy. In so far as they could they introduced adult male suffrage, which was assuredly an indication of democratic good faith; but the broadening of the popular basis of government did not mean any increased confidence in the organs of government. The great organ of democracy was the partisan association of good Democrats, which was wrought chiefly for purposes of negatively controlling the official government rather than for the purpose of using it, after possession had been obtained, for any positive purpose. Organized Democracy became more than ever a machinery for limiting and paralyzing government by men. State constitutions were made more easily amendable, chiefly to enable the Democracy to impose more elaborate prohibitions upon the exercise of official discretion. In spite of a manifest disposition to attribute to the state legislatures a kind of residuary sovereignty under the name of the police power, legislative action was submitted to a constantly increasing burden of specific and general restrictions. The exercise of the police power was made subject to the scrupulous supervision of the courts. The executive veto was strengthened. On the other hand, the executive authority itself was disintegrated by being distributed among a number of elected officials, ostensibly responsible to the people at large, but really to the party by which they were nominated. Thus in every respect the tendency, betrayed originally by the state constitutions, to weaken and disintegrate government and impair the responsible and effective expression of the individual and the collective will in the supposed interest of the Law and of Democracy, was conspicuous in the whole process of state constitutional revision undertaken by the Jacksonian Democrats.

The underlying object, as well as the net result, of these constitutional changes was to drive in a wedge between the Law and its administration. The Law itself was stupendously magnified. Its administration was systematically and ruthlessly emasculated. By these means did the Democracy seek to create a political system which would possess cohesion but avoid the delegation of positive official responsibilities or opportunities. The strength of the Law must not be imparted to its administration, because a strong administration might be too strong for the Democracy. The men by whom the Law was administered, and who were supposed to be controlled by it, really owed their allegiance to a very different lord. Their masters were the unofficial partisan Democratic organization, which derived its strength from their weakness, and was indifferent to the character of the Law, provided its administration could be controlled. Hence general laws were confided to the execution of local officials, responsible to a constituency wholly different from the one whose will was embodied therein. Hence the executive power was torn apart, so that no one executive official would be powerful enough to wax independent of the party, and substitute his will or his interpretation of the Law for that of local partisan opinion. Hence the legislature was dominated by the party caucus and was divided up into administrative committees — any one of which would be less likely to escape control than would the whole body. Hence the judiciary was made elective, so that the courts could be subordinated to the Democratic partisan machine; and the trial judge, who is the primary instrument of a firm administration of justice, was placed under the thumb of jury and counsel.

These peculiar methods of democratization could not be as successfully applied to the central government as they could to that of the states. The Federal system was characterized by great inherent strength and a tenaciously independent vitality. It was, indeed, the very tendency to independence on the part of the Federal Law and government which had been so disconcerting to the Democracy, and which had much to do with the creation of this unofficial partisan government supplementary to the official system. It could not disintegrate this Federal organization, but by heroic efforts and drastic measures it could reduce it to much more effective control. It could elect a Democratic administration and by the power of partisan allegiance keep it after election under tolerable subordination. By virtue of this subordination the administration could be very much weakened. The adoption of the principle of rotation in elective offices and the application of the spoils system to appointive offices did much to injure the independence of the Federal system and to impair its integrity. The local partisan organization named the Federal officials and took care that they served their real rather than their ostensible master. Thus the Federal government was tamed by the local Democracy, if not entirely subdued.

The fundamental motive of their work of official and unofficial Democratic reorganization was not a preference for government by Law over government by men, but the conviction that government by Law should not be allowed to become dangerous by its administration at the hands of the other kind of men. The subordination of administrative and legislative officials to the Law was accompanied by the increasing emancipation of real Democratic leaders from the Law. Within the partisan association the organization was based upon mutual confidence and the exercise of practically unlimited discretion by the chosen leaders of the party. Within the official organization every arrangement presupposed mutual suspicion and was inimical to the exercise of individual responsibility. Thus the new organization of democracy was determined fundamentally by very human motives. The Democrats were willing to place a great deal of trust in a certain kind of men, with whom they could associate on equal and familiar terms, whereas they instinctively distrusted other or less familiar classes of men.   Fundamental economic and social conditions determined both these antipathies and sympathies.

The Democracy still represented, no less than in the days of Jefferson, the pioneer farmer — the man who had recently taken up the land, who sought above all to capitalize the future possibilities of his acreage, whose horizon did not extend beyond his own geographical surroundings, and who was accustomed to doing things in his own way.   The quickest possible gratification of his immediate economic interests demanded a national Law which was firmly established but feebly executed.   The firm establishment of the Law tied society together and prevented its feeble administration from degenerating into anarchy.   But by virtue of its feeble administration individual and local economic interests were allowed great latitude of action. The Law could be enforced or relaxed or even ignored according to the dictates of local convenience; and the local groups testified to their convenience through the agency of their local partisan organization.

Thus the first body of conscious American Democrats accepted the constitutional system as a bond, but did their best to neutralize it as a leaven.   They needed a strong legal anchorage, in which their economic enterprises could find a safe refuge, and to satisfy this need they submitted to an impersonal legal dictatorship.   But they could not permit this dictation to become too active, because in that event it might interfere with their dominant interest

— which was the quickest possible *of* appropriation and development of the natural resources of the country. Not that they had any fundamental objection to the use of governmental agencies, as such, in the interest of local economic interests. They were quite willing to exhaust the credit of their state governments in the effort to provide highways, canals, railroads, and the other necessities of local economic development. But when the Federal government acted, its decisions seemed to be dictated or at least modified by those classes whose interests demanded expert and centralized economic control and whose tendency was to interfere with local needs and methods. And as the Federal government was possessed by an instinctive tendency to positive action, good Democrats must be organized for the purpose of rendering this action inoffensive.

Thus a negative do-nothing Democracy inevitably became inimical to the administrative aspect of government. Good administration consists in the adoption of the most efficient available methods for the accomplishment of an accepted policy. It is essentially active, functional and purposive, and depends for its success upon the accuracy and extent of its available supplies of knowledge and equipment. Its standards, consequently, are scientific, technical and special, yet with a specialism that always tends towards coördination. In its search for the most economical method and in its tendency towards centralization, it overrides local interests and local habits. The pioneer Democracy instinctively disparaged and distrusted exacting administrative standards. In its own economic and social life it needed alertness, adaptability and energy far more than it needed special equipment or comprehensive plans. It was disposed to secure immediate temporary local results rather than relatively permanent and inclusive results. Whenever it sought to accomplish anything that needed careful planning and skilful execution, as it did in this case of its projects of state internal improvements, its flagrant administrative ineptitude was immediately revealed. You might as well ask a social club to operate a life insurance company.

The one apparent exception to Democratic administrative ineptitude consists in its highly successful partisan organization; but this exception is more apparent than real. The Democratic partisan organization has always been based rather on common interests, common sympathies and common antipathies than on common purposes. Thus it has usually been deprived of that the most effective and fruitful source of human association, which is coöperative effort on behalf of a disinterested public object. Of course many individual Democrats and many groups of Democrats have cherished disinterested public objects, but as soon as they have done so, they have found their previous party allegiance more of an embarrassment than a help. If they have been sincere, they have usually in the end been obliged to break away. The essence of the partisan Democracy has consisted in the lively personal sympathy existent among millions of pioneers, who shared common experience and interests and who organized for the benefit of their class domination. In order to become and remain dominant, they had to impose upon one another a drastic system of party discipline, which, in the absence of other effective motives, was enforced by the application of personal rewards and punishments. He who obeyed and served waxed mighty in the land. He who disobeyed and proved disloyal was dismissed and dishonored. On this basis the organization became immensely powerful. For as long as a national policy of do-nothingism prevailed, it constituted the real government of the country.

The Whigs, whose early aggressiveness had instigated this new formulation and organization of Democracy, were never able to offer any effective opposition to it. A national party whose life depended upon its ability to unite on an enterprising positive assertion of the public interest, was placed on the defensive and was unable even to maintain its own early achievements. Its National Bank was abolished. Its protective tariff . was reduced almost to revenue basis. A national plan of internal improvements was never adopted. Thus the Whigs were beaten all along the line. They were beaten, not only because the Democrats represented the more vital phase of contemporary American life, but because the latter were more thoroughly united and more effectively organized. The Whigs were obliged to adopt both the organization of their opponents and the peculiar Democratic methods of enforcing party discipline; but in the case of the Whigs the new methods did not succeed so well. They lacked the social homogeneity characteristic of the Democrats. Their interests and experience contained a greater diversity of material, and demanded a more comprehensive and purposive basis of unification.

The clearest indication of the weakness of the Whigs is that they allowed the Democracy to determine for them their attitude towards the Constitution. For them also the Law became a bond rather than a leaven — a source of security rather than of development. Having failed in their effort to consolidate the Union, they began to fear that the Union was in danger — as, indeed, it temporarily was as the result of their premature and one-sided attempt at centralized economic organization. They were terrified also by what seemed to them the lawless tendencies of the new Democracy and its reassertion of a hybrid popular sovereignty. They appraised the Democracy as a disintegrating and demoralizing social force, against the dissolving effects of which the Constitution formed the only sufficient protection. They became, consequently, its appointed defenders. By the force of their reiterated panegyrics they did much to surround the monarchy of the Law with a more radiant halo of sanctity, which under the circumstances may have had its uses; but they certainly carried their worship of the Word too far. The traditional system was explicitly transformed into a permanent constructive political dogma. The impersonal dictator, which the Democrats respected but proposed partly to control, the Whigs accepted as a political Providence, which should be allowed to develop according to the forms of its internal purpose, irrespective of the will and wishes of its living subjects. Their doctrine became one of unqualified non-resistance to the monarchy of the Word.

The one certain way of killing any specific expression of the national spirit is to identify it with dogmatic conservatism. The temple in which the Constitution was enshrined became the mausoleum of the Whig party. The national ideal had to find a new expression, which it soon began to do under more promising conditions. During the Middle Period the time was not ripe for a comprehensive nationalism. The Democrats constituted the substance of the national life. The Whigs represented an essential aspect of its formative ideal. The two could not coalesce, because the two economic classes which they represented were not ready to coöperate. The commercial and capitalist Whigs were always raising obstacles to the diversion of any more capital and labor than could be helped to the development of the western lands. They objected to stimulating the exploitation of the natural resources of the country, because industry did not immediately benefit from such exploitation and because in their opinion no stimulation was really necessary. The opportunities were so abundant and accessible that the government in the interest of a well-balanced economic system should rather discriminate in favor of industry and commerce. The Democrats, on their side, while they were not able to secure from the central government all the encouragement for agricultural development desired by them, waxed powerful enough to overthrow much of the existing discrimination in favor of industrial and financial centralization. The outcome was really a deadlock. The Democrats, after they had become dominant, could not put their authority to any positive use; and the Whigs were impotent to accomplish their inadequate program. The two parties consented to travel in the same train; but they refused to mix and they were aiming at different destinations.

Thus during the Middle Period the different classes of American popular interest and opinion could not be united for the realization of a positive national economic policy — except in so far as such a policy was already embodied in the Constitution. Still more was it impossible to bring about any positive relation between the better aspirations of the American people and the realities of their political, social and economic system. Throughout this whole period the underlying democratic and social ideal was becoming explicit, radical and self-confident as it had not been in 1789. An intense and widespread intellectual, moral and social fermentation set in, which took possession of many of the more ardent spirits. But the fermentation proved to be fruitless, partly because of the dearth of appropriate special disciplines and methods of expression, and partly because these moral adventurers could not become enthusiastic on behalf of the established system and were neither sufficiently qualified nor sufficiently enlightened to attack it. The fermentation had an outlet only in one direction. The Law was affording its powerful protection to a palpable and corrupting violation, not merely of a liberal social ideal, but of the ideals of individual liberty consecrated by the Fathers of the Republic. A legal system which permitted human slavery could not make for social righteousness. The American conscience, as soon as it began to take stock of its national possessions, was bound to protest strenuously against such ugly hypocrisy and the consequent lack of national integrity.

On the whole, however, the political innovation and achievement of preponderant importance during this period was the enormously increased power and efficiency obtained by organized political parties. Through these organizations thoroughgoing political democracy obtained its first wilful and masterful expression — an expression which had to be as masterful as it was wilful, largely because sectional feeling, individual and class interests, and other centrifugal social forces were so aggressive that despotic control was necessary. Partisan organization became, consequently, a nationalizing influence second only to that of the Constitution and in some respects more effective than the Constitution. The democratic leaven was working, although within the bonds of the Law. The American democracy became conscious of the need and the power of self-government. It had demanded and obtained a certain freedom and efficiency of associated action. Its achievements were extraordinary. If it had not been for Democratic party discipline, the rebellion might have occurred before the North could be sufficiently united for its suppression. If the Republicans could not have borrowed and appropriated an efficient partisan organization, they could hardly have fought the war to a successful conclusion. But the partisan system could not be made powerful enough to accomplish its appointed work without becoming too powerful for its ostensible master. Developing as it did into the government of the country, it necessarily insisted on confusing party with public spirit; it necessarily organized an elaborate and insidious system of partisan taxation; and it necessarily began to use its power more and more for its own perpetuation. It always paid the most elaborate verbal and ceremonial deference to its official superior, but this deference was merely the homage which any mayor of the palace must pay to a crowned king, upon whose formal authority but actual weakness the upstart is really subsisting.

CHAPTER IV

THE OLD ECONOMIC NATIONALISM

THE strong partisan organizations which were developed during the Middle Period have been described in the last chapter as a nationalizing political agency of the utmost importance. The description need not be retracted; but the work of nationalization accomplished by such agencies was limited both in its scope and its effectiveness. The two parties were national in the sense that they occupied the whole national territory and tied the scattered sections, classes and individuals together for the sake of effective joint action. They were not national in the proper sense of embodying constructive national purposes and ideals. Both of these partisan democracies were necessarily spellbound by the Constitution. They had been wrought for the work of satisfying certain political needs which the official system was powerless to meet; and they naturally shrank from tampering with a political mechanism whose weaknesses rather than whose strength determined their organization and function.

The waxing anti-slavery agitation placed both the Whigs and the Democrats in a peculiarly embarrassing position. Slavery was indubitably constitutional, yet it was essentially inimical either to a territorial national organization or to any positive national ideal based upon human welfare. The attempt to nationalize slavery and to denationalize freedom would destroy the ideal ingredient in the American political system. The attempt to denationalize slavery and to nationalize freedom would endanger the legal fabric of American political life. There arose a conflict between constitutionalism and nationalism which neither of the existing national parties dared to meet, yet which no really and constructively national party could afford to ignore.

In seeking to evade the issue, the two geographically national parties were true to their own natures and to the necessities of their situations. Neither of them could act, although for different reasons. The pioneer Democrats, as we have seen, had been organized in order to oppose any positive action on the part of the central government to effect a desirable national policy. Stephen Douglas did not care whether slavery was right or wrong or whether it was voted up or down. His conscience and his creed as a Democrat were satisfied in case local political bodies enjoyed full opportunities to vote upon it. Popular sovereignty meant to him the autonomy of local political groups, whose only bonds of union consisted in the Constitution and a Democratic partisan organization. The worst violence which could be done to such a Democracy was the dictation of one part of a community to another part. It made no difference whether this dictation was or was not enlightened by a sound conception of the national interest and made ultimately for national integrity. In an analogous way Webster cared much less whether slavery was right or wrong, or whether it made for political unity or political distraction, than whether it was constitutional. The most awful impiety which the American people could commit would be to tamper with the Constitution. The sacred Word must not be doubted, and it must not be supplemented. Thus an irresponsible individualist and particularist Democracy reached substantially the same conclusion as an irresponsible and merely constitutional Unionism.

A new era began in American politics with the formation of a national democratic party. The Republicans proposed to use the general government as the instrument of a policy which sought national integrity by means of the assertion of a humanized democracy. For the first time in our history democracy was conceived by an effective political organization as possessing an essential human interest which had not already been defined and protected in the fundamental Law and which could not be left to irresponsible individual and local action. The great contribution of the Republican party to the development of American political democracy consisted in this. While accepting and utilizing the extra-official democratic political machinery contrived during the Middle Period, it imposed upon the American people a national policy which aimed at the enhancement of human life and which demanded the use of active and efficient collective agencies. It gave to the nation a cause to work and to vote for, as well as matters of business to vote upon. Thus the sectionalism of which the Republican party was constantly and not unjustly accused did not prevent it from being our first national party as distinct from the first general party. By seeking to denationalize slavery and to nationalize freedom without rending the Union, it was using its power over American public opinion for the accomplishment of a policy which associated democracy rather than mere constitutionalism with political righteousness. Humanity was placed above the Law.

The organization of a party devoted to a national democratic anti-slavery policy implied the possibility of invigorating and emancipating the policy of the central government in other respects. The conditions had finally become ripe for a closer alliance between the two dominant economic classes. No positive national economic policy was possible during the Middle Period, because, as we have seen, the agricultural and capitalist interests, although united in desiring security for property, were divided as to the best means of encouraging its production and acquisition. This division resulted from the diffused and local character of American economic organization. The industrial and commercial communities obtained their subsistence and raw materials usually from their own neighborhoods. The pioneer farmers were dependent, much against their will, largely on local markets, and could rarely obtain the cash which they needed and the credit to which they believed themselves to be entitled. These conditions were changing. By the middle of the fifties a large percentage of the pioneer settlers of the Ohio and Mississippi valleys had arrived. They had opened up communications and accumulated actual money. Inasmuch as they had capital invested in their farms and an improved standard of living to satisfy, they needed more abundant and secure markets for the sale of their increasing products. To the west another generation of pioneers was occupying the territory beyond the river, but under the wholly new conditions created by the railroad. They were never isolated as their predecessors had been. To the east the increase of commerce and industry deprived the older states of their economic independence. Owing to the accumulation of capital, the improvement in means of communication and the actual settlement of so large a part of the best American farm land, the economic system had been at once diversified, generalized and consolidated.

For the first time in American history a political and economic alliance was possible between industrial and agricultural promoters. The two fundamental aspects of the national economic life had passed out of the stage of precocious childhood and had celebrated their comparative maturity by recognizing their interdependence. Eastern industry had come to need western minerals for its factories, western timber for its buildings, western meat and grain for its food supply. Western agriculture began to demand a vast quantity of special products which could be produced only by a concentrated factory system. Midway between the agricultural west and the industrial east was situated the middle west, which was becoming both industrial and agricultural and which mediated effectively between the two sections. The alliance immediately had a profound influence upon the economic policy of the general government. The pioneer Democracy began to realize that there was such a thing as a national economic policy. Heretofore it had employed state authority in the interest of economic development and had recognized the contribution made to the same process by the association in the fundamental Law between personal liberty and private property; but it had regarded the central government chiefly as the incipient enemy of its positive economic interests. Now, however, the general government began to be conceived as the possible friend of popular and agrarian economic interests rather than the probable enemy. Stephen Douglas himself was the first conspicuous political leader who proposed national grants of land in aid of railroad corporations. The industrial states of the east sold to the agricultural grazing and mining states of the west the public domain, and claimed in exchange a high protective tariff and every possible encouragement of industrial development.

The system was not fully matured until some years after the war, and in its final shape it was very complete and very efficient. The strong constitutional guarantees of the security of property were based on the supposition that the individual and the social economic interests substantially coincided. But if it was so desirable that the Law should protect the right to property, why should not the Law be used to promote its acquisition? Why should not the economic theory underlying these clauses of the Constitution be converted into a positive national economic policy? These questions were soon answered in the affirmative. Public assistance was bestowed upon almost every essential economic interest. The Homestead Act furnished free land to the farmer. The Timber and Stone Acts gave to the miner and timber man unrestricted access to the rich mineral resources of the public domain and to its vast stores of merchantable wood. The railroad construction necessary to the quick utilization of these gifts was stimulated' by land grants. The range was turned over to the cattle barons. Manufacturers drew up the tariff schedules to suit themselves. Corporation laws and railroad rates were made chiefly by their beneficiaries and in order that we might have a bountiful crop of corporations and railroads. The economic system of the country was conceived as a vast coöperative productive enterprise, in which the social or the public economic interest was promoted by energetic and promiscuous stimulation of productive agencies in private hands.

The disfavor with which the results of this system have recently been regarded, particularly among progressive democrats, has contributed to a widespread misinterpretation of its meaning. Its critics claim that the Republican party, which began its career by associating democracy with national righteousness and by asserting that human values should not be subordinated to the Law, did not remain true to these standards. It almost immediately became the victim of special economic interests, and devoted its power to the establishment of a privileged and undemocratic economic system. That the economic nationalism of the Republicans ceased after a certain length of time to make for human welfare is undoubtedly the case, but its eventual perversion should not prevent us from placing a correct estimate upon its original meaning. In its economic policy the Republican party was not merely giving positive effect to the economic theory underlying the Constitution, but it was entering upon a program of constructive democratic legislation, as democracy was then understood. Both its opposition to slavery and its stimulation of economic production were intended to enhance human values. In respect to slavery it sought to divorce the policy of the government from the limits imposed by the Constitution, and to assert by virtue of congressional action, but without violation of the Constitution, that negroes should be treated legally as human beings. In the case of the economic system it fastened upon the government the active realization of an object which had always been considered essential to American democracy — the object of accelerating the production of wealth, and of increasing the economic independence and, consequently, the moral opportunities of American citizens. No previous American party had possessed, or could have possessed, the courage to demand the active purposive enhancement of human values by the central government, either with or without the sanction of the Constitution.

At present the effect of this Republican economic policy seems to many of us very far from contributing to the enhancement of human life; but I am not dealing with the ultimate effect of the system: I am dealing with its im-

mediate object. Americans had always associated and
rightly associated the enhancement of human life with the
abundant production of economic goods. The apparently
inexhaustible resources of a virgin continent offered to them
an opportunity to distribute a larger amount of economic
independence over a wider area than had been offered
any people in history. Their whole legal and political system was wrought for the purpose of keeping the
work of appropriation by individuals at once secure and
unrestricted. Their constitutions surrounded property
rights with guarantees as definite and complete as human
ingenuity could devise, and their governments, which had
been made strong and stable in order to protect property,
were weakened in administration by the Democrats themselves, wherever their strength indirectly tended to hamper
the utmost freedom of economic activity and the quickest
accumulation of economic goods. The pioneers had,
indeed, accepted the Constitution, because it left them
secure and free to appropriate and develop the natural
resources of the country for their own benefit, which was,
of course, considered identical with the welfare of the
American democracy as a whole. A fair inference from
the erection of the impregnable legal fortress by which
the rights of property were defended was that the most
active possible exercise of those rights contributed to the
public welfare practically in proportion to their activity;
and under the conditions prevailing in this country the most
active possible exercise of those rights depended upon the
encouragement of the general government. That govern-

ment controlled the undeveloped natural resources of the nation, and by its policy with respect to the distribution of these resources, it could give a largely increased value to the property rights enjoyed under the Constitution. The Republican party took the additional step of committing the government to the policy of giving to these rights this maximum immediate value. In adopting the policy it acted in good faith, and on the highest prevailing authority.

The fact that any such policy could be adopted was an indication not merely that American agriculture, industry and commerce had become much more unified and interdependent, but that the American people had ceased to be afraid of the Constitution and of the general government. The extra-official organization of the Democracy, which had been gradually completed during the Middle Period, was beginning to have its effect. In all probability the local democracies would never have consented to the increase of power and responsibility of the central government which the Republican national economic policy brought with it, had not the voters been supposed to possess an extra-official means of control. This control had become so effective that the local democracies were no longer apprehensive of being betrayed or even very much interfered with by the central government. For the Republicans had appropriated in its essential particulars the popular partisan organization originated and elaborated by the Jacksonian Democrats. It is true that the Republicans, being composed of different economic classes, were lacking in the quality of being socially homogeneous, so characteristic of the pioneer Democracy, but the lack of unity of feeling was more than made up by a more effective unity of purpose. The Republicans were associated for the attainment of a joint policy; and they could use the same effective means for enforcement of party discipline as could their predecessors. As time went on, the machinery was perfected and the partisan organizations obtained a still firmer grip upon the effective government of the country. Their control of the official machinery became complete. The old suspicions almost completely faded away. The parties owned the government, and the people were supposed to own the parties. Why should the people fear an increase in authority and activity of its own agent?

If it had not been for the memories of the Civil War, another era of good feeling might have ensued. In spite of various ebullitions of discontent among agrarian borrowers and in spite of the occasional eruption of reforming agitations, the American people seemed for a generation to be very well satisfied with the nature and results of their political and economic system. Its machinery not only worked smoothly, but, as an incident of its operation, uttered loud and seductive verbal harmonies. The platforms of the two dominant parties declared the unextinguishable devotion of their numbers both to popular rule and to the Constitution and government of the country. The Republicans forgot that they had once placed human welfare above the Constitution, and became as well satisfied with that instrument as the Whigs had been before them. The Democrats forgot that the Constitution and its government had once seemed dangerously independent of local public opinion and outdid the Republicans in its praise. The two parties, like their predecessors before the war, could not but be affectionately devoted to a body of Law and a government which so enhanced the value of their own services, and which left them so completely the masters of the situation. Government by Law was emphatically and universally extolled, not so much for its own sake as because of the kind of personal partisan government with which it was necessarily associated. All this worship of the Law was considered to be entirely compatible with the utmost contempt for its conscientious administration. The enthusiasm for government by Law would have been very much mitigated in case the laws had been actually enforced. The economic effects of adding to the protection of the Law the encouragement of the economic activities thus protected satisfied public opinion. It was a period of industrial pioneering on a large scale, and its accomplishment was prodigious. Wealth was created and accumulated more quickly than ever before. The public domain was appropriated at an accelerated rate. Industries multiplied throughout the east and the middle west. The American people were enjoying much prosperity and were mad for more.

Nevertheless, beneath the satisfactory superficial results of the system and the apparent complacency of public opinion serious trouble was brewing. Party leaders and party platforms continued to repeat the old formulas and to flourish the old shibboleths; but the actual facts of the political and economic situation had taken on a wholly new meaning. When the Republicans had converted the earlier negative policy of emancipating economic production into a positive policy of comprehensive stimulation, they were apparently doing nothing more than develop an existing system. But in truth the development had been tantamount to transformation. Both the capitalist and the agricultural classes had come to depend for the satisfaction of their interests, not merely on the protection afforded by the Constitution, but on the vigorous stimulation provided by the government. They had profited by legislation in their favor, which, in case it were withdrawn or not supplemented when necessary, might subject them to severe losses or prevent them from making large additional gains. They had not been content to remain within their constitutional fortress and accept the good things which might accumulate automatically for their benefit. They had ventured outside their walls and occupied certain lucrative fields in the neighborhood which could not be so easily and strongly defended. By these means they had largely increased their acquisitions, but they had also become very much more vulnerable. Their acquisitions had to be protected by a mobile army, the creation and provisioning of which created a serious problem for a propertied interest whose resources were enormous, but whose numbers relative to those of the whole population were small.

The disadvantages of the situation were appreciated very slowly, because an exposed position did not seem to be dangerous as long as a serious attack was not threatened. No large part of the American people seemed to object to the most effective possible employment of existing opportunities, natural and artificial, for the acquisition of wealth. Whatever hostility menaced the capitalists did not come so much from the voters as from the extra-official political machinery, whose coöperation had been an essential condition of the adoption of this policy of economic stimulation. From their position behind the breastworks politicians could see how vulnerable the whole system was, not merely to a strong popular attack, but to the raids of casual mercenary bands. They themselves organized raids of this kind so as to compel the capitalist interest to furnish means of defence. They even encouraged the occupation of constantly more advanced but dangerous positions, in order that they might profit from the defensive measures which necessarily followed. In this way an active alliance was created between a certain class of political leaders and a certain class of economic leaders for the sake of occupying as much fertile territory as possible outside the legal and political fortress of the Constitution and of dividing the fruits of the occupation. Both parties to the alliance were the more willing to venture upon this apparently hazardous enterprise, because, if they were caught out, they counted on being able to retire behind the protection of the friendly and impregnable legal defence.

That any such situation could have developed beneath the seductive exterior of the American political and economic system is a sufficient proof that something was radically wrong with the nature and operation of the system itself. Its underlying economic and political assumptions were steadily losing their former serviceability. The central government had been stimulating individual and corporate economic production on the supposition that every economic class was benefiting equally from the stimulation, and that an access of social welfare was an inevitable result. The people had consented to the governmental aggrandizement which accompanied this positive national economic policy, because the success of popular partisan organizations and the control which could be exercised over the official machinery had relieved them of their former suspicions concerning the government. In point of fact the stimulation of productive economic energy no longer contributed necessarily to the public welfare; and the two partisan organizations were no longer instruments of democratic rule. At the very moment when the body of the system was becoming unprecedently huge, its supporting legs were being weakened and were giving way under the burden.

The assumption of a substantial identity between individual and social economic interest had been sufficiently true under the pioneer conditions antecedent to the war. It had, perhaps, been sufficiently true during the two

decades after the war, in which the American industrial
system continued to be essentially in the pioneer stage.
As long as the natural resources of the country remained
disproportionately large compared to the demands which
were being made upon them, the man who developed
them and was paid for his work by their appropriation
was a valuable public servant. The pioneer, in spite of
his aggressive uninformed individualism, was essentially
a good citizen. He was building a society, and he was
himself a social benefactor. His individual purposes had
not betrayed him into an anti-social attitude towards his
fellow-countrymen. His feeling towards them was expansive and generous. He was genuinely though crudely
interested in the enhancement of human life. Until the
last twenty years the system built and maintained by
him did have a large balance of human value to its credit.
The vast hunting-ground of the new continent had provided room for all. The hunter could pursue his quarry
unscrupulously. After slaughtering all the game he
needed, he could, if necessary, burn down the forest in
order to cook his dinner without necessarily doing his
fellow-countrymen any harm. Competition was keen;
but it was competition less for subsistence than for the
largest killing.

Just in proportion, however, as this appropriation and
development of the natural resources of the country
tended, even in a very small degree, to limit the opportunities remaining to other and future adventurers, the unscrupulous individualism of the pioneer was deprived of

its social value.   The enhancement of the life of the conquerors, particularly when the conquerors appropriated
far more than they really needed, brought with it an impoverishment of the lives of those who did not succeed,
or who in the future would not have the same chance to
succeed.   And such a contradiction between the individual and social interest would appear as soon as the element of scarcity value was introduced into the pioneer
economic system.   As a matter of fact, comparative scarcity in certain parts of the country of some essentials of
economic production was apparent even during the pioneer
period; but the effect of the intrusion of scarcity values
was little noticed as long as abundance still existed elsewhere.   Not until the last two decades of the nineteenth
century did the unwelcome visitor begin to knock sedulously on the door.   By the end of the century he had
partly forced his way into the peaceful living room of the
American economic system.   Once inside he knew no
more peace.   Harmony between industrial and social
interest could no longer be automatically created merely
by stimulating individual economic enterprise within the
limits of a few self-executing rules laid down in advance
by society.   Any such harmony, if it were to be attained,
must be patiently contrived by the discriminating exercise of the national will and intelligence.

Thus a system whose dominant policy was the stimulation of economic production no longer contributed to
the enhancement of human values.   A certain proportion
of the American people continued to enjoy its benefits

H

and to live more emancipated lives by virtue of its assistance; but a constantly larger proportion did not. The majority was becoming wage-earners rather than large or small proprietors. The opportunities of securing independence, which had been offered by the exploitation of the public domain to the energetic man without capital, were being restricted, not merely by the increasing scarcity of the physical resources and general economic opportunities, but by the larger capital needed for their sufficiently economic development. The really essential strategic points in the battlefield of business had been appropriated — with the result that their proprietors had obtained an advantage over present and future antagonists. A system which had intended to scatter the benefits of special economic privileges over the whole surface of society, had resulted in the piling up of these benefits on certain limited areas. The attitude of democratic public opinion towards such an economic and political system could not remain acquiescent. Mere stimulation of the production of wealth, which was being distributed in so unequal a manner, was no longer a nationalizing and socializing economic policy. Persistence in such a policy would not help to unify and consolidate the American people. It would, on the contrary, drive them apart by creating real and irreconcilable antagonisms between class and class. If the American democracy proposed to continue its attempt to enhance the value of its citizens' lives by bestowing on them economic security and independence, it must adopt other than the traditional methods.

If the assumption of the national system in the region of economics had broken down, the basis of its political structure was proving to be even more untrustworthy. The partisan organizations, which were created to be the safe, sensitive and efficient agents of popular rule and which were to mediate between the people and their alien government, had ceased to perform any such work. Instead of using the parties to democratize the government, it was becoming necessary to use the government to democratize the parties — to force upon them obedience to the will of their own members. Thus the feeling of mutual confidence which had justified the primitive system of partisan representation, and which contrasted so curiously with the entire lack of confidence in official representation and leadership, faded away. The huge arbitrary power wielded by the heads of the local machines, which was apparently so contradictory but really so inevitable an outcome of government by Law, was being used for the benefit of themselves, their immediate followers and the owners of the largest and most exposed business enterprises. The partisan leaders justified the opposition which the theoretical enemies of any effective concentration of political power have always offered to such concentration. They betrayed their trust.

The Republicans in taking over the system of partisan organization and discipline originated by the Jacksonian Democrats had neglected to remould it and its correlative official machinery in conformity with their own imperative needs. They neglected to convert the whole system into a proper instrument for the realization of their national program. It was all very well for the Democrats, who were united fundamentally by class feeling and similarity of experience and interest, and whose social and economic life was localized and diffused, — it was all very well for the Democrats to organize for the purpose of strengthening the Law and weakening its administration. They had no positive economic and social program to accomplish, and an irresponsible, inefficient and disintegrated administration was an advantage to the party, even if a disadvantage to the nation. But the Republicans were united rather by a positive program than any similarity of feeling, experience and interest. They were seeking to bring together diverse interests, standards and experiences on a comprehensive national platform. Instead of taking community of spirit for granted, they had to build it up and consolidate it by the use of energetic and varied means. Thus an administrative disintegration which was natural and innocuous to a do-nothing individualist democracy was embarrassing and contradictory to a nationalizing democracy. National democracy is tied to the task of supplementing the preëstablished automatic action of the Law by a constant readjustment of official methods, organization and creeds to the needs of its positive purpose; and such a work cannot be accomplished without the assistance of discriminating and responsible expert administrative agencies. The Republicans attempted to carry out a top-heavy, carefully balanced policy of general economic privilege by means of the same machinery that the Democrats used in allowing an automatic and presumptively unprivileged system to realize itself. The strength of the administrative organization and the level of its technical standards were wholly inferior to the requirements of their declared party policy.

In truth the national democracy of the Republicans always remained a hybrid. The party was attempting to accomplish the purposes of a humanized democracy with the machinery of a legalized democracy. It sought to impose a constructive democratic policy on the nation without eradicating a large residue of negative, democratic methods and ideas in its own composition. It built up a national economic system beyond the fortifications of the Constitution; but it wanted that system to enjoy both the privilege of unlimited expansion and the shelter of impregnable and definite walls. Of course the attempt failed. The national economic system cannot be both conquering hero and a timid and cautious dependent on legal bulwarks. It must maintain a progressive outlook and spirit or else lose its vitality and fall back into the merely defensive attitude of constitutional conservatism.

By pushing a national economic policy as far as it did, the Republican party quite unconsciously was both building and destroying better than it knew. Its enterprise was bound to have revolutionary results. The balance between the Law and the government established by the preceding Democracy was upset. A negative do-nothing government was the natural companion of an inaccessible and self-righteous body of public Law. The

government, having been confined by the Law to tasks
of minor importance, did not need to be strong, expert
and efficient. The necessary control did not need to be
exercised by the people directly, but could be handed
over to party organizations which subsisted on this weakness. But the Republicans, as a result of their economic
legislation, bestowed upon the government onerous responsibilities and considerably increased powers. While
the Law still remained technically supreme, the government had really become at least a coördinate power, which
was accomplishing purposes no less essential to the national welfare by the exercise of enormous discretionary
authority. At the same time the instruments whereby
this government was to be controlled in the popular interest, viz., the party organizations, had themselves largely
escaped the popular will. How was this new government,
which the Law continued to control in so far as it threatened the vested rights of property-owners, to be controlled in so far as its action affected popular interests?
Should the balance be restored by a retreat to a do-nothing government, which would work harmoniously with
an inaccessible and autocratic body of Law? Or should
the Law be made less inaccessible and autocratic in conformity with the spirit and needs of an enterprising government? And if the second alternative be adopted,
how was this formidable machine, which became possibly
dangerous to the individual and national interest just in
proportion as it was possibly serviceable, — how was this
machine to be controlled in the interest both of human
welfare and ultimate popular political responsibility?

CHAPTER V

THE NEW ECONOMIC NATIONALISM

I HAVE indicated at the end of the preceding chapter some of the reasons for the eventual collapse of the Republican national economic system. Based as it was on the indiscriminate stimulation of the productive energies of the country, in the benefits of which industry, commerce and agriculture were all supposed to share, it worked sufficiently well so long as the undeveloped and unappropriated natural resources of the country remained comparatively abundant. A steady supply of fresh land, new mines, virgin timber and the like prevented the privilege of appropriation from becoming excessively remunerative. But just as soon as the undeveloped natural resources began to be scarce and to increase considerably in value, the number of people who could take advantage of them became fewer. The system no longer could pretend to accomplish the economic results traditionally associated with American popular government — a socially desirable distribution both of wealth and of economic responsibility, and a steady improvement in the general standard of living.

The system rested on an alliance between the farming, commercial and industrial classes, which had been made economically possible by the advent of the railroad. The members of each of the producing classes were supposed to benefit in substantially equal measures from the stimulation of the economic energies of the country. But at least one of the three classes was in part never satisfied with the fairness of the distribution. The farmers in the newer states, whose industrial development was still rudimentary and who were obliged both to buy and sell in remote markets, were constantly protesting against their economic dependence. During the Middle Period the pioneers fought for and obtained the utmost local independence, but as time went on the later pioneers realized that, even though they had preserved their local political independence, they were losing their economic independence. They were entangled in the meshes of an increasingly centralized economic system, over which they and their state governments could exercise no effective control. Their railroads were owned in the east and managed with frequent disregard for local interests. Large industrial corporations were looming up, which ruthlessly suppressed local competition and at least partially determined prices. Above all, the national credit and currency system was not adapted to their needs. It encouraged them to borrow during periods of prosperity and forced them to pay during periods of depression. The trans-Mississippi farmers could not work their land and profitably dispose of its product without the use of more capital than was necessary to their predecessors. The opportunities offered to them of obtaining loans usually occurred during a semi-speculative boom; and when the debt subsequently fell due, after the boom had subsided, its payment frequently meant the loss of the farm.   The farmers of the newer states were, consequently, never satisfied with the results of the old economic nationalism. The Greenback, Granger, Populist and Silver agitations were the expressions of their discontent.

The phase of the progressive movement formerly known as Republican Insurgency was a final development of the discontent of substantially the same class. In its later form, however, it received a much cooler and more considerate expression. In 1909 when Insurgency gathered to a head, the farmers of the west and northwest had become very prosperous, and their revolt was not due to their own pressing needs. It was rather a natural result of altered economic conditions. The special privileges for which the farmers had traded the artificial stimulation of manufacturing and commerce had been deprived of their former value. The desirable agricultural land having been entered, homesteading ceased to be profitable. The pioneer by disposition could no longer sell his improved but partly exhausted farm and move on to virgin soil. The other rights connected with the public domain, in which the small producing agent had formerly been interested, had become more valuable to the industrial promoter than to the pioneer locator. On the other hand, the corresponding privileges enjoyed by the capitalist class had prodigiously increased in value. Its members had been able to take the utmost advantage of the protective tariff, the lax corporation and railroad laws, and the general disposition to give a loose rein to business. They were appropriating a large share of the benefit which should have gone to the other classes. As soon as the mining and timber rights tended to become scarce, they passed into the hands of capitalist promoters, while capitalist organizers were able, by virtue of a certain control over prices and rates, to make extremely large profits. The stronger, abler and better organized member of the partnership was gradually absorbing most of the benefits of the association. No wonder the free-holding democracy raised a standard of revolt.

Such being its origin, the Insurgent phase of the progressive movement naturally received a negative emphasis. It aimed fundamentally at the correction of abuses, the equalizing of opportunity and the eradication of privilege. The expectation was that if the concentrated economic system could be checked and disintegrated, small local producers, both agricultural and industrial, would have a much better chance of prosperity. The Insurgent program aimed, consequently, at the destruction primarily of the existing centralized organization of industry and commerce. Where destruction was not possible, it accepted the alternative of checking any future development of the tendency and of regulating its still surviving manifestations. Some means were to be found of breaking up large business organizations just in so far as size interfered with the freedom of competition. The tariff was to be revised so that it would no longer divert capital and labor from the land and from local industries into artificial channels whose maintenance was a great burden on the community. The schedule of railroad rates was to be transformed in the interest of local rather than centralized industry. Finally, the grip which the organized capital had obtained upon the banking and credit system of the country was to be loosened, in order that the accumulation of capital would not be invested chiefly for the benefit of any one interest. Associated with this economic program was a group of political reforms, the general object of which was to enable the people to exercise a more effective control over their government.

Although Insurgency originated among the Republicans, a large part of its program was inspired rather by a revival of the older Democratic tradition than by any attempt to reconstitute Republicanism. The Democrats had always upheld the Jeffersonian formula of equal rights for all and special privileges for none as the foundation of a just economic policy. The Republicans had rather sought to build up a comprehensive system of special privilege, in the benefits of which all American citizens were supposed to share. The Insurgent program was primarily an attempt to do away with privilege rather than an attempt to make privilege socially useful. It possessed close analogies to the anti-Whig program of the Jacksonian Democrats. Just as Jackson and his followers in alliance with the Southerners destroyed the National Bank, repealed the tariff of abominations and broke the power of the legislative caucus, so the new Democracy is attacking the money trust, other forms of centralizing capitalist power, a high protective tariff and machine rule — the object being in every case to release local popular political and economic energy from the constraint imposed upon the many by the privileges of the few. The implication is that if these constraints are removed, the mass of the American people will be able by their own efforts and without any artificial assistance to enter into a sufficiently large share of the economic heritage of the country. No doubt parts of the Insurgent program, such as its comparative hospitality to administrative regulation for certain purposes, require a different explanation; but the analogy traced above is significantly close. It helps to explain why the carrying out of this part of the progressive program has been confided to Democrats rather than to present or former Republicans.

The foregoing program, useful and necessary as it is in certain details, does not constitute a sufficiently radical revision of the old national economic system. It shares with that system one fundamental assumption which is the cause of many of our serious difficulties and which a really national economic system must abandon. Both of them assume that the unfettered exercise of those rights of appropriation which are secured to individuals by the Constitution are bound to result in national well-being. The controversy between them really turns upon a choice between two methods of promoting the free, fair and full exercise of the right to acquire and to hold property. The Republicans believed that they could stimulate the exercise of all these privileges to an approximately equal extent. The Insurgents and the Democrats rightly object that the accepted policy of stimulation has been operating much more favorably for some classes than for others. The latter propose, consequently, to get rid of this favoritism, but the equality of right which they wish to restore is an equality which can only operate in favor of the small economic producer and the small property owner. They assume, just as much as the Republicans, that no necessary privilege attaches to property as property, that a system of equal rights wrought in the interest of property owners can be kept an essentially unprivileged system by withdrawing the active encouragement which the government has been granting to specific productive agencies. They ignore in the theoretical statement of their general economic policy the existence of a class to whom the right conferred by the existing legal system to become proprietors is of comparatively little value.

In so far as the old Republican system is confronted by Insurgency and the "New Freedom" of the Democrats, the conflict is merely one between two classes of property owners and capitalist productive agencies. The contemporary descendants of the old territorial democracy have recovered from the illusion that they can enter into a close partnership with the large industrial and banking interests for the exploitation of the opportunities of economic profit. The advantages of such a partnership are largely in favor of the capitalists. If a localized economic system wishes to hold its own against a centralized economic system, it must take care to strip the agencies of big business of every shred of governmental favor. Nay, considering the favors which those agencies have enjoyed in the past, and the grip which they have obtained upon the vitals of the American economic system, they must be discriminated against and reduced to comparative impotence. The American territorial democracy have awakened to the necessity of such a policy in their own class interest. They can, furthermore, make out a strong case on behalf of a large part of the "New Freedom" as a matter not of class but of public interest. Nevertheless, in so far as their policy is dictated by the class interest of the small local producer, both industrial and agricultural, it must be scrutinized carefully and not be allowed to impose itself on public opinion as a comprehensive national policy.

The owners of highly organized industries are usually supposed to be the greatest beneficiaries of the economic changes of the last ten years; but in truth the descendants of the pioneer democracy, just in so far as they remained property-owners, have benefited in much the same way. The value of agricultural land actually doubled from 1900 to 1910; and the increase, so far from being due to more efficient methods of cultivation, was fundamentally speculative. Good agricultural land had become comparatively scarce, and its proprietors, particularly in the case of unusually fertile farms, began to taste the pleasures of rent and often to live the life of a *rentier*. The fraction of the total economic product absorbed by rent is much larger than formerly — a fact which is at least associated with the increased cost of living. "Higher prices," says Professor Simon N. Patten ("Reconstruction of Economic Theory," p. 55), "show that the national income is being transferred from profits to rent and also that localized differential advantage is growing at the expense of centralized wealth. Industries are centralized, in which case their return remains profits; or they are localized, in which case their return is mainly rent. Profit and rent represent two opposing tendencies and from the opposition there developed comes the acutest problem of modern civilization." Again he says, "There is a real opposition of interest between centralized industries whose gains are profits and the localized industries where income is mainly rent. It is possible to aid Illinois farmers at the expense of Pittsburg profits or New York landlords at the expense of those of smaller towns. Neither group, however, has any right to claim that they represent the people. To transfer dollars from New York to Wisconsin is no more to the public interest than a movement in the other direction. Local advantage is absorbed in land values."

Thus the policy of the territorial democracy in attempting to destroy the privileges enjoyed by organized capital cannot fairly be described as one which seeks to abolish all privilege. Rather is it an attempt to do away with one particular kind of favoritism in order that another particular kind of favoritism, which operates in the interest of a larger class, may be released from inconvenient encumbrances. The attempt to accomplish this result may or may not be justifiable; but certainly it cannot be justified by the rule of equal rights for all and special privileges for none. Privilege is none the less privilege because society merely recognizes instead of stimulates its exercise. Local advantages are quite as much a matter of privilege, in their effect upon their proprietors and society, as is an exclusive franchise or a protective duty. Privileges of this kind are an essential part of any system of private property.

Economic reformers of different schools contend, of course, that by means of the single tax or some similar device, all privileges can be eliminated from the economic system. I shall not pause for any careful discussion of this claim. Economic privilege is so plainly the result of a combination of inequalities in individual ability and the institution of private property, and the institution of private property, as we now have it, has its roots buried so deep in the average human nature, that no partial alteration in economic mechanism can possibly eliminate privilege. The single tax reformers and their like ignore or pay too little attention to the human factor in the problem. Unquestionably the institution of private property stimulates human cupidity, particularly under the conditions prevailing since the industrial revolution. A modification of that institution will itself tend to socialize human nature. But to modify is not to eliminate; and as long as private property endures, as it must for a long time, it will carry with it a certain substantial measure of economic privilege. The exclusive possession of any instrument of production bestows upon its owner a necessary advantage over those to whom such possession is denied.

Democrats, who are firm believers in private property, and yet who insist upon the rule of special privileges for none, are the victims of a flagrant self-contradiction. The Republican rule of special privileges for all is less contradictory and promises much more useful results; but in so far as it implies that privileges can be distributed equally as well as generally, it rests on a baleful illusion. The recognition of a necessary inequality and injustice in the operation of the existing institution of private property, coupled with the recognition that the immediate abolition of private property would be both unjust and impracticable, constitutes the foundation of any really national and progressive economic policy. Political agitators are and will remain reluctant to accept this conclusion, because it is always easy and often remunerative to charge their opponents with being friends of privilege; but sincere progressives cannot afford to indulge in the hypocrisy of indicting their opponents for a crime of which they themselves are as plainly, if not so flagrantly, guilty. Neither should progressives even by implication recognize and advertise a principle which is wholly barren as a source of constructive social action.

The notion of the possible existence of an equality of privilege arises from the habit of considering privileges merely in their legal aspect. A right enjoyed under some legal rule should, of course, be declared by the courts without any shred of favoritism; but, while the equal protection of the laws is one thing, their equal operation is a wholly different thing. American democrats have usually hugged the illusion that equality of right would automatically bring with it equality in the exercise of rights. When the result of the exercise of presumably equal rights has been gross inequality of benefit, they seek constantly to repair the damage by abolishing or attenuating rights which seem to be fruitful of inequalities. They argued at first that, inasmuch as the whole field started from the same line, the whole field had had an equal chance to win. When it was found that the fleetest runners were always winning, the privilege of starting with them from the same line seemed to be a poor consolation for constant defeat. The natural inference followed. If the great object of the running was the prize of victory, and if all deserved an equal opportunity of winning the prize, the only fair race was the handicap. Instead of starting equally and finishing unequally, they should start unequally in order that they might finish equally. The sting of inequality was to be assuaged with the salve of promiscuity. Indiscrimination was declared to be the proper antidote to discrimination.

If, however, privilege is conceived from a functional point of view, rather as an opportunity of achievement than as a right of possession, it assumes a different significance. Attention is then fastened upon the human performance rather than the material result. A large amount of inequality and essential injustice has to be accepted for an indefinitely prolonged future in the distribution of material

opportunity; but in the meantime privileges can be gradually socialized in the manner of their exercise.   Instead of
vainly seeking to impose what is intended to be a completely socialized system on a very incompletely socialized
society of men and women, the opportunity is taken of using
the operation of what is in reality an unsocial system in order
to more completely socialize its human instrument.   Those
who enjoy privileges as the result of existing institutions or
of natural gifts must, for the most part, be allowed to keep
them, because their forcible dispossession would merely
be to substitute one injustice for another.   But the privileges which they are allowed to keep they must be educated
or forced to earn.   Society is undoubtedly interested in
affording everybody an opportunity to win prizes in the
race; but it is still more interested in arranging for a fast
race, a real contest and an inspiring victory.   If for the
present a large part of the spoils must belong to the victors,
it is the more necessary to insist that the victors shall be
worthy of the spoils.

The Republican system was, then, justified in frankly
accepting economic privilege as the basis of a democratic
national economy.   Its mistake consisted, not in seeking
to pass privileges around, but in failing to make sure that
every class obtained its full share of these natural and artificial economic opportunities, and in failing to insist that
society as a whole had as much interest in the way in which
privileges were exercised as individuals and classes had
in the way in which they were distributed.   A genuinely
national economic policy will, consequently, seek to modify

the prevailing system in two respects. It will seek to revise the distribution of privileges in the interest of those classes, if any, which are at present economically disfranchised; and it will seek to create a system of special discipline, coextensive with the system of special privilege, the object of which will be the assurance, as the result of its operation, of socially desirable fruits.

As a matter of fact the old economic system failed to recognize the independent existence of one of the major economic classes in the community — that of wage-earners. The early American democracy was, as we have seen, made up of people who possessed or expected to possess property. Its legal system assumed that in safeguarding the rights to property the state was adopting the most effectual possible means of promoting individual independence and social amelioration. It aimed at enhancing human life by increasing the number and security of the property-holders, who were taken to be substantially coextensive with the community of thrifty and laborious men. The notion that the wage-earners as a class would not benefit to any considerable extent from the free and equal exercise of the right to hold and acquire property did not occur to the early American democrat. The wage-earner was conceived to be an economically independent individual, who negotiated with his employer on substantially equal terms and who had the same interest that his employer had in the scrupulous protection of freedom of contract. The legal rights which safeguarded the proprietor in the enjoyment of his property safeguarded the laborer in the enjoyment of the fruits of his labor. These assumptions are now very generally recognized to have erred somewhat on the side of optimism. The actual economic situation of the wage-earner does not correspond with the legal formulas. The wage-earner as an individual has to be satisfied with a share of the economic product apportioned to him by a system over which his fellows exercise little control, — a share which in the case of three-quarters of the adult males and nineteen-twentieths of the adult females in the United States amounts to less than $600 a year. This unimpeachable fact sufficiently indicates the attitude which in the long run wage-earners are bound to adopt towards a system which proposes to enhance human life merely by encouraging the acquisition of property.

In the past the assumption of the traditional system in respect to the wage-earner had more truth in it than it has at present. He was, indeed, always obliged to accept pretty much the reward which the economic system generously granted to him; but for a while the economic system permitted him, if not real independence as a wage-earner, at least a chance of escape. Under the influence of free land and the abundance of economic opportunities, the class of wage-earning laborers interpenetrated constantly with the class of freeholders. Every provident and steady wage-earner carried the title deeds of a farm and of economic independence in his hat. Of late years the same change in economic conditions which has broken the alliance between the agrarian and the capitalist interests has also been dividing the freeholder from the manual worker. Farms have to be bought.

Thrifty wage-earners confide their money to the savings banks. When they take a farm, it is usually as tenant rather than as proprietor. But they rarely take a farm. They have become much more definitely classified in fact and in their own mind as employees. They are now demanding recognition from the legal and economic system of the country as a class to whom equal rights in the possible acquisition of property does not under existing conditions offer the promise for the future traditionally associated with the American democracy.

The claim is confidently made by the advocates of the "New Freedom" that its group of general economic reforms will benefit the wage-earner no less than the local producing agent; but such a claim cannot be sustained. While the wage-earner may benefit in some measure from the revision of the tariff and the promotion of competition, one of the chief causes of high prices is, as Professor Patten points out, the increasing burden of rent which a localized economic system necessarily carries. He will not in the long run obtain his necessities of life any cheaper from a localized than from a centralized economic system; and he will not obtain a higher rate of wages from many small than from a few large employers. On the contrary, a group of small employers are more difficult to coerce or to convert in the interest of a high minimum standard of wages than are a few comparatively large ones. What the wage-earner needs is not the equalization of an existing system of privilege, but the construction of a new system which will repair the inadequacies and redress the grievances of the old.

The aim of the whole program of modern social legislation is at bottom the creation of a new system of special privilege intended for the benefit of a wage-earning rather than a property-owning class. Its assumption is that freedom of contract and the development of a merely competitive system to its highest possible point of fairness and efficiency leaves the wage-earner exposed to exploitation by his employer. If his condition is to be improved, society must interfere in his favor. It must protect him against the accidents of work and life which prevent him from attaining to a higher standard of living by virtue of his own efforts. It must assist him to organize, so that the employer will not have to deal with the comparatively helpless individual, but with much more independent union. Finally it must, so far as practicable, impose upon the industrial system certain minimum standards of security, health, education and remuneration which are necessary to the enjoyment of a wholesome human life. The creation of such a new system of privilege has only just been begun. Many of its methods are still experimental. The extent to which it can succeed in accomplishing its object may still be a matter of reasonable doubt; but there is no doubt at all about its necessity and about its guiding and inspiring purpose. It seeks to modify the economic system so as to substitute for the method of enhancing human life by the automatic operation of an acquisitive motive another method, which makes sure that a sufficient amount of acquisition really occurs, is really earned, and is serviceably distributed.

The creation of this new group of privileges will necessarily require the modification in certain respects of the traditional system of privilege. The better chance of economic emancipation which the wage-earner will enjoy must be purchased in part by a gradual revision of the rules which determine the existing distribution of the economic product. Nevertheless, the new system of privilege will be added to the old rather than substituted for it. The two contain many active and latent possibilities of hostility, which are now and will continue to be troublesome. But the hostility will be irreconcilable only in case privilege continues to be conceived chiefly as a promissory note written by society on behalf of individual and class interests. Such a conception of privilege will provoke an indefinitely prolonged class conflict, which will end in the triumph of the physically strongest and the bankruptcy of society. A privilege is, it is true, a promise to pay, but only for value received. Society is to be made to pay larger and more widely distributed benefits to its constituent class and individuals; they in their turn must provide a sufficient fund from which the payments can be made.

The different groups of economic privilege will never be reconciled merely by being established side by side in the legal system. A genuinely national system must possess unity as well as inclusiveness; and the unity can be obtained only by the active coöperation of its different parts for the realization of a common purpose. The common purpose which must determine the activities of a democracy is the enhancement of human life. The whole system of rights and the whole system of educational discipline which must accompany the exercise of the rights, must be continually appraised and reappraised in reference to their effects on human nature. The problem has become the perfectly concrete one of so arranging the economic and political system that men and women shall neither be deprived of economic benefits nor overloaded with them, and that in any event they shall be worthy of their salt. The conclusion inevitably follows that, in so far as they are not worth their salt, they must be helped, trained and sometimes coerced to become so. Society cannot afford to treat men and women better unless the men and women themselves deserve the better treatment; and society itself as well as men and women individually must take measures to redeem this responsibility.

We shall consider at a later stage of this discussion some of the specific measures which must be undertaken in order to make the American property owner and wage-earner worthy of his hire; but before we discuss the nature of this necessary social discipline, attention must be called to the political consequences of the creation of a system of economic privilege which includes all classes and submits all classes to analogous requirements. Each of the several historical phases of the American economic and legal system carried with it a corresponding modification of the political system. The new phase, which is being so plainly foreshadowed by the prevailing economic and social fermentation, will necessitate similarly radical changes in political ideas and organization.

American political organization will have to be adapted to the accomplishment of affirmative rather than of negative public purposes. The fundamental duty of the state will not be merely the protection of a group of previously defined personal rights, but the conscientious extension of the area of privilege, and the equally conscientious solicitude for its proper exercise. Inasmuch as the well-being of the state will depend primarily upon the manner in which these grave responsibilities are performed, the active part of the political organization should no longer be subjected to the passive part; the government should no longer be subjected to the Law. The economic and social experiments of the past three generations have most assuredly taught the futility of attempting to establish an automatically complete legal and political mechanism. The state lives and grows by what it does rather than by what it is. Its integrity must be a creation rather than a permanent possession; and the work of building up the integrity of its own life is becoming more onerous and more immediately necessary. Precisely because the industrial revolution has imparted such an enormously increased momentum and efficiency to the exercise of existing individual and class rights, a corresponding efficiency and momentum must be imparted to the instruments of social policy, — to the active law-making and law-administering functions of society. An irresponsible democracy and a definitive system of economic privilege are certain to prove incompatible. A responsible democracy and a definitive system of economic privilege will also prove to be incompatible. Equally incompatible will be an irresponsible democracy and a progressive system of privilege. On the other hand, a responsible democracy and a progressive system of privilege may prove to be compatible, but only on condition that their coöperation is faithfully and deliberately brought about by voluntary and well-equipped individual and collective effort.

The Republicans started the work of giving positive economic and social functions to American government; but they did not carry it very far. They could not carry it very far, because they tacitly accepted the traditional assumption of a substantial coincidence between the property-acquiring interest and the public interest. Nevertheless the economic and social policy of progressivism is in a very real sense a development of the Republican system. Republicanism began with the assertion of congressional authority in the interest of a democratic purpose as contrasted with passive constitutionalism. It has used the active powers of the government somewhat unscrupulously for the promotion of what was considered to be a national policy. Although the attempt to realize this policy suffered from the administrative irresponsibility inseparable from its partisan tradition, the increasingly sincere desire to secure the accomplishment of a more national program has of late years resulted in a real improvement in the efficiency of its administrative methods. In all these respects Republicanism has been prophetic of progressivism, but its advance was checked at a certain point by the limitations of its underlying traditions. It refused to go beyond a certain point in subordinating a passive constitutionalism to the superior authority of an active, responsible and efficient government. American parties had been organized to work with the Constitution, and to supply the deficiencies of that document as an instrument of democratic policy. The organization of a strong official government would not only render the Constitution of less importance, it would also tend to dethrone the party machines. It would imply that the government itself was by way of being democratized, and that the democracy no longer needed to depend upon partisan organizations to represent popular purposes. The emancipation of the government from the Law brings with it the emancipation of the democracy from its bondage to partisan organization. The government itself, rather than the parties, is to be responsible for the realization of the popular will.

The history of American economic development in its relation to American political development points to a concomitant and correlative reorganization of both the economic and political systems. A national economic policy of comprehensive but carefully disciplined privilege demands a strong government as its instrument. Such a government could not be controlled by party organizations whose strength depended on the weakness of the official mechanism and which were bound to be weakened just in proportion as the government itself is strengthened. But if the parties cease to be the trusted servants of the American democracy, in what way is the democracy to control this formidable machine which is so steadily and so remorselessly being constructed? May not a government which is strong enough to accomplish the social policy essential to the welfare of a democracy, be too strong for individual, class and popular liberties? The American democracy accepted in the beginning an inaccessible body of Law and an uncontrollable mechanism of government, because the Law promised property to all, and because a government organized to perform such negative functions did not need to be rigidly controlled. This old balance between a negative government and a loose control having been destroyed, how can there be substituted for it a sufficiently complete and safe popular control of an essentially energetic and affirmative government?

Such, in brief, is the situation in which we are left by our historical survey. The remainder of this book will be devoted for the most part to the task of answering the question just propounded; but before beginning that answer, we must pause for a while and consider more closely the existing political and economic situation. Just what is meant by the phrases which have been used in the preceding paragraphs? There is nothing that the ordinary conservative regards with more consternation than any departure from the constitutionalism of the past. If progressivism does bring with it some such departure, how far will it go and what will be left of the traditional Monarchy of the Law? How will the new system provide for the stability, the impersonality, the combination of flexibility with orderly process, which was characteristic of the old? Finally, what human values are involved in the transition? What has been the effect of the traditional system on the individual and the national spirit? And how will the individual and national spirit have to be transformed, in case the Law is to be subordinated to the government instead of the government to the Law?

CHAPTER VI

THE LAW AND ITS BENEVOLENT ADMINISTRATION

IN the foregoing historical sketch I have traced the process whereby a democratic people came to accept a comparatively undemocratic system of law and government. The acceptance of such a system was not, however, equivalent to entire submission to its discipline. In various ways the undemocratic system of law and government was gradually modified at the bidding of democratic convictions, which steadily became more conscious and more insistent. The work of modification has finally reached a stage in which the very foundations of the traditional system are being undermined, and which have created a real conflict between democratic progressivism and legal conservatism. It is time to consider the issues of this conflict more upon their merits; but before we come to such a consideration one more preliminary task remains to be accomplished. Our sketch of the development of the American political system in its relations to the American economic system was not exhaustive. There were neglected certain special aspects of the political system, which must be discussed and understood as a condition of understanding the real issue between current progressivism and current conservatism. We must pause for a moment to consider our political tradition from this somewhat different point of view.

In 1788 the American people could not have digested and did not need more than a slice of democracy. Democracy itself, both in the old world and in the new, was very much of an experiment. It aroused more apprehension among the angels than it did conviction among the fools. It seemed to be and possibly was incapable of providing the stable and orderly government necessary to the successful distribution among the American people of the benefits of their abundant economic heritage. At the same time no foundation existed upon which any government could be built, except one which technically derived its power from the people. The Declaration of Independence had asserted the principle of popular sovereignty. Prevailing political theories endowed the new sovereign with all the prerogatives of the old. The omnipotent ghost once having been prefigured, it was noisily worshipped and most abjectly feared. There must be a throne for the omnipotent people; but the throne and its occupant must be surrounded by a cage. The practical stability and security which the Fathers of the Republic could not find in the democratic principle, they sought for and found in the traditional English reverence for law. Constitutions were established which derived their powers from the popular will, but were chiefly concerned with the establishment of limitations on the source of their authority. The Federal Constitution in particular was framed in order to escape popular control and to substitute the safe sovereignty of the Law for theoretically irresponsible and capricious popular despotism. The irresponsible despot meekly submitted. Demos was so thoroughly scared by his own ghost that when later he sought greater freedom of movement, he obtained his end without disturbing the forms of his bondage.

Rarely, however, has any political contrivance proved to be such a considerable success as the Constitution of the United States. It accomplished the work for which it was established. It has proved to be the centre of gravity of the American political system. "The Constitution has done for us," says Judge Amidon, "what custom, tradition, established order and historic life have done for the nations of the old world." Says President A. Lawrence Lowell still more emphatically: "The Constitution was to us what a king has often been to other nations. It was the symbol and pledge of our national existence and the only object on which the people could expend their new-born loyalty." It is, I think, almost literally true that the Federal Constitution has served the American people in the same way that their national monarchies served the peoples of Europe. During a period in which patriotic feeling was weak and distracted, in which no habit of national association and of mutual good faith had been formed, and in which economic interests were localized and individualized, the Federal Constitution bound the American people together. It provided not merely a flexible framework for their expanding national life and an effective source of political authority, but, as its services became appreciated, an object of veneration and obedience. We need not be surprised that in the end

K

veneration became superstition. The modern democrat, no matter how much he may believe that the limitations imposed by the Constitution have become more disintegrating than binding, should render the most generous recognition to the contribution made by the Constitution to the building of our national political edifice. Whatever the purpose of the Union, the major consequences of its gradual triumph were beneficial to the interests of democracy in America.

The modern democrat should also recognize that the least democratic article in the Constitution contributed effectively to the desirable stability of the early American political system. The machinery of amendment provided by the Constitution did more than anything else to emancipate that instrument from popular control. Its revision required such an emphatic preponderance of approving public opinion that no proposed amendment could be carried by any one political group. All parties understood the futility of inserting amendments in their partisan programs. Proposed changes in the fundamental Law rarely became a matter of practical political discussion. American political controversy was condemned, consequently, to an unedifying superficiality; but there was one great compensation. When Solon imposed a new constitution on Athens, he wanted the original instrument to have a fair trial. He decreed that it should remain unchanged for ten years. The early American law-givers had a plausible excuse for desiring an analogous period of political conformity during the early years of the new Republic. A feeling of security was peculiarly desirable during the first two generations — more desirable, perhaps, than was a greater sincerity and intensity of political experience. The Constitution was really king. Once the kingdom of the Word had been ordained, it was almost as seditious to question the Word as it was to plot against the kingdom. A monarch exists to be obeyed. In the United States, as in other monarchies, unquestioning obedience was erected into the highest of political virtues.

That the American people should have submitted so readily and so patiently to the kingdom of the Constitution is certainly an extraordinary fact. They were predisposed to insubordination rather than subordination, and the centrifugal political forces were insistent, pervasive and powerful. A complete explanation of this fact would afford¹ the guiding clew to American political history, and would carry us far beyond the necessary limits of the present discussion; but the decisive importance of one agency of reconciliation seems sufficiently clear. The American people were reconciled to obedience partly as a consequence of the admirable administration of the new kingdom. By virtue of such administration the possibly remote, rigid and arid monarchy of the Word was converted into a benevolent human dominion, in such wise that this government by Law really became government by a peculiarly qualified body of men. Government by Law, it is true, was supposed to dispense with the need of any such highly responsible human agency. In theory all officials and even all citizens were both equally the servants of the Law, and equally free to place their own interpretation upon its meaning. But in practice this interpretation of the system deprived obedience of its essential quality. The monarchy of the Law could not be worked without the assistance of an administrative aristocracy, who made an exposition of the Law the excuse for mediating between its rigors and prevailing popular needs and opinions.

The early American law-givers, both Federalist and anti-Federalist, were united in their purpose of making the American political system the embodiment of reason and justice. They were fully possessed by the conviction that they could embody in the Law certain principles of natural right, conformity to which would mean salvation for any political body and the opportunity of personal fulfilment for its citizens. When, however, these principles of natural right were definitely formulated, they read, as we have seen, very much the same as did the traditional rights which English citizens had enjoyed under the common law; and as a consequence of this fact American law-givers were confronted with the necessity of solving a momentous and difficult problem. These traditional English rules were intended to protect English citizens against certain specific methods used by the executive to injure their personal liberties. But they were never intended to forbid all the methods which an ingenious and resolute legislative body might use to impair the free enjoyment by the individual of his possessions; and as any such impairment was considered to be as dangerous to natural right as was executive usurpation, the following question had to be answered. By what machinery could legislative bodies be prevented from destroying democracy by plunging it into essentially unjust and unsocial behavior? This question was not answered all at once; but manifestly there was only one way in which it could be answered. In addition to these specific prohibitions, which were inherited from the common law, certain general rules which would affirm the essential principles of natural justice must be established, and these general rules must be declared and applied by the courts in reference to every doubtful exercise of the legislative power of the state.

A tendency to the use of some method of moralizing legislative action was to be observed long before the American political system reached maturity. A number of state courts, during the years immediately succeeding the Declaration of Independence, began to realize the need of general rules of political good behavior, and of an agency to enforce them. These courts declared acts of legislative and administrative authorities of no effect, because such acts were supposed to violate principles of natural right. Principles of natural right had, it is true, never been legalized by any declaration of the sovereign; but the early American jurists were not deterred by any such technical objection. They did not fear to place themselves, as the custodians of these principles of "legal morals," in a position of superiority to the sovereign power in the state, and they could assume such an attitude because of the very general acceptance of a political philosophy which bestowed supreme rational authority over the consciences of good citizens on abstract rules of justice.

The attempt, made by the early state courts, to read their own interpretation of general political principles into the actual law was immediately confronted with most vigorous resistance. The growth of democratic conviction was so rapid that such a flagrant defiance of popular sovereignty could not have prevailed. But while the controversy was still active and undecided, the Federal Constitution was proposed and adopted; and the Federal Constitution, while it afforded no necessary support to the doctrinaire expounders of legal morals, resulted almost immediately in an increase of the power and prestige of the courts. The Federal legal system was not only concerned with the relation between the individual citizen and the general government, but between the general government and the separate states. Federal authority was paramount within its own legitimate sphere of action and powerless beyond. No certainty existed, however, as to the precise limits of its legitimate sphere of action. A large number of questions arose almost immediately concerning both the power of the general government to perform certain specific acts and the power of the states to use their legislative authority in certain ways. In the beginning public opinion was far from being united as to the agency which should be used for the settlement of these controversies.

The Federal Supreme Court, as the authoritative interpreter of the Constitution, was naturally the most conspicuous claimant for the office of final arbiter; but its pretensions were vigorously contested. Jefferson and his followers objected more persistently and energetically to this claim than they did to any other aspect of the Federalist system. They protested not merely in the interest of the states, whose reserved rights might be insidiously impaired by leaving the interpretation of a Federal system to a branch of the central government, but in the interest of the American people. They declared that by this means the political destiny of the nation would be placed in the hands of the Supreme Court. Jefferson was an ardent advocate of the theory that the Constitution was intended to establish three departments of political power coördinate and independent, that they might check and balance one another, and he feared that such an intention would fail, in case any one of them exercised the right "to prescribe rules for the government of the others." "The Constitution," says Jefferson, "on this hypothesis is a mere thing of wax in the hands of the judiciary. It is an axiom of eternal truth in politics that whatever power in any government is independent, is absolute also. Independence can be trusted nowhere but with the people in mass."

In spite of the embittered vigor with which the Jeffersonian Democrats protested against what they considered to be the usurpation of the Federal courts, they made no attempt, after they assumed power, to alter what had already become an established practice. The bestowal of this function on the Supreme Court proved to be every bit as important as Jefferson anticipated. It made the Supreme Court the guiding influence in the national political development; but the Democrats never did anything which looked in the direction of vindicating ultimate popular political responsibility from ʼattenuation at the hands of the judiciary. On the contrary, the subsequent representatives of partisan Democracy, the inheritors of the Jeffersonian tradition, became the warmest and most unqualified advocates of a judicial decision of fundamental political controversies. Their acquiescence was merely an emphatic indication of the existence of a real necessity for an aristocracy of the robe in a legalistic democracy. A system which tends to erect the Law into a permanent and righteous expression of the sovereign will, tends to convert questions of political policy into cases to be decided by a court according to its interpretation of the meaning of the supreme Word.

In the meantime the claim originally advanced by the state courts that they were entitled to declare whether the action of the state legislatures did or did not conform to the principles of natural justice had to be abandoned. The local democracies, which were becoming yearly more assertive and self-confident, would not allow their legislative will to be nullified by the courts except for reasons which could be derived from the state constitutions. In the case of the Federal system, they began to accept with comparatively little hesitation the guidance of the Supreme Court, because in that region popular political responsibility was necessarily equivalent to national rather than local political responsibility. But in their own special bailiwicks they wanted, at least for a while, freedom of collective action; and they would not brook any interference with the clearly expressed local popular will — except that which followed from the exigencies of the Federal system. As a result of these general tendencies, the police power of the state legislatures, under which these bodies became the dominant branch of the state government and enjoyed a large range of legislative discretion, was very much developed.

The results of the assertion by the state legislatures of large discretionary authority indicates, however, that any such assertion was inimical to the spirit of the traditional system. The police power of the legislatures, after having reached a certain development, did not hold its own and began to be attenuated. The state courts little by little reasserted their claim to submit the exercise of legislative discretion to certain tests. They did not derive these tests, as they had formerly, from the principles of natural justice. They managed most ingeniously to deduce them from two or three provisions of the bills of rights; and by this means they vested their reassertion of judicial control upon popular authority. The bills of rights contained certain general rules, the meanings of which were ambiguous and elastic — such, for instance, as that no citizen should be deprived of life, liberty or property without due process of law, or of the equal protection of the laws. These rules had certainly never been framed for the purpose of curbing legislative action. They were intended in the beginning to guarantee to English citizens whose liberties might be threatened by the arbitrary power of the executive, the protection of certain legal forms. The injured citizen obtained thereby his day in court and a full hearing before a magistrate. Or he secured judicial protection against any discrimination by executive officials in the enforcement of the laws. But whatever their original meanings, the state courts used them as a sufficient legal pretext for submitting legislative acts to tests derived from the abstract principles of justice. Under the authority of these rules, the police power of the state legislatures was emasculated; and the system of government by Law at the hands of a judicial aristocracy was perfected.

The desire of the legal profession to protect the property of their clients from damage by adverse legislative action had much to do with the particular development of American jurisprudence; but no such economic motive affords any complete explanation of it. There was logic in it and good intentions as well as special economic interests. There was logic in it, because the unchecked assumption by the legislature of such a considerable discretionary authority would have made that branch of the government paramount over the other branches; and this result would have been wholly obnoxious to the principle of the separation of the powers. The traditional system was not intended to permit the exercise of a paramount legislative authority. There were good intentions in it, because this curb on legislative authority was at least in part desired for the purpose of rationalizing and moralizing the political behavior of the state. In case legislatures had possessed the legal power to commit flagrant acts of economic injustice, all the guarantees of the American system would have been meaningless. For these reasons American public opinion sustained the courts in the assertion of their authority. The manner in which the legislatures actually employed the police power of the state convinced public opinion that its unrestrained exercise was dangerous, and should be checked by a free use of both an executive veto and that of the courts. The American people have never respected and trusted their legislative bodies to anything like the extent that the Englishmen have trusted Parliament; and our American legislatures have rarely deserved the trust.

No matter, consequently, how much such phrases as due process of law and the equal protection of the laws were tortured in order to serve as legal pretexts for judicial control over legislation, the logic of traditional political system demanded that they should be broken upon the rack. That system, according to its original presuppositions, could not survive unless it were rationalized and moralized. The attempt had been made to rationalize it by embodying what were supposed to be fundamental principles of right in the very constitution of the system; and it necessarily followed that the active branches of the government, such as the executive and the legislature, must somehow be subordinated to these rules of justice. When it was found that the specific phrases which were supposed comprehensively to define essential individual liberties, still left to the legislatures so much discretionary authority that the exercise of it would erect them into the paramount branch of the government, it became necessary both to check their tendency to self-aggrandizement and to find warrant for the interference in the bill of rights. The warrant was found, but only with some difficulty and

only by trusting to the courts a discretionary power almost
equal to that which the legislatures had assumed. The
angel of due process of law hovered over the dragon of the
police power and prevented him from becoming the scourge
of the land.

In this way the American system escaped the threat
of legislative omnipotence, but only at the expense of
making another branch of the government preponderant.
The courts could not be said to be omnipotent, because
they were a passive branch of government, and were supposed to decide particular cases rather than to establish
general rules binding on the legislature. But they could
not live up to the responsibility which they had assumed
without attempting to develop constructive principles, to
which subsequent legislative and executive action would
in practice have to conform. As a consequence of their
power to establish these principles and of the acquiescence
therein by public opinion and the active branches of the
government, the American judiciary began to exercise a
positive political function. In relation to all matters of
fundamental importance their opinions came to have a
decisive influence on the policy of the state. Of course
their political influence was exercised in the name of the
Law and was supposed to possess the higher sanction which
the Law in its majesty possesses over the arbitrary action
of the human will; but in point of fact the American people
were not living under a government of laws. What they
had done was to prefer government by one class of
men, viz. the class of lawyers, to that of another class,

viz. the political leaders. This choice was made in obedience to the real necessities of their political system, which bestowed upon the legally trained man a privileged political position and a latently representative character. There is much to be said in its favor; but well as in certain respects it has worked, government by lawyers must not be confused with government by Law. In so far as it was successful, its success was due to the fact, not that it reduced the personal element in government to a minimum, but that it bestowed enormous political power upon a group of specially qualified men.

That so grave a political responsibility should have been intrusted in a democracy to a body of men not specifically elected for a political purpose, constitutes convincing testimony to the almost universal acceptance of certain underlying political convictions by the American people. They allowed the judges to decide political questions for them, only because the judges were supposed to represent the achieved results of political reason. American political welfare was dependent on political dogma. The dogma was embodied in the Law. The Law in its turn needed to be interpreted by a rule of reason. The rule of reason must emanate from the courts, because judicial decisions are determined by reasoning rather than merely by wilful choice. The courts could enforce their decisions with coercive measures only by the coöperation of the active government. They were disinterested and independent. Inasmuch as the American nation possessed an official political creed which required an authoritative exposition, the courts inevitably assumed the function of providing the regular version. The duty of expounding a political philosophy was never, indeed, expressly granted to them. The exercise of such a grave responsibility was without precedent in the English law or in a public law of any other nation. Yet the American courts assumed it for several generations to the apparent satisfaction of American public opinion. Their decisions upon constitutional cases have been filled with dissertations on political science which are of as much interest to students of politics as they are to possible future litigants. These philosophical jurists were actually possessed of an unique power which might have aroused the envy and admiration of the philosophical dogmatists of all ages — the power of making a real world conform without protest to their own ideas of what a world ought to be. They uttered words based upon a free rational interpretation of other words, and lo! men bowed their heads and submitted.

CHAPTER VII

THE LAW AND ITS REACTION

IN the preceding chapter the process whereby the politically privileged class of lawyers succeeded in adapting the kingdom of the Law to the ideals and needs of the American people has been roughly traced. That kingdom proved to have, like other kingdoms, a large element of human discretion in its composition. Its success was due less to the wisdom of the original formulation of the Word than to the ability with which the Word was adapted by the courts to national and local needs. In consequence of this benevolent administration of the Law, the American people cheerfully accepted its supremacy. Of that there can be no doubt. But even though the fact of acquiescence be fully recognized and even though it be admitted that the submission was based on solid reasons, certain grave questions remain to be asked — questions which concern the effect of their submission upon the American people and American public opinion.

Has our benevolent constitutional monarchy had the same reaction on our people that the national monarchies of Europe have had on theirs? The latter have in the long run not merely conferred upon their citizens the blessings of political stability and protection against foreign aggression, but, as an indirect result of these improved political conditions, the European nations have gradually succeeded in obtaining and in usefully exercising an increasing measure of self-government. Have the American people been prepared by the kingdom of the Law for an analogous increase in popular political responsibility? Or is it just as necessary as ever to subordinate the active expression of the prevailing popular will to tests derived from presumably righteous political dogmas and applied by an aristocracy of lawyers? In short, what is the permanent political value of this kingdom of the Law? Must it continue indefinitely to grind out righteous political conduct for the American people? Or has its function been educational as well as practical? Have the American people submitted to their benevolent monarchy, as well-behaved children submit to a schoolmaster, in the expectation of ultimate emancipation? Or has the increasing political maturity of the pupil availed nothing to make future tutelage less necessary?

The foregoing questions are critical and decisive. They should be considered with care and answered with caution. The current issue between conservatism and progressivism hangs upon the nature of the answers. If the traditional system has not been educational in its reaction on American public opinion, the conservative adherence to it in all its essentials becomes nothing other than obscurantism. But · if its reaction has been educational, has not the inevitable result been to make the indefinite perpetuation of some of its specific safeguards less necessary? If the political education of a democracy does not authorize an increasing measure of popular political responsibility, what kind of an education has it been?

When the Fathers founded the Republic and incorporated in its Constitution what they considered to be the fundamental principles of right, they were not seeking to establish a system of popular political education. They believed, on the contrary, that the legal and political machinery would continue to grind out social righteousness, and that this machinery would be as necessary and salutary in the year 2000 as it was at the end of the eighteenth century. But since their day this particular kind of social mechanics has fallen into disrepute. An educational standard has come to prevail. The traditional system is defended, not because it makes popular political education unnecessary, but because it contributes thereto. Progressivism on its part makes analogous claims. The great object of progressives must always be to create a vital relation between progressivism and popular political education. If such a relation cannot be brought about, progressive democracy becomes a snare and an illusion.

Superficially the progressives seem to have the better end of the argument. They can begin by admitting, not that the traditional system ever embodied a permanently valuable formulation of the principles of right and a perfect mechanism of government, but that it did embody a useful working compromise between democracy, the common law and the eighteenth-century ideal of social justice. The monarchy of the Constitution satisfied the current needs and the contemporary conscience of the

American nation. Its government was at once authoritative, national and educational. It instructed the American
people during their collective childhood. It trained them
during their collective youth. With its assistance the American people have become a nation. They have been
habituated to mutual association and joint action. Their
union has been consolidated by a frightful Civil War.
It has been consecrated by a multitude of sacrifices. It
has been symbolized in a succession of national heroes.
Established as it is in the nervous system and in the hearts
of the American people, its composition is similar to that
of the older European nations. Having reached, collectively speaking, a mature age, are not the American people
entitled to a more considerable assumption of their own
political responsibilities? To be sure, an adult is in need
of education quite as much as is a boy or a youth; but he
needs education of a different kind. Has not our royal
Constitution accomplished in this respect the larger and
better part of its work? Should the king and his attend-
ant aristocracy be willing to sacrifice some of their responsibilities and privileges in the interest of their pupil's
further advance?

Educational, moreover, as the monarchy of the Constitution has undoubtedly been, it has been in some respects
educational in spite of itself. If it had been merely a
machine for the grinding out of political righteousness, as
it was usually conceived to be by the Fathers, its effect
would never have been edifying. The American people
were learning quite as much from their own unofficial ex-

periments in democracy as they were from official instruction in the Word. The education which they obtained was the result of an attempt to combine democracy with the rule of a righteous Law. The combination was, as it happened, essentially external. Democracy and a moralistic legalism were both developing, and developing in relation one to the other, but the development was taking place along parallel lines rather than from a common centre. Nevertheless, even under the monarchy of the Constitution, the American people profited by a genuine experience in democracy — enough surely to deprive a more completely democratic polity of its former experimental character. Although the people have never fully exercised their ceremonial power, their supposed actual sovereignty, they have had the illusion of its exercise and their successes have been called the triumph of democracy. They have become more, than ever democratic by conviction, and associate their future as a nation with the success of the democratic ideal.

The very means, however, which were adopted to nationalize the monarchy of the Word and make its effect upon public opinion formative, necessarily restricted the scope and value of its educational contribution. We have seen in the previous chapter that the kingdom of the Law, as a specific and comprehensive formulation of political righteousness, early broke down. In order to protect the monarchy from the aggrandizement of the legislature, it became necessary to call in the assistance of the courts. The interpretation which the Law received at the hands of the courts, rather than the law itself, constituted the effective vehicle of the rule of reason. What the courts were really interpreting was not merely the written Word, but the ideal of justice, which the written Word was supposed to embody. As long as public opinion was agreed upon the general nature of the ideal of justice, it submitted without protest to the interpretation placed upon that ideal by the courts. But whenever serious differences developed in public opinion in respect to the contents of the ideal of justice, the duty of the courts became much more difficult and its dicta much less educational. Such differences raised an embarrassing question which had theretofore been successfully evaded — the question of a possible conflict between Demos and the traditional monarchy. What would happen in case the ideal of justice cherished by popular opinion began to diverge from that particular formulation of justice which had been worked out by the Fathers, which had been sanctioned in the bills of rights, and which had dominated the long and intricate process of judicial interpretation and amplification?

As a matter of fact a divergence of this kind has been growing. The ideal of individual justice is being supplemented by the ideal of social justice. When our constitutions were written, the traditions of the English law, the contemporary political philosophy and the economic situation of the American democracy all conspired to embody in them and their interpretation an extremely individualistic conception of justice — a conception which practically confided social welfare to the free expression of individual interests and individual good intentions. Now the tendency is to conceive the social welfare, not as an end which cannot be left to the happy harmonizing of individual interests, but as an end which must be consciously willed by society and efficiently realized. Society, that is, has become a moral ideal, not independent of the individual but supplementary to him, an ideal which must be pursued less by regulating individual excesses than by the active conscious encouragement of socializing tendencies and purposes.

An inevitable result of this transformation or enlargement of the ideal of justice has been an increasing circumspection in the use by the courts of their discretionary authority. The police power is being emancipated from the restrictions under which it has until recently been exercised; and an increasing responsibility is being thrown upon the legislative machinery. This is as it should be. It indicates clearly that the American democracy is entering upon another phase of its career, in which its further advance in political education will be the result more of a systematic effort to realize its own collective purposes, and less of the benevolent protection of the courts and of their reasonable discourses and rulings. This does not mean necessarily that the legislature will be substituted for the courts as the preponderant branch of the government. It does mean that the government will effectively dictate the Law and that, if possible, the people will effectively control the government.

Now that a plain tendency exists to emancipate legislation from judicial control, the serious practical weakness with which this aspect of the traditional system was afflicted should not escape scrutiny. The rule of reason which it was supposed to bestow on the American nation was based upon passive acquiescence rather than an active and discriminating popular choice. The public opinion which sustained the law was stupefied rather than invigorated by its own acquiescence. If words are to be educational in the highest sense, they must be closely connected with purposive action. The words of the judges, which were uttered in the name of the people, but without their express understanding, could have no permanently and sufficiently formative effect on public opinion. The foundation of the vast and complicated system of public law, which was gradually erected as a safe and dry shelter for the American nation, has necessarily remained verbal, technical and professional. Public opinion has accepted it on trust and from tradition. The American people confided to the courts the duty of thinking over their political system, on the ground that the work of thinking it out had already been satisfactorily performed by the Fathers. Why need a good American ponder about fundamental political problems? The only patriotic and respectable goal of such an exertion was the reward of a foregone conclusion. Inevitably Americans have applied a less shrewd and patient consideration both to the working of their official system and to their actual political experience than they would have done in case the system itself had been supposed to be less consummate. They have become in this respect intellectually irresponsible — which is the one reason why the traditional system required as a condition of its successful operation such a large amount of patriotic exhortation. In spite of the substantial unanimity with which the system was accepted by public opinion, its more intelligent friends have always been conscious of the fundamental insecurity of its foundation. The people bowed their heads to the authorized version, but they were passive in their acceptance, and there was no guarantee against a sudden revolt and the adoption of an unauthorized version. Thus the rule of the Word became the fruitful source of more words. Public opinion had to be assiduously beguiled with praises of the perfection of the system. It had to be assiduously terrorized by threats of the awful consequences which would inevitably result from its impairment or destruction.

The practical weakness was the result of the imperfect relation which was established between democracy and the rule of reason. The democracy was subordinated to the rule of reason in order that its behavior might be moralized and rationalized. Its behavior was made comparatively correct by this device, but correct conduct is a poor substitute for positive good-will. In truth, the traditional system was seeking to escape from the conditions and limitations of its own origin. It was afraid to trust the necessary sources of its own power. Democracy does not consist of a devouring popular sovereignty to which all limitations are essentially obnoxious. Many severe limitations are imposed upon it as a condition of its own self-expression. But democracy as a living political system does demand the effective recognition of ultimate popular political responsibility. The serious criticism which can be directed against the traditional system is that it did not provide a sound and candid method of making popular political responsibility real and effective. The people are to be made responsible, not by acquiescence in a benevolent monarchy of the Word, but by their own disposition and power to prefer the public good. If democracy is to endure, its own essential good-will is the function which must be fortified; and its good-will can be fortified, not by the abdication but by the exercise of its own proper activity. The traditional system cannot permanently reënforce the function of popular self-government. In effect it asks the popular will to express itself in the act of renouncing certain essential political duties. To comply with the demand would in the long run be suicidal to a sincere democracy.

Many friends of the traditional system do not scruple to declare that the real guarantee of political stability and social progress in a constitutional democracy consists in the good-will of a considerable majority of the voters. "We are naturally," says President Lowell ("Essays in Government," p. 126), "in the habit of ascribing to the courts a sort of supernatural power to regulate the affairs of men and to restrain the excesses and curb the passions of the people. We forget that no such power can really exist and that no court can hinder a people that is determined to have its own way; in short, that nothing can control the popular will except the sober good sense of the people themselves." Chief Justice White in a recent speech supplies testimony to the same effect. He says: "The wonderful step in democracy which our fathers took was that they builded the government on the character of the American people. All the restraints which they created of constitutions, of which so much has been said, are, in my opinion, but the superficial view of the subject. The great thought which they conceived, the great thing which they executed, was to bring into being a government which rested on the power of men to restrain themselves." And President Hadley contributes the statement that the real limitation to the unbridled power of majorities is to be found in the habit of the American people of governing themselves by tradition and reason.

The founders of the Republic did not build the government, as Chief Justice White declared, on the character of the American people. Their basic idea and intention rather was to create a system which would make for liberty and justice in spite of the want of character of the American people. The Chief Justice's statement is the result of our subsequent experience with democracy and not of the historical intention of the Fathers. But it is true in substance if not in form. The foundation on which our government has come to be builded is unquestionably the character of the American people, and consequently the really decisive question about the monarchy of the Law concerns not so much what it has done or what it is intended to do, but its present reaction upon popular character and intelligence. The future of American constitutional conservatism depends upon its ability to demonstrate that the continued subordination of the democracy to a specific formulation of the Law, as interpreted according to the light of reason by the courts, will make for popular moral integrity and improvement.   The future of democratic progressivism depends upon the truth of its claim that the emancipation of the democracy from continued allegiance to any specific formulation of the Law, and its increasing ability to act upon its collective purposes, is far more likely to contribute to the moral stamina and the collective enlightenment of the people.   Can there be any doubt as to which of these claims is supported by what we know about the effect of political institutions on human nature?

Let us suppose that a rich man had two sons between whom in his will he proposed to divide his estate.   The elder of these sons, John, was granted by the will complete and undivided control of his half of the property.   The other half was bequeathed to James, the second son, but James's inheritance was placed in trust.   James had the spending of the income of the trust, after the expenses of the trustees and the fees of the lawyers had been deducted, on the condition that he agreed to obey certain rules.   The principal was placed in the hands of the trustees with power to determine the character and the amount of all investments.   As a matter of courtesy and prudence, they consulted James, because he had something to say about the appointment of new trustees, but they were not obliged seriously to consider his opinions.   Indeed in the event of a decisive difference of opinion, it was almost their duty not to follow his advice.   Were they not appointed to protect

James against his own ignorance, inexperience or possible levity?

What would be the inferences which could be fairly drawn from the terms of such a will? What would be its effect upon the characters of John and James? Did the disposition of James's inheritance warrant the inference that in his father's opinion he was possessed of much self-control and character? And might not its effect eventually be to undermine what character he possessed? Would he not be likely to devote more time to the spending of his income than to the management of the inaccessible principal? Would he not inevitably try to evade the rules under which the income was supposed to be spent? And would not the trustees in order to prevent this evasion multiply the specific restraints contained in the rules? Finally, at the end of twenty years who would probably be the better man, John or James? John, it is true, might have squandered his fortune and be penniless, while James would still possess intact both his principal and his income. But I repeat, penniless or not, who would probably be the better man? Who would have lived the braver life? Who would be more likely to possess character, self-control and a lively sense of responsibility?

The Fathers of the Republic intentionally placed the American people in a position resembling to a certain extent that of James. They did not trust him. They could not absolutely guarantee him against the consequences of his own misbehavior, but they could protect his inheritance of ideals and actual or accruing property by placing them beyond his immediate control. James consented, because he really had very little confidence in himself. The trust deed allowed him, not only more liberty than he had enjoyed during the lifetime of his father, but as much liberty as at that time he needed. The opportunities which were offered to him under the trust seemed to be abundant. As a matter of fact they were liberal, considering the day on which the bond was signed. They were sufficiently liberal to enable James to lead during his youth a useful and an invigorating life. But a rule whose restrictions looked liberal, compared to the rigor of a previous tutelage, may after some years of growth become irksome and confining. A rule obedience to which may build up the character of a youth may have a demoralizing effect upon that of an adult. Under such conditions would not the adult express his character, not by meekly submitting to the rule but by energetically striving to throw off the bonds?

The benefits which the American people have derived from their long period of tutelage, and which have been already admitted, could not be purchased except at the cost of certain drawbacks. While they were being treated as juvenile and were in some respects as juvenile as they were being treated, they also had to be treated in some respects as adult. They have been the beneficiaries of a fund, but not its custodians. In respect to the spending of the money they had some responsibility. In respect to its safety they have had very little. For practical purposes they have spent the income much as they pleased without being allowed to touch the capital. This combination of responsibility and irresponsibility has had peculiarly equivocal results. The very security of their political capital has tempted them to waste their political income. They have been accustomed to handle large sums of money; but they have not felt the necessity of saving any part of it or of learning how properly to invest it. They have been boys with some of the responsibilities of men. They have been men subject to the same tutelage as boys. Compared to other historic peoples, they have been at times almost preternaturally good — as good as the best boy in a big school, who earns one hundred per cent in all his studies and goes home with a conscious halo around his head. But after having been very good in school, they have felt so sure of salvation that for the rest of the day they have often been more than usually bad.

Herein is to be found the explanation of that peculiar combination of law and lawlessness characteristic of the American political and economic behavior. The very supremacy of the Law and the domination of the lawyers in respect to the more essential political functions has encouraged lawlessness in respect to less essential activities. In regions effectively controlled by the Law the American democracy has submitted so obediently that as soon as it was free from control it felt authorized to disregard mere legality. In the open prairies beyond the fences the law was everywhere and nowhere. Business of all kinds, public and private, was conducted under a perpetual suspension of the rules. In party politics, for instance, the eagerness of a majority to browbeat a minority has only been equalled by the eagerness of a minority to usurp the functions of a majority. The discretionary powers confided to the legislatures have been systematically abused. They have been wholly unable to earn the respect of their constituents by imposing rules of procedure upon themselves which contributed to the efficient transaction of public business and safeguarded essential public interests. The whole system of popular partisan politics has been little more than a conspiracy to evade the restrictions of the official system and to substitute for it the unprincipled authority of a partisan organization. The American people have been suffering without knowing it from the division of purpose between their democracy and their Law. Although by virtue of the Constitution they have been instructed in citizenship, and although by virtue of their extra-official experiments in popular rule they have been instructed in democracy, a mutually helpful relation has not been created between the civic and the democratic ideals. Their citizenship has lacked energy and conquering power. Their democracy has lacked vision, principle and dignity.

The results of too much Law and too little principle in American economic life have been similar to the results in the region of politics. The rights which were guaranteed by law to the individual existed to be exercised. According to the spirit of the system, their exercise should not be hampered, it should be encouraged. Their value should be increased by permitting the private appropriation of every part of social income. The beneficiary under the trust was licensed to get all he could for himself. To take advantage of the license was almost a public duty, because the trust was intended as much to stimulate the distribution of the social income as it was to guarantee the integrity of the social capital. The one public duty more important than that of exercising a beneficiary's rights under the trust was that of protecting the trust against assailants. As President Wilson says: "The law is not automatic; he [the American citizen] must himself put it into operation, and he must show good cause why the courts should exercise the great powers vested in them." The great public responsibility thrown upon the individual by the traditional system is that of bringing law-suits against anybody who would hamper the legalized distribution of the social income. The expenditure was justified by the trust and needed no more specific sanction. As already indicated, some further rules were drawn up, but the spirit of the system countenanced the evasion and the defiance of these supplementary regulations. If private appropriation of the fund were not in the interest of its beneficiaries, why surround private rights with so many legal guarantees? The licenses were issued to be energetically used. The pioneer and the exploiter in their relation to the public domain, the manufacturer in relation to the tariff, organized business in relation to the corporation laws, small tradesmen in relation to honest weights and measures — in all these and in many similar respects, our fellow-countrymen have felt themselves relieved of any responsibilities except for the accomplishment of a certain result. They have pursued their ends and broken rules in

the course of so doing as sedulously and almost as inno-
cently as boys do out of school.

As a consequence of this general situation, we must be-
ware of attaching too much importance either to the characteristic aberrations of the old American democracy or
its characteristic virtues. Its irresponsibility was that of
a young man who did not feel the necessity of taking life
too seriously, but who was not corrupted by his own wild
oats. With all his vagrancy and wilfulness he remained
pure at heart and eager to learn. His recklessness was at
least in part the result of his irresponsibility. Partisan
politics has been despotic and corrupt, because it was a
substitute instead of a supplement for an effective system
of popular government. The business development of
the country has been lawless, because in the prevalent
confusion between public and private interest the great
American exploiter felt within him the overmastering
impulse of a Higher Law. Such offences against political
sobriety and economic thrift should not be used as an argument against the assumption by the people of a more complete responsibility. In part, at least, they are themselves
the result of an incomplete responsibility. After having
encouraged James to be extravagant by confiding to him
an enormous income and by assuring him in his own despite
of the safety of his principal, we cannot urge mere lavishness
of expenditure as a proof of his inability to undertake the
custody and management of his own fortune.

If his wild oats have not deprived him of his innocence,
neither has the tutelage deprived him of his hardihood and

self-respect. In spite of the admonition of his official tutors, his spirit has not been impoverished. They have done whatever they could to make him apprehensive. They have been assiduous in reminding him that he has learned to swim in shallow water and according to rules which were exhaustively expounded by a procession of pious instructors. They insist with entire truth that his admitted skill in paddling around the pool is no testimony to his abilities as a swimmer in the deep. Swimming in deep water requires courage, endurance, and a readiness to meet unforeseen emergencies which cannot be learned under the eye of a master and under the protected conditions of a pool. Fortunately, however, the democracy has paid very little attention to these admonitions. James has exhibited a certain amount of enterprise even in shallow water. In spirit he has been a great adventurer, and that spirit has persisted. The best promise that the American nation will succeed as a deep-water swimmer consists not so much in its long schooling, beneficial though that has undoubtedly been, but in the confidence with which it stands ready to take the indispensable and irrevocable plunge.

The very act which, from the conservative point of view, indicates either foolhardiness or depravity becomes, from the progressive point of view, the best proof of its own necessity, the best prophecy of its own success. James is claiming the custody of his own political and social inheritance. He is doing so on the ground that the operation of the deed no longer contributes either to the safety and wholesome growth of the fund or to the welfare of its beneficiary.

M

Evidence has been accumulating that the effect of legislative perversion, partisan tyranny and business lawlessness was becoming really poisonous, and would assuredly in the end deprive the American people of the beneficial results of their laborious work of national consolidation. For a long time it was believed that these evils could be checked by the changes in the laws governing political and business behavior and by an improved enforcement of both the new laws and the old. But the multiplication of statutes and even the strengthening of their administration makes the operation of the system more rigorous without providing any remedy for its essential defect. Its essential defect is that of treating the spiritual property of the nation as a fund to be protected instead of a fund to be increased by the manner in which it is employed. It is not a money treasure which is held in trust by the Constitution. It is the life of the American nation. Its rules and its organization can derive their force only from their congruity with the national will and from the vitality of the national will itself.

CHAPTER VIII

THE LAW AND THE FAITH

THE preceding chapter closed with the statement that the very act of democratic self-assertion which from the conservative point of view indicates either a foolhardy or a malign spirit becomes, from a progressive point of view, the best proof of its own necessity and the best prophecy of its own success. Let us look a little further into the meaning of this contrast.

The contrast depends on the widely different value placed upon different methods of either encouraging or sustaining popular political character. Sensible conservatives and sensible progressives agree that no democratic or semi-democratic political system can succeed without the possession on the part of the people of what is known as character. What, then, determines the character of a people? Is it fundamentally a quality of the blood, which deteriorates only when the blood deteriorates and can be improved only with an improvement of stock? Or is it fundamentally a moral quality which conforms rather to the conditions of moral growth and decay? If the latter, what ambiguity about the conditions of moral growth and decay opens the door for such a radical difference of opinion between progressives and conservatives as to the best method of building up popular political character?

The questions raised by a purely physical conception of popular political character are important; but they are irrelevant to our present difficulty. Both progressives and conservatives assume that national traditions, institutions and ideals can and do have a decisive effect in moulding popular political character. The consistent conservative must insist that no matter how excellent the stock from which a democratic people is derived, it cannot dispense with the supremacy of a righteous Law. The progressive must insist that the attempt to impose a specific formulation of the Law upon a democracy in the name of political righteousness will tend, in the long run, to national moral relaxation rather than to national moral vigor. Both parties, that is, are seeking to build up popular political character by means of political institutions and ideals, but one would accomplish this result by making the national will the servant of a specific formulation of the principle of right, while the other would convert the Law into a sensitive and efficient instrument of the national purpose.

Those who would subordinate democracy to the Law must believe in the existence of certain permanent constructive principles of political conduct, to which society must conform and conformity to which is both the evidence of political character and its necessary means of discipline. Those principles not only protect the integrity of society against its enemies, but supply the necessary forms for the free growth of political character behind the legal bulwarks. On the other hand, those who would subordinate the Law to democracy object to the attribution of permanent authority to any particular formulation of political and legal principle. Such social bulwarks become comparable, not to an ordinary fortress, which could be occupied or abandoned according to the exigencies of social policy, but to a great Chinese wall of Law. Its function would be completely to enclose the sacred community, — to constitute a permanent partition between a civilized and a barbarous democracy.

Any such means of protection is very much more successful in keeping civilization from expanding than it is for preventing the inroads of barbarism. No wall is so high and thick and so well defended that the barbarians cannot break through; but the more complete the apparent protection, the more it circumscribes the movements and determines the policy of the company of the elect. The sacred community loses its initiative. Its members in their conceit boast that they are effectually protecting civilization against the inroads of barbarism, whereas in truth they are barring admission to the seeds of growth, and impairing their power of exploring and conquering the supposed wilderness beyond. A nation which needs the protection of walls for any but temporary purposes soon loses the power of conquest. Its expeditions degenerate into mere raids. The wall, which can be nothing more than a temporary convenience, becomes symbolic of a divided will and an apprehensive outlook on life.

The Chinese have not been the only members of the animal kingdom who were the victims of their own means of defence. According to Bergson, a very grave danger threatened the evolution of animal life in its transition from lower to higher forms. At one period a strong tendency existed to incase the animal in a more or less solid sheath, so that it might enjoy permanent protection against its possible enemies. This tendency was itself the result of the increasing mobility of animal life and consequently the increasing ability of animals to destroy one another. But he adds: "This breastplate behind which the animal took shelter constrained it in its movements and sometimes fixed it to one place. It was even condemned to partial slumber. That the arthropods and vertebrates avoided this fate is due to the expansion of the highest forms of life. They supplemented the insufficiency of their protective covering by an agility which enabled them to escape their enemies and also to choose the offensive. A progress of the same kind took place in the evolution of human armaments. The heavy hoplite was supplanted by the legionary; the knight clad in armor had to give place to the light free-moving infantryman; and in a general way, in the evolution of life, just as in the evolution of human society and of individual destinies, the greatest successes have been for those who have accepted the heaviest risks."

Without pushing the analogy too far, may it not be fairly urged that American conservatives want to trust the safety of the nation too much to an external legal

barrier and not enough to its own mobility and its conscious devotion to its own positive ideals? Is not the
conservative element in public opinion likely to encourage
a condition of partial slumber in the body behind the
legal barrier? Does not the most effective protection
which any man and any nation can enjoy consist in faith
in the purpose of their own life and freedom to employ every
method and every instrument required for the realization
of their ends? In short, does not the exaggerated value
which has been attached to constitutional limitations,
and the apprehensive and reactionary state of mind
which has in consequence possessed many patriotic Americans, tend to undermine the foundations in human nature
and human will upon which the whole superstructure
of a progressive democratic society must admittedly be
built?

The character of a nation, like the character of an individual, is wrought not by submissive obedience to the
Law, but by the active assertion of the needs and purposes of its own life. Every conscious formulation of a
really valuable phase of human experience tends to erect
itself into an authoritative Law, and so seeks to bend
the living human will to its dictates and demands. When
the living human will, individual or collective, asserts
its own necessary superiority to such dictation, it is always accused of a more or less impious defiance of salutary traditions and experience; but none the less the
living human will, if it is to continue to live, must continue to assert itself. It cannot derive vitality from any

Law of Salvation. Its vitality depends, that is, not upon knowledge or reason, but the only possible substitute for knowledge — which is faith.

The assurance which American progressivism is gradually acquiring, and of whose necessity it is finally becoming conscious, is merely an expression of faith — faith in the peculiar value and possible reality of its own enterprise, faith in the power of faith. A democracy becomes courageous, progressive and ascendant just in so far as it dares to have faith, and just in so far as it can be faithful without ceasing to be inquisitive. Faith in things unseen and unknown is as indispensable to a progressive democracy as it is to an individual Christian. In the absence of such a faith, a democracy must lean, as the American democracy has leaned in the past, upon some specific formulation of a supposedly or temporarily righteous Law; but just in proportion as it has attained faith it can dispense with any such support. "Before the faith came," says St. Paul in his Epistle to the Galatians, "we were kept under the Law, shut up into the faith, which should afterwards be revealed. Wherefore the Law was our schoolmaster to bring us into Christ, that we might be justified by faith. But after that faith has come, we are no longer under a schoolmaster."

In the foregoing passage St. Paul is addressing a group of Christianized Jews who were seeking salvation by conformity to the traditional Law rather than by faith in the person and mission of Jesus. He is arguing that the

Law, which represented the definite formulation of the Jewish national experience, and the observance of which constituted such a large part of the Jewish national religion, had merely an instrumental and educational value. It had constituted the necessary preparatory discipline for a higher flight of religion. As a result of the consecration of the Law, they had developed not merely a personal but an intensely national religious consciousness, which had made religion the very foundation of public order and the most essential part of their collective life. By virtue of this national religious experience they had become a religious community, qualified for the freedom of a higher justification. The Law, as written in the books and as expounded by the holy doctors, had been their schoolmaster, for whose instruction during their national religious adolescence they might well be grateful; but once Christianity was revealed, the schoolmaster lost his peculiar authority. Thereafter the highroad to salvation was traced by an uncompromising faith, the constructive effect of which was incomparably greater than was conformity to any Law or the study of its learned commentaries.

A similar formula may be applied to the relation between the past and the present of the American democracy. The self-confidence which might be impertinent, presumptuous and foolhardy in a boy or a youth, becomes merely a necessary attribute of the dignity of manhood. While its possession does not mean that a man will succeed, it does mean that without it he can hardly be worthy of success. Of course, if human nature is so essentially erring that it will certainly go astray unless it continues to be personally conducted along the highroad to civilization, then the Law and the schoolmaster constitute our only hope of salvation; but in that case the less said about the character of the American people the better. A political system based upon such a conception of human nature would imply an essential and permanent lack of character on the part of its beneficiaries.

It cannot, however, be too clearly and emphatically stated that the kind of faith which gives dignity and character to a progressive democracy affords no guarantee of the success of the enterprise. The faith which must sustain a democracy is faith in human values, individual and social, not in the accomplishment of specific results. The assumption of a large and a genuine risk is inseparable from a loyal participation in the enterprise; and any success which may be secured will have to be purchased by sacrifices as considerable and as genuine as the risks. Faith is necessary and constructive, precisely because the situation demands both risks and sacrifices, and because the readiness to incur the risk and make the sacrifices is an essential part of political character in a democracy.

No doubt a strong argument can be made in favor of a thoroughgoing experiment in political and social democracy as a really prudent method of meeting modern political and social problems. A manifest tendency towards democracy is beginning to dominate the life of all civilized nations; and the resolute attempt to oppose this tendency seems to be attended with quite as much risk as the resolute attempt to see it through. The risk of failure and the necessity of sacrifice are not confined to progressive democracy, and the assurance of salvation to which American legal conservatives attach so much importance is largely an illusion. Considerations of this kind, however, while they are of some importance, are not decisive. A prudential democracy would be a democracy without power, without character and without ascendancy. It would be a democracy, charged not for action but for reaction, which would be easily discouraged, and whose career would be a series of petty crises and petty remedial expedients. Such a democracy would either have to acquire faith in its own purposes and value, or else become something other than a democracy.

The opponents of a thoroughgoing democracy are justified in scepticism as to the future of the democratic experiment. The political experience of mankind, in so far as it throws light upon the matter, indicates the probability of failure. Very little ground for encouragement can be found in the political history of civilized peoples. By what narrow margin and at what cruel cost have the more civilized people secured the bare essentials of political order and a certain measure of crude justice! How easy will it be to throw away our costly heritage of individual liberty and social security and plunge back into the exhausting and degrading rhythm of despotism and anarchy? How can human nature be expected all of a sudden to attain to the high ideal of individual and collective life implied by progressive democracy? Does the behavior of an American crowd on the night of a presidential election lead one to place any additional confidence in popular self-restraint and sense of responsibility? Nay! let the progressive democrat search his own heart and ask himself whether, in case the larger proportion of his fellow-countrymen were raised to his own exalted level, they still might not fall short of the necessary standard? The refusal to ask too much of human nature in politics should not be confused with an entire lack of confidence in popular political character. Is it unreasonable to believe that our fellow-countrymen will have a much better chance of national political fulfilment, in case they will only remain satisfied with the more modest and safer program to which they are committed by their established system of law and government? That system is based on the firm foundations of the most emphatic success which has been attained in the political experience of our race. Why risk accrued and substantial benefits by a hazardous attempt to overreach the probable limits of successful political achievement?

No entirely satisfactory answer can, I believe, be returned to the scepticism of the preceding paragraph. Precisely because the risk which a thoroughgoing democracy must take is a real risk, the satisfactory demonstration of its probable success, based upon the past political experience of mankind or any existing knowledge of social law, is impossible. In the absence of such a demonstration, a certain amount of judicious scepticism is not unreasonable. The real answer to this sceptical attitude turns upon its suicidal character. It is quite as fatal to the traditional system as to any proposed substitute for the traditional system. The past success of that system is no proof of its ability to meet the critical needs of the immediate future. The political problems of modern nations have, as all must admit, been profoundly altered by changes in social and economic conditions; and these changes have to a certain extent compromised the essential character of the traditional system — that is, the balance it preserved between individual liberty and social coercion, between rights to property and social needs, between the fundamental Law and the government. Changes must be made. Risks must be incurred. It is only a matter of degree. Politics is so far from being an exact science that plausible prudential reasons can be urged against any experiment; but such reasons are not and cannot be conclusive. If our knowledge of politics does not permit us to predict the success of a thoroughgoing democratic experiment, neither does it permit us to prophesy its failure. We have a right to be sceptical of any attempt to reduce political theory to a science of causes and effects. The success of a thoroughgoing democracy is not to be prophesied. It is to be created; and in the process of creation an uncompromising faith in the moral value of democracy is the essential thing.

The acceptance of the progressive democratic faith, consequently, is based on a critical attitude towards certain popular attempts to formulate social knowledge. In renouncing the support of a law of social cause and effect, of any prophecy of probable success, it also renounces allegiance to such a law. A loyal progressive democracy is emancipated not merely from the authority of a legal formulation of social righteousness, but from bondage to a mechanical conception of social causation. The beauty of faith consists in the freedom with which it endows the faithful. Belief in a Law means that we can escape being the victims of the Law only by becoming its conscious servants. The progressive democratic faith means a stubborn insistence upon the conformity of social facts to a social ideal. Those who are to become the chosen people must choose themselves for the distinction and the work. The national will is to make the difference between the social present and the better social future.

The two different formulations of the Law from which the progressive democratic faith will liberate a community are closely allied. The peculiar value which has been attached to the traditional legal and political system of the United States has, indeed, always implied loyalty to an ideal as distinguished from a law of social righteousness; but the significance and the power of the ideal element in the system has been obscured by its identification with a specific formulation of individual rights; and this specific formulation of individual rights, while its immediate origin was historical, was reënforced by its identification with an abstract system of natural law. If the Constitution had not been supposed to embody a

code of socially righteous behavior, it could never have
been erected into a permanent guide to social conduct, and
of course the righteousness of this code in the eyes of its
advocates depended less upon its infusion of ideal social
aspiration than in its boasted formulation of authoritative political and social truth.

When in the nineteenth century a more serious attempt
was made to formulate the necessary laws of social behavior on a scientific basis, the new group of economic
laws resulted in much the same practical political policy
as did the political and social rationalism of the eighteenth
century. The foundation of both of them was an individualistic conception of society, which assumed an
essentially automatic harmony between individual and
social interests. Such was the assumption of the American legal system, because it was willing to trust the social
welfare to the free expression of individual and class economic interests. Such was the assumption of the earlier
economists, who anticipated admirable social results from
the enlightened selfishness of individuals. Both of these
systems recognized the plain fact that individuals were
not always enlightened in the expression of their interests,
and that a certain amount of social correction was required. In so far as the social interest was asserted
against the individual, it necessarily assumed the form
of imposing restraint upon his actions; and thus the
power whereby the government attempted to promote
a specific social interest became known by the utterly
perverted name of this police power. But any such neces-

sity was due merely to lack of knowledge. In so far as the individual economic interest was really enlightened, social welfare could be trusted to its unrestricted action. Social progress resulted automatically from conformity to economic law.

Dogmatic individualism, consequently, entangled the social consummation in a causal process, which condemned it, on the penalty of utter failure, to seek social results by means of conformity to economic law. Conscious attempts to improve social condition by legislation were futile, because, just in so far as they were successful, they would encourage population to multiply up to the improved means of subsistence. From this conclusion scientific individualism passed over into a similarly "scientific" socialism, which proclaimed that the very processes upon which the individualists depended for a social result would accomplish that result only by social revolution. After this social revolution was over and individual rights to property abolished, social amelioration would be brought about, not by trusting everything to individual economic interest, but by trusting nothing to the individual economic interest. Thus the "scientific" forms of both individualism and socialism rest finally on a dogmatic economic determinism, which presumes to define the laws of social causation, and whose ideal necessarily consists in the submission of the individual and social will to the conditions of the social process.

The progressive democratic faith carries with it the liberation of democracy from this class of social pseudo-knowledge. Democracy must risk its future upon the assertion of an express and positive social ideal. The ideal is not, as we shall see presently, unenlightened and blind. On the contrary, it is associated with an increasingly better understanding of the nature and meaning of the essentially social process. But it can never be embodied in a Law which operates independent of the wilful choice of the community. That choice and that choice only gives reality to the Law. In emancipating the democracy from the Law, the faith imposes a responsibility upon the social will commensurate with the degree of emancipation. Thereafter a democracy must choose and manage somehow to be good.

The reader must not assume, however, that because the progressive democratic faith is necessarily based on the primacy of the social will, it brings with it any disparagement of the proper use of the individual and social reason. It does, of course, involve such a disparagement, in case the attempt to rationalize the social process ends in the promulgation of social laws, such as those proclaimed by political rationalists of the eighteenth century and by the earlier economists and sociologists, which either must or should determine the social consummation. The establishment of the progressive democratic faith as the primary creative agency of social improvement necessarily gives to any specific formulations of social law a merely temporary and instrumental value. They have their use for a while and under certain conditions. They constitute the tools which the social will must use in order

N

to accomplish certain specific results or to reach a useful temporary understanding of certain social processes. In this sense democracy is necessarily opposed to intellectualism and allied to pragmatism.

But the brand of intellectualism which sought to prescribe authoritative or necessary forms of social behavior was never really reasonable. It consisted in an attempt to impose permanent rules and laws upon a social process which was too complicated and too wilful to submit to any such dictation. Whenever these laws or rules were made specific, as they were to a very considerable extent by the earlier economists and later to a still greater extent by Karl Marx, social development had a disconcerting way of falsifying their predictions. Whenever they were made extremely vague, as they were by the earlier sociologists, their very generality and vagueness deprived them of significance and fertility. The result of these experimental generalizations of social process and social conduct indicated that the method which these innocent intellectualists had used to subdue the social process to the human reason was in itself unreasonable and inadequate.

I have already referred in some detail to one flagrant example of this inadequacy, but a further examination of the same critical case will help us to understand the contributions made respectively by the will and the reason to human government and the social progress. In a preceding chapter we have seen that government by an essentially authoritative Law, which is based fundamentally on the ability of the reason to formulate the natural laws of social righteousness, has actually to be realized in government by a particular class of men, viz. the lawyers. The prohibitions contained in the constitutions against the violation of specifically formulated individual liberties were soon found to be insufficient. Legislatures could always devise new ways of using the police power, which escaped the grasp of these specific prohibitions, and when as a result the legislatures threatened to become superior to the Law and the dominant branch of the government, the courts intervened to restore the balance. The state courts based their interference on the due process of law and the equal rights clauses of the state constitutions. The Supreme Court used the vague interstate commerce clause of the Federal Constitution or filled out its specific provisions by means of the doctrine of implied powers. The value of these clauses and doctrines to the courts consisted precisely in the ambiguity of their meaning. They could be used as an excuse for the exercise of the courts' judgment as to the meaning or the merits of a piece of legislation. In the exercise of this discretionary power, they were, of course, obliged to make their decisions square with precedent, and they were obliged to consider in each case a group of concrete facts; but not even the warmest advocate of the judicial review will claim that the decision was the automatic result of the application of precedent to a concrete case. The concrete case always provided an opportunity for the exercise of a large amount of discretion in construing the rule and the precedents.

The point is, however, that government by Law was made reasonable, benevolent and human not by the immaculacy or the adequacy of the declared principles of right, but by their interpretations at the hands of the judges. The aspiration for political good behavior, in which the bills of rights had originated, had to be renewed and refreshed by the good-will of the judges and by their ability to throw out concrete expression of this good-will, which proved acceptable to public opinion. The rule of reason was not, consequently, dependent on the reasonableness of the rule; it was dependent upon the reasonable application of the rule. In so far as the rules were reasonably applied, their rationality was, to a really decisive extent, the result of the good-will of the judges; and, of course, in so far as the rules were unreasonably applied, their irrationality was due to judicial malevolence or ineptitude. In either event the reason was born of a specific interpretation, and the reasonable interpretation was the result of a combination of good-will and of some kind of a pertinent rule applied with discrimination to a group of concrete facts.

Professor Roscoe Pound says in this connection: "In a much-quoted case of the fourteenth century, counsel reminded the court that if it did not follow its own decisions no one could know what was the law. One of the judges interposed the suggestion that it was the will of the justices. 'Nay,' corrected the Chief Justice, 'law is reason.' In this antithesis between law and reason we have the root of the matter. Mere will as such has never been able to maintain itself as law. There is no device whereby the Sovereign, whether King Rex or King Demos, may put mere will into laws which suffice for the administration of justice." It is certainly true that mere will as such cannot maintain itself as law. But is it not also true that reason divorced from the will is equally barren in the domain of law? Reason divorced from the will might assure certainty to the law in the sense of repetition or monotony, but justice it would not secure. The attainment of justice in concrete cases implies the exercise of the will to interpret the law in the interest of justice. It implies a conscious desire on the part of the judge to make the rule and the precedent serve the cause of justice. Such is the origin of judicial novelties, of judge-made laws, of the contribution made by the courts to the development of jurisprudence. Such development, when it takes place, is the result neither of the will alone nor of the reason alone, but of a combination of the two. That in the form taken by the decision the essential contribution made by the will is obscured by a screen of reasoning from rules and precedents, must not blind us to the fact that in so far as there is any judge-made law the constructive result is derived from the judge's will as well as the judge's reason.

Such is particularly the case with the part played by the judges in the development of our American constitutional system. The defenders of our benevolent judicial aristocracy claim that judicial decisions, constitutional or other, have no authority except that based on reason. "Decisions," says President Hadley, "furnish precedents, and precedents secure unquestioned acquiescence, because the reason which dictated the first decision still holds good with those who examined the matter impartially in subsequent instances." Be it admitted that government by the courts has contained as large an infusion of reason as the political exercise of that faculty is likely to obtain. The series of fundamental decisions upon which the prevailing construction of the Federal Constitution is based, may fairly be described as the most imposing example of the faithful, discreet and public-spirited exercise of the reasoning faculty offered by the political history of mankind. But in so far as the judges themselves have made any contribution to this admirable structure, their contribution must be derived in part from the arbitrary exercise of the will. It is the will which chooses, insists and dares. The Constitution provided certain limits within which the national development was to take place; but in other respects it offered only ambiguous counsel. Under the leadership of Chief Justice Marshall the Supreme Court selected a specific route along which the nation has ever since continued to travel. The selection was accepted because it proved to be both a safe and a serviceable road. If the choice had been left directly to public opinion, a less safe and serviceable road might well have been selected — although in that case public opinion would have learned more about the national itinerary. But the point is that in making the selection the Supreme Court did not reason merely from precedents. It selected policies. If it had not performed this essentially political function, the Court would never have served, as it has been supposed to do, as the effective promoter of political order and progress.

The conclusion is that you cannot obtain a reasonable human government by enclosing reason within a rule. A reasonable human government must recognize the limits within which precedent and knowledge can be made serviceable to mankind. We cannot derive policy from knowledge alone. On the contrary, social knowledge has been and will be to a constantly greater extent the fruit of policy. Hence the function and the necessity of this progressive democratic faith. It must have the courage to select and to insist and to dare, in the hope that its insistence and daring will make the difference between adding something and adding nothing to the social consummation. Such is the sense in which faith is indispensable to social progress. It is the spiritual possession wherewith a democracy will convert the necessary mechanism of society into the veritable instruments of its needs, and by the use of these instruments, not merely to accomplish, perhaps, certain useful results, but add to the energy and the wealth of its own life.

CHAPTER IX

THE INDIVIDUAL AND SOCIETY

IN the preceding chapter the faith necessary to the fulfilment of the progressive democratic ideal was characterized as implying two sharply distinguished attitudes towards two different types of political and social knowledge. It implies a thoroughgoing scepticism of the attempt to reduce social processes to mechanical law, but it constitutes a sufficient compensation for the lack of any such social knowledge. Scepticism as to the reality of the value of this kind of social knowledge does not involve scepticism of all social knowledge. It is very far from involving either a blind or an unenlightened attitude towards the problem of social progress. The ability to live by and in the progressive democratic faith is the source of the really illuminating social knowledge — of a knowledge which is not merely useful, but binding and regenerating.

The journey which humanity is undertaking towards a completer fulfilment of individual and social life may be helpfully compared to the journey of a company of pilgrims in the dark over a rough and dangerous country towards a goal which is as remote as it is desirable. The journey was begun in response to a forward impulse which was instinctive rather than conscious. Our forbears took to the road uninspired by any understanding of the nature of the goal and undeterred by any anticipation of the difficulties and dangers of the journey. For many centuries they groped their way in the dark and made but little headway. They were constantly being caught out on impossible roads, running up into blind alleys, falling down over disastrous precipices and suffering cruel and terrible losses. But urged on as they were by a vital impulse, they persisted; and their persistence was rewarded. They acquired little by little some familiarity with the more obvious and recurring difficulties of their journey. The repetition and memory of their experience stimulated ingenuity. They began to invent tools which diminished the labor and eased the sufferings of their journey, and which finally enabled them occasionally to pause and consider the nature, object and cost of their enterprise. They began to cherish the illusion or reality of knowledge.

In the mythological history of humanity the birth of knowledge is associated with the birth of sin. The association must be accepted. Good and evil were born at the same time. Before knowledge came the travellers were united by a blind vital impulse, which kept them to the road in spite of the best reasons in the world for discouragement and exhaustion. The birth of knowledge destroyed this vital unity. As soon as the travellers began to learn something about their journey and to reflect upon its circumstances, its cost and its objects, they inevitably regarded the business from different points of the view.

The early instinctive unity of feeling was destroyed, and the continuance of the journey was imperilled as the result of the invention of serviceable instruments for its facilitation.

The most diverse opinions began to be entertained both as to the circumstances of the journey, its cost and its value. Many travellers were so fascinated by the access of light that they proposed entirely to abandon the advance and spend their time in contemplation of its beneficent rays. Others it filled with a sense of personal pride and power. The knowledge which had been acquired so slowly and by the exertions of so many contributors was appropriated and used to sustain flights of individual prowess. Still others were profoundly discouraged. The rays of light were so feeble, the surrounding obscurity so dense and so vast, the journey was so costly and the goal so remote that they protested and refused to proceed. Thus the people who overvalued and those who undervalued the knowledge which their fellows had been acquiring reached the same conclusion. They both declared in substance that the game was not worth the candle, and that they and their fellows would gain nothing from continuing to pay its price, which they could not gain by remaining where they were and contemplating or objurgating their store of knowledge.

The divisions which the birth and development of knowledge had introduced into the company of travellers were, however, less important than the seceders themselves imagined. Knowledge had brought evil with it only because it had also brought good. It was a fundamentally social product. It had been born of the exigencies of social intercourse quite as much as the exigencies of the journey. The recording of experiences and their comparison with other experiences had not stifled invention, but had kindled it. The consequence was that better knowledge of the road, improved instruments of travel and an increasing depth and scope of social interpretation all went hand in hand. If the onward movement of the host was sometimes interrupted by those to whom knowledge had become a stumbling-block, the temporary loss of motion brought with it certain compensations. Although the travellers learned less of the road, because of the arrested motion, they learned, for a while at least, more about one another. When the journey was resumed, as it eventually was, the travellers brought with them an increase of profoundly valuable social experience.

The resumption of the journey meant that the travellers, as the result of an exhaustive contemplation and discussion of the reasons for their hesitation, discouragement or excessive pride, had come to understand better the nature and value of their new instrument of knowledge. The understanding resulted in humility; but the humility did not necessarily justify discouragement. The light of knowledge did not penetrate very far into the surrounding obscurity. The illumination which it afforded, like that of a torch, was limited by the intrinsic power of its rays, and by the actual situation of the torch-bearer. It added little to the enlightenment of the travellers, as long as they remained in one place. The inference was, however, not that the torch was useless, but that the journey should be continued. The torch had been invented primarily as an instrument of travel. Small wonder that if the journey was arrested, the torch ceased to be of very much use. The company must continue to travel, in case they would continue to learn.

As soon as the journey was resumed the travellers began to acquire knowledge at an accelerated rate. The more the torch was used, the more serviceable it became. With the increase of serviceability its duties were multiplied. It began to throw enough light upon the surroundings to permit the drawing of rough maps. Aided by the maps, the travellers began to plan for the immediate future an easier and better itinerary. Roads and bridges were built. Means of subsistence were accumulated. Thus the torch began to serve as something more than the mechanical servant of an onward-moving vital impulse. By virtue of its assistance the blind forward impulse has become a more or less definite and a more or less useful program. The will itself has acquired some enlightenment. It is dedicated not merely to forward movement, but to forward movement informed by a purpose which claims to exercise a temporary authority over the behavior of the travellers.

The transformation of the torch into an immediately practicable itinerary and program tempted some of the travellers again to overestimate its value. They assumed that these temporary itineraries were in reality maps of the whole country, which assured to the travellers a safe journey, uninterrupted progress and a specific and desirable goal. In so doing they not only forgot that their program still remained, and must always remain, only a torch, but that if it did illuminate the whole landscape, the journey would lose its most alluring aspect. A country which is completely explored and charted, an itinerary which is definitely traced and perfectly safe, lose the better part of their interest. The novelty and the adventure cease. Every new day looms up as the confirmation of justifiable anticipations. In a sense the company must continue to travel in order that it may continue to learn, for its knowledge is only an indefinitely prolonged itinerary, but what it learns is merely a confirmation of what it already knows. The journey, as a consequence of losing its novelty, loses its value. Ever since they had attained to a consciousness of the good, the travellers had been sustained in their journey by the will to make the good prevail. They had been inspired not only by the impulse to travel, but by the passion to improve. The conversion of a merely temporary itinerary into a complete map made improvement meaningless and unnecessary.

The specific program which may determine the itinerary of the travellers at any one time can never claim to be quite authoritative. At best it is a plausible guess as to the road which ought to be adopted in the immediate future. The travellers will not be united in its support. Equally well-informed and well-intentioned men may differ as to its availability. What really unites the travellers is not the immediate program, because there will always be many torches, and they can never be improved and fused into a sun which shines for all — for China as well as for Peru, for the future as well as for the present, for the Philistines as well as for the Children of Israel. They are united rather by the conviction that however imperfect the instrument of travel, the journey itself is worth while — by a conscious and loyal preference for the adventures, the penalties, the hardships, the experiences and the compensations of the road. A conviction of this kind if not authoritative is at least binding. It is born of the necessities of a dangerous journey in company with other people through the dark towards a goal which is both inaccessible and valuable. It converts such a journey into a pilgrimage, and it ties the pilgrims together with the bonds of a common faith.

In the absence of such a faith the pilgrims will be lacking in a sufficiently tenacious bond. Individual pilgrims or groups of individual pilgrims can live spiritually upon the will to realize some specific social program and purpose. Unless there were men and women to carry these flaming torches, the work of exploration would cease. But the community as a whole, and the individual pilgrims in so far as they constitute part of the whole community, cannot live spiritually on any such meagre fare. Individual pilgrims frequently make the attempt. They will have nothing to do with their fellow-travellers who prefer different roads. They jeer at the alien torch-bearers and often seek their destruction. It looks sometimes as if the enterprise would be wrecked by such divisions, that the pilgrims would never reach the holy city, because they persisted in quarrelling about the route. If they are kept steadfast, it is by virtue of their faith in the holiness of the city, and they are kept together by being kept steadfast. They may continue their rivalry as to the character of the most available itinerary, but they will not allow the competition fundamentally to divide them one from another. Their rivalry will be subordinated to a sense of unity derived from their faith in the holiness of the city.

Thus in so far as a nation adheres to the progressive faith, it is hitching its wagon to a star. The star does not pretend to shed any light upon the conformation of the country or on the proximate difficulties and dangers of the pilgrimage. For all such illumination the pilgrims must still depend upon their torches—upon definite but tentative programs, prepared by courageous and competent leaders. But the light which the star affords shines steadily and brilliantly, even if it does not illuminate the landscape. By virtue of the faith which its steadfast ascendancy inspires, it helps to create another kind of light and another kind of knowledge. It illuminates because it binds. Travellers who are united by a common and a steadfast faith come to feel peculiarly responsible one to another. The common faith sanctifies those who share it. All the brethren become objects of mutual solicitude. A fellow-feeling is born, which helps and prompts the pilgrims to reach a better mutual understanding.

Thus faith in the unique value of the pilgrimage becomes a profoundly socializing influence. Its substitution for the earlier vital and instinctive homogeneity of the travellers could not be attained without centuries of cross-purposes, misunderstanding, disenchantment and frequent enfeeblement. Cross-purposes, misunderstanding and disenchantment will continue. But cross-purposes are preferable to no purposes. Misunderstanding may be a thorny path to understanding. Disenchantment is frequently a necessary discipline. The conscious bond of a common faith makes not for an indiscriminate fusion, but for a genuinely social union, constituted both by individuals and by those smaller social groups which give direction to so much of individual life. The bond stimulates mutual understanding and is itself strengthened thereby.

As soon as politicians and statesmen divined that the bond of a common faith was a socializing influence, they could not let it work itself out. The faith which in its integrity was a means of emancipation was converted into a means of bondage. Since it tied men together when freely adopted, why should it not be equally efficacious in case it were not freely adopted? The increased sense of mutual responsibility began to assume the form of a co-ordination of conviction. They began to redeem the responsibility by bringing pressure to bear on their less emancipated or more stubborn fellow-pilgrims to accept the faith. The faith had become a necessary social institution, which if it were not accepted must be imposed. The recalcitrant must be coerced into submitting to the discipline and the duties which it involved — coerced not necessarily by force so much as by social constraint of one kind or another.

Such social constraint was probably necessary. It was

certainly efficient. Whatever else it did, it economized the time of the pilgrims, made their journey easier, helped to assure their subsistence, improved their itineraries and enriched their store of inventions and knowledge. But it constituted none the less a perversion of the faith, for once again it attached the faith to a specific program and made of it a torch carried by a few rather than the star which not only binds the pilgrims together, but tends to equalize the bond. The faith can only reach its final ascendancy and its true dignity, in case it is disengaged from the coercive aspect of social construction, and identified with a free recognition of the spiritual value of the holy city and a pilgrimage thereto; and this free acceptance must apply to all. Not until the faith becomes democratic can it be finally emancipated. Its association with democracy means an indefinite extension among the faithful of human sympathy and human understanding.

The pilgrims in the course of their adventurous and dangerous journey towards the holy city are acquiring two kinds of knowledge. They are acquiring a practical knowledge of the road, which assumes the form of temporary and only semi-authoritative itineraries; and they are acquiring a still more evasive and difficult moral and social insight. It sometimes seems as if these two classes of knowledge were mutually independent or perhaps even mutually hostile — as if preoccupation with moral and social truth interfered with the success of the journey, or as if the journey had sometimes to be suspended in order that the pilgrims could reconcile their moral differences

o

and so increase their social knowledge. In truth, however, they are really supplementary, and as the area of knowledge increases they become increasingly dependent. Moral or social knowledge, like knowledge of the road, will fail to increase, should the journey be permanently discontinued; and no matter how useful the torch of practical knowledge may be, the journey will have to be discontinued unless its progress is accompanied by a completer mutual understanding among the pilgrims. Better-prepared itineraries impose upon the travellers more rather than less responsibility, because such itineraries are impossible without the use of tools of all kinds; and this access of mutual responsibility quickens insight into human nature and purposes. A sounder and more adequate individual and social psychology is the necessary agent and friend of an improving social standard.

An adequate individual and social psychology is still a most remote and elusive achievement; but some advance has been made. The knowledge of individual and social life which we crave has an essentially moral character. It can never be attained by describing, analyzing and comparing existing or past individuals and societies one with another. Much can be achieved by means of this process of description, analysis and comparison; but the synthetic ideas upon which the comprehension of this raw knowledge depends must be born of morally and socially creative purposes. Individuals and societies are not natural facts. They are wilful processes — moral creations. Both words are essentially verbal nouns, and mean something which is going on and must continue to go on. Society is the process of socializing. Individuality is the process of individualizing. Neither of these processes is a matter of monotonous repetition. Both of them are consummations and fulfilments, which necessarily carry with them the risk of failure as well as the chance of success.

What we need above all to understand is the relation between these processes of individualizing and socializing. The nature of this relation has constantly been confused by the treatment of individuals and societies, in the forms in which they actually exist, as if they were the real and final subject-matters of social knowledge. When we examine a particular social group, the only component parts thereof which we can actually see are separate individuals, who superficially might or might not be formed into this or any other society. It was inferred, consequently, that society resulted from the mere accretion or combination of individuals, and that if individuals were to be socialized, the chief agency of socialization must be external restraint. The notion that genuine individuals were formed by being separated out from a social complex had no influence on these speculations. The analysis of the situation was completely dominated by the illusion of physical individuality, and by the consequent necessity of merely inferring the existence of other individuals from the testimony of certain physical symptoms. Of course these individualist psychologists recognized the existence of social instincts and emotions, but their general psychological presupposition did not permit them to attach much importance to such instincts. They never recognized the existence of sociality as a primary psychological fact. They never understood that consciousness was as much social as it was individual, and that the existence of other individuals is given in consciousness in the same sense that the existence of the individual is given.

The social process wore a different aspect and assumed a different significance as soon as psychology itself was made essentially social. Individualist psychology necessarily inferred that the social relation could not add anything new to the contents and the meaning of individual minds. Society was constituted by a relation among individuals, which was subject to precise definition. But if consciousness was essentially social, the possibility at least was established of social or collective growth. The association of different minds might result in the creation of something new, which was not given in the contents of the mental partners to the association. The novelty which was added as the result of association could not have existed unless the individual minds had combined, but neither could it have been predicted by any analysis of the ingredients of the combination. Something had been created which possessed the same kind of reality as had the original elements.

One particular school of philosophical idealists had always been attributing, on what were essentially pragmatic grounds, this kind of reality to social combinations. Society was as real to certain of the idealists as were individuals, because the reality of society was a necessary consequence of individual moral needs.   But it has been reserved for recent social psychologists to give a concrete account of the way social minds are formed, and consequently to bring the idea of social minds into relation with the fundamental idea of society as a process.   A society is not made up primarily of individuals.   It is made up of an innumerable number of smaller societies.   Men and women become associated together for the accomplishing of an infinitely large and various number of purposes, and each of these different associations constitutes a society, whose reality is deter- mined by the tenacity and the scope of the purposes which have prompted the association.   Every church, every club, every political and military organization, every labor union, every family, even every temporary social gathering, constitutes a society of a kind.   As the work of socialization progresses, these centres of association tend to become more numerous, more various and more significant, but social- ization none the less does not consist merely in multiplying the objects and enlarging the machinery of association. The societies necessarily seek some form of mutual accommo- dation and adjustment.   They acquire joint responsibilities and seek the realization of common purposes.   Out of these joint responsibilities and common purposes a social ideal gradually emerges.   Society comes to be conceived as a whole, with certain permanent interests and needs, into which the different centres of association must be fitted.

Correlative with this emergence of society as a whole, a different conception of individuality also comes to the surface.   From the point of view of social psychology, the individual, merely in the sense of a man who inhabits a certain body and possesses a certain continuity of organic sensations, is largely an illusion. The individuality of the uncivilized man is merged in that of the societies — the clans, religious sects and the like — to which he belongs. Genuine individuality is also essentially an ideal which does not become of great value to men and women except in a society which has already begun to abstract and to cherish a social ideal. The sacred individual and the sacred community were born of a similar process of abstraction and grow in response to a similar sentiment of loyalty to ideal values.

As the words individual and society, however, are ordinarily used, the value which can be legitimately attributed to individuality and sociality as ideals is constantly being attributed to the merely incipient individuals and societies which are actually participating in the struggle for existence. Both the individual and society are tacitly assumed to be finished achievements instead of formative ideals; and the attempt to define their relation is falsified as a consequence of this initial misconception. The relation between an individual who is only in the process of being individualized and a society which is only in the process of being socialized, is entirely different from the relation between the individual and society conceived as finished products. If both or one be conceived as finished products, the result is a tendency either to sacrifice the individual to society or society to the individual. The interdependence of the two can be conceived only in terms of dependence one upon the other. But if the individual and society are both conceived as formative ideals, which are creating centres of genuine individual and social life out of the materials offered by human nature, then a relation of interdependence can be established between the two, which does not involve the sacrifice either of the individual to society or of society to the individual.

If, then, the progressive democratic faith is to have any meaning, society is not merely a result of the harmony or the conflict of individual interests or wills. It is an end in itself, as is the individual, and correlative with the individual. The individual and the social welfare must both be willed and won from a reluctant world which, if left to its own action, would go ahead regardless of one as of the other. The individual has the best chance of giving integrity to his life in a society which is being informed by the social ideal. The social ideal cannot mould society to its own needs, unless individuals are seeking to give ascendancy to their own lives. But their interdependence does not carry with it any necessary harmony between the individualizing and the socializing process. Although individuals can obtain a higher integrity of life in a formative social medium, they will never be saved merely as a result of social salvation. Although an advance towards social salvation will be accelerated by increasing individual integrity, society will never be saved as a consequence of the regeneration of individuals. The two ideals cannot become sufficiently interdependent without retaining a large measure of independence.

The faith which a progressive democracy needs does not become effective, consequently, through the agency of individual ideals. It becomes effective through the agency of a social ideal which differs from and is independent of any collection of individual ideals. The existence of an effective social ideal is none the less real because it has no specific habitation as concrete and as visible as the individual body. A habitation it has in the whole group of political and social institutions which have been wrought as the instruments of its purposes; but in spite of this residence, it always requires an effort of the imagination to conceive the social mind and will as possessed of just as much reality as individual minds and wills. The social will is creating an increasing and an ascendant society out of the material afforded by human nature, just as the individual will creates individuals out of similar material.

CHAPTER X

The Ideal and the Program

THE conception of individual and social fulfilment briefly sketched in the preceding chapter, consisted in only a general formula. The application of this formula to the actual situation and problems of the American democracy remains to be considered. The American nation is not society in general. It is a particular society with a history, traditions, achievements, resources and purposes of its own. If we assume that the American nation, in so far as it accepts the ideal of progressive democracy, is obliged to live by faith, we must consider how far a faith of this kind has an ancestry in the national tradition and how far it can discover any available instruments in the national organization and institutions.

The extent to which a nation may dare to live by faith will depend upon the extent of its past political and social attainments. The impulse which urged the human race forward during the early part of the journey was, as we have seen, chiefly instinctive. After many centuries of blind striving and after many calamities and failures, a conscious faith began to emerge as a result of the reflection of the more enlightened peoples upon their own experience. Such a faith once having been proclaimed, it became as a star in the heavens. But its immediate value to any particular group of pilgrims depended upon their ability to profit by it. It burns bright or dim, and saves or betrays, according to the ability of the pilgrims to see the light, to cleave to it and to share it. Just as the Christian faith cannot regenerate an individual savage, and must be embodied for the savage's benefit in specific rules, which are authoritatively interpreted by priests or by some other method of tutelage, so a democratic faith cannot regenerate a nation, unless that nation has been gradually educated by its own national experience up to the required level. The most luminous and the most soaring expression which the progressive democratic faith has ever received was uttered by the Italian Mazzini; but the Italians of his generation were not prepared to live by it. It had never been wrought into their national consciousness as a result of the educational effect of their national experience. If they had scorned the kind of monarchical tutelage to which they were accustomed by their political traditions, and which helped to establish them in the confidence of their European neighbors, they might have eventually succeeded in founding a social democracy, but only after convulsions and tribulations analogous to those which have beset the career of the French democracy.

The national experience of the American people has prepared them to live by faith. Their political and economic education has reached a stage which necessitates, as a condition of any further national advance, the emancipation of the national will from specific tutelage, and the frank reliance for the building up of the national life upon the good faith with which, collectively and individually, they seek to realize the national or, if you prefer, the social purpose. Perhaps the most fruitful lesson taught by modern psychology is that men do not act well merely because they are enlightened, but that they are in a large measure enlightened because they act well. The lesson applies to nations no less than to individuals. If the American nation is gradually to become more enlightened, its enlightenment must be, to a large extent, the fruit of collective and coöperative action, directed and inspired by the ideal of social democracy.

When in a previous chapter the American nation was compared to a youth, who under experienced guidance had grown to maturity, and who as the result of his experience could and should dispense with the former tutelage, the analogy had a foundation of literal truth. Sound social psychology enables us to attribute to a nation which has made sacrifices on behalf of its own national unity, a higher degree of reality than can be attributed to the great majority of its individual citizens. American nationality has been created by virtue of the binding effect of the attempt to realize certain common political and social purposes. Four generations ago the nation was really immature, because it lacked the consciousness of its own essential common objects and because the instruments necessary for their realization had not been forged. It possessed, on the one hand, a vague aspiration for social righteousness. It possessed, on the other hand, extraordinary op-

portunities for contributing to the economic welfare of
its citizens. The aspiration for social righteousness or
betterment was, consequently, expressed in an energetic
and single-minded effort to increase the total economic
income and to distribute it over the widest possible area.
This task was thoroughly, comprehensively and constructively national. It was imposed upon the new body politic
by its social ideal, by its partially popular political institutions, by the nature of its geographical and physical
environment, and by the expectations of its citizens. The
possession by the nation of a vast but wholly undeveloped
domain constituted the decisive fact. The public lands
abounded in sources of individual economic independence,
which could be made available and appropriated only as
the result of national policy. Yet the nation which had to
work out this policy had only just been born. It had taken
over at the beginning of its career a most exacting ideal
and had assumed a most onerous responsibility. It was
obliged to work out an immediate method of redeeming this
responsibility, which did not conflict with the prevailing
formulation of social justice.

The result was the concealment of the novel social purpose under a traditional legal and economic mechanism.
The paternal solicitude of the nation for the economic
welfare of its citizens was disguised under the official pre-
tence that the individual was earning by his own efforts
the share of the national property and income which he
could appropriate; but as a matter of fact the average
American citizen from the outset owed more to the oppor-

tunities freely conferred on him by the nation than he did
to his own exertions. The system of law and government
was organized not merely to prevent any harm from over-
taking the individual, but to secure the general dissem-
ination of wealth. Property was rigidly protected, but
only in the confident expectation that it would be widely
and wholesomely distributed. Liberty was glorified chiefly
because it was intended and expected to result in equality.
Thus the American nation, in spite of its parade of individualism and in spite of its individualist legal and economic
methods, was fundamentally more socialized in purpose
than were the European countries.

The American nation was really young, because its underlying national purpose was novel, and because the methods
whereby that purpose was to be realized had not been
tested and developed by experience. For the time being it
had the same kind of reasons for accepting tutelage that
the Italians had fifty years ago. Until the habit of national association had been established, until the natural
resources had been developed, until a preliminary adjustment had been reached among the distracting interests
of classes and sections, until a national consciousness,
capable of assimilating national experience, had been
formed, the American people wisely leaned for support and
counsel upon the political and social experience of other
peoples. It accepted a specific legal formulation of this
experience and agreed to be guided and ruled by its
spirit and letter. Thus it became the first complete
prig in the history of nations. As George Santayana

says,[1] "America is a young country with an old mentality;
it has enjoyed the advantages of a child carefully brought
up and thoroughly indoctrinated; it has been a wise child.
But a wise child, an old head on young shoulders, always
has a comic and unpromising side. The wisdom is a little
thin and verbal, not aware of its full meaning and grounds;
and physical and mental growth may be stunted by it and
even deranged."

As a matter of fact, the nation's physical and mental
growth was not stunted by its mental precocity, because,
as we have already seen, the wise child forgot a good deal
of his wisdom as soon as he was out of the schoolroom.
His precocity was not due to any lack of vitality. He began immediately to make experiments of his own in politics
and economics, the nature of which was, indeed, partly
determined by the doctrines of the school, but which had
also an independent value. By these means the growing
child did something to form his character and to accumulate
a fund of personal experience. He acquired self-confidence;
he learned to know the land in which he lived; he learned
to use the tools and machinery necessary for its cultivation;
he began gradually to contribute to his own support. Thus
little by little he reached the stature of a man — leading in
the meantime a dual life and purchasing, as we have seen,
by his good behavior in school the right to be somewhat
unruly outside.

If as a consequence of the division between his will and
his intelligence any deterioration of character or derange-

[1] "Winds of Doctrine,' p. 187.

ment of the emotions had taken place, the derangement resulted not so much from the fact of the tutelage as from its undesirable prolongation. Instead of being diminished as the pupil became older, the supervision and the instruction had a tendency to increase, because in so far as the wise youth was left to himself he was not behaving wisely. The pupil did not very much object to the increasing supervision. A large part of his time was still spent outside of the schoolroom in legally irresponsible occupations; and he was willing to pay for an increasing irresponsibility after school hours by an increasing tutelage during those hours. He had acquired certain bad habits. He had become accustomed to taking life too easily, to depending overmuch upon the repetition of sacred words, and to concealing an actual lawlessness of behavior with a mock homage to the forms of law. He was ceasing to be a prig and threatening to become a hypocritical libertine. During the last quarter of a century general relaxation of American moral fibre has unquestionably been taking place; and in spite of the increasing use of disciplinary measures, the process of relaxation has not as yet been fairly checked.

The effective way not merely to check but possibly to cure it, is to release the pupil from the school and to bestow upon him the responsibilities of a man. The American nation must have a man's opportunity to determine his own life, to make his own mistakes, and to learn his own lessons. If the long period of tutelage has not prepared him for the responsibilities of manhood, he never will be prepared, and the confession should frankly be made that the method of education adopted by the Fathers has been a failure — that the attempt to enlighten the national will has resulted only in its enfeeblement.

Progressivism testifies and insists that the national will, in spite of certain tendencies to relaxation, has not been enfeebled. The nation, after an enervating course of too much rich food and strong wine, is trying to pull itself together for a new attack upon the problems of its life. That is the salutary fact. In the very attempt to pull itself together and to release its collective life from the bondage to bad habits, it is obliged also to throw off the apprehensions with which its bad habits were associated. The effort itself, in so far as it is sincere and enlightened, will be liberating. The prig, we may anticipate, will be buried in the same grave as the libertine. The national will and the national intelligence may be brought into mutually helpful rather than mutually hostile relations. The American democracy, instead of depending for its integrity upon a submissive attitude on the part of its collective will to a specific formulation of previous social and political experience, is to make its own integrity the fundamental object of its conscious effort. It is likely to misinterpret the experience of others, unless it seeks an equally valid experience of its own. The national will has the responsibility of being the custodian and the creator instead of the servant of the national ideal.

The national ideal in its essential aspect has consisted not in the specific formulation of legal and economic individualism which was wrought into our constitutions, but in a much vaguer demand for a righteous political and social system. The distinctive feature of the American political body is the presence of such a demand for social righteousness as a formative influence at the foundation of the Republic. European nations were the result far more of accidental historical forces, and their unity is still dependent upon fidelity to arbitrary historical traditions. But American nationality was associated at its birth with the attempt to create a righteous political and social system. In the course of four generations this ideal of social righteousness has been gradually disentangled from the specific formulation in which lawyers and political thinkers embodied it at the end of the eighteenth century. The bondage of the national will has been due, not to the existence of the ideal, adhesion to which would always be binding and liberating, but to the sacredness attached to a particular method of applying the ideal, which was the result of a genuine and valuable but limited and, in part, superseded phase of political and social experience.

Coincident with the demand that the American nation should be dedicated to social righteousness, there emerged an equally peremptory demand for effective popular political authority. The attempt of the jurist to give explicit expression in the law to the ideal of social justice occurred in the closest historical proximity with the democratic affirmation that all fundamental law must be expressly validated by the popular will. The association was not accidental. The ultimate problem of democracy was clearly propounded. Popular political authority must be real and it must make for social righteousness. How was the socially righteous expression of the popular will to be brought about?

In framing the traditional political system the Fathers believed they could guarantee the righteous expression of the popular will by a permanent definition of the fundamental principles of right, by incorporating these specific principles in the fundamental law and by imposing obedience to these principles on the organs of government whereby the popular will was expressed. Considering the prevailing conceptions of the nature of political sovereignty and the function and powers of the human reason, they could hardly have adopted any other method. But another method did exist and continues to exist. It is bound to be tried by the political enterprise of an age which possesses a different conception of the nature of political sovereignty, which has abandoned the innocent yet pedantic rationalism of the eighteenth century, and which can build on the results of four generations of national political experience.

The alternative method is fundamentally educational instead of fundamentally pedagogic. The American nation is no longer to be instructed as to its duty by the Law and the lawyers. It is to receive its instruction as the result of a loyal attempt to realize in collective action and by virtue of the active exercise of popular political authority its ideal of social justice. The attempt can be made more safely now than it could four generations ago, because the ideal of justice and the habit of orderly procedure have been

wrought into the American national consciousness; but
safety is not its peculiar virtue. It is the one method
which may be able to call up moral and intellectual resources needed by a progressive democratic society. If the
ideal of social righteousness is to be realized at all, it can be
realized only in a thoroughgoing political democracy.
The socially righteous expression of the popular will is to
be brought about by frank and complete confidence in its
own necessary and ultimate custodian. This faith is in
itself educational in the deepest and most fruitful meaning of that word. However unsatisfactory its immediate
results may be, it is a challenge to human nature to put forth
its best behavior. The value of the social structure is
commensurate with the value of the accompanying educational discipline and enlightenment. A better society may
be built up, but only in so far as better men and women
are called forth by the work. Human beings are at once
the designers of the house, its artisans, its materials, and
its fruits.

Progressivism means a relation between political and
social democracy which is both mutually dependent and
mutually supplementary. Thoroughgoing political democracy is unnecessary and meaningless except for the purpose of realizing the ideal of social justice. The ideal of
social justice is so exacting and so comprehensive that it
cannot be progressively attained by any agency, save by
the loyal and intelligent devotion of the popular will. If
democracy is aiming at anything less comprehensive and
ultimate than the ideal of social righteousness, this limited

task would be capable of more precise definition and might conceivably be imposed upon society by Law. But if democracy is aiming at the ideal of social righteousness, the will of the whole people can be the only possible custodian and creator of so momentous and exacting an enterprise. The people are made whole by virtue of the consecration of their collective efforts to the realization of an ideal of social justice..

The close connection exhibited in the recent history of the progressive movement between the increase of popular political power and of social legislation is an evidence of the necessary formative relation between political and social democracy. Political democracy is impoverished and sterile as soon as it becomes divorced from a social program. A social program becomes dangerous to popular liberty, in case it is not authorized by the free choice of the popular will. There is nothing to be gained by emancipating popular political power, and by providing it with adequate instruments for the realization of its purposes, unless this emancipated will is consecrated to the establishment of worthy moral and social purposes. But a social program which is to be carried out by an increased use of legislative and administrative power cannot be allowed to escape popular control. Effective popular control was not considered necessary under the traditional system, because a supposedly do-nothing government was not dangerous. Even so, as has been pointed out in the historical introduction, the supposedly do-nothing government soon began to assume active and positive functions and was balanced by the organization of a free partisan democracy. But a social program ,demands much more powerful and efficient government instruments than did the old national economic program, and such instruments must be kept in the most intimate possible relation with the popular will.

The Fathers were entirely justified in believing that the devotion of the people to the ideal of social righteousness could not be taken for granted. Their lawful children at ,the present day are equally justified in protesting against the extent to which political democrats do take some such devotion for granted. One of the great weaknesses of professional democrats in this country has been their tendency to conceive democracy as essentially a matter of popular political machinery. From their point of view the way to assure the preservation of a democratic social system was to enable the people to vote upon the qualifications of the maximum number of public officials and the maximum number of public measures. They did not pretend that the people could not go wrong; but they conceived democracy as an air-ship with an automatic balancing and stabilizing mechanism. The free use of the ballot box was sufficient to render it proof against fools and knaves. This conception of democracy, precisely because it fails to associate democracy with the conscious realization of a social ideal, always assumes a negative emphasis. Its dominant object is not to give positive momentum and direction to popular rule. It seeks, above all, to prevent the people from being betrayed — from being imposed upon by unpopular policies and unrepresentative officials. But to indoctrinate and organize one's life chiefly for the purpose of avoiding betrayal is to invite sterility and disintegration. Any such negative formulation of the democratic purpose is in point of fact derived from the alliance of the old American democracy with a system of Law which had usurped the essential responsibilities of the popular will, and which had communicated to democracy its own underlying atmosphere of suspicion and apprehension.

If the devotion of the popular will to the ideal of social righteousness cannot be taken for granted, neither can we assume that social righteousness can in the long run be attained by any agency, save by the free conscious and loyal devotion to it of the popular will. At different times in the past benevolent governments, both political and ecclesiastical, have imposed social benefits upon subservient people; but such benefits could never go very far. In proportion as the program of social benefaction has attained scope and integrity, its wholesome realization has become dependent upon a more active and a more general support from popular public opinion. The amount of assistance which a people can wholesomely receive from the government depends upon the amount of public interest and public spirit which the governmental mechanism and policy demands of them. A government does not become undesirably paternal merely as a consequence of the scope of its social program. The policy or the impolicy of its fatherly interest in the welfare of its citizens depends less upon the extent of its active solicitude for them than upon the extent to which this active solicitude is the result of a free and real choice of the popular will. The political system of the United States, even when the government was most limited in its activities, was always extremely paternal, because it was always seeking to guide the American democracy in the path of righteousness by means of the monarchy of the Law and an aristocracy of the robe, but without any effective consultation with public opinion. A political system in which the government was more active and yet more responsive to the popular will, might be essentially less paternal than was the American system when its advocates were most loudly and fondly celebrating its repudiation of paternalism. The more conscious, the more comprehensive and the more enlightened the ideal of social righteousness becomes, the more completely must it be sustained by the explicit, reiterated and loyal expression of the popular will.

Inasmuch as the connection between the ideal of social righteousness and the popular will cannot be taken for granted, it must be created. It is being created by the faith which underlies progressive democracy. Progressive democracy can no more get along without it than an airship can dispense with an engine. Its value should be as widely and as persistently inculcated in a democracy as the worship of the Constitution formerly was, for it is the foundation not only of the liberty of the American people, but of their ability to convert civil and political liberty into a socially desirable consummation.

But the verbal affirmation and inculcation of a faith is only the beginning. The loyal devotion to an ideal of social

righteousness will not as the mere result of its own affirmative power bring into being social righteousness. The
ideal must be embodied in a temporary program. The
program must be realized by legislative and administrative action. The governmental action must conform to
certain conditions which will serve to make of it an honest
step towards the ideal of social democracy. It must be a
genuine expression of the popular preference, and it must
be adapted to the efficient accomplishment of its immediate
purpose. If it conforms to these conditions, it will be
constructive not merely in the obvious sense but in the
sense of being educational. A nation which does not act
sincerely and intelligently in the interest of its collective
purpose will not learn much from its own experience.
Societies will never be socialized out of scripts, speeches,
exhortations and creeds, unless their interest has been
aroused, their attention concentrated, and their will disciplined by loyal action on behalf of the social ideal. The
attempt to redeem by practical action a comprehensive
social responsibility derives its peculiar value less from
the probability of any emphatic immediate success than
from the demands which it makes upon its supporters.
Every specific program which is honestly intended to
work for social betterment issues a challenge to its advocates for careful preparation, for disinterested self-devotion,
and for a candid appraisal of any possible results. The
popular will cannot be sincerely expressed in such a program without also being strengthened and enlightened.
A social atmosphere will be created of enterprise, of accom-

plishment, of moral earnestness and of inexhaustible curiosity, which will help to make the systematic inculcation of the faith really fruitful.

Progressive democracy is bound to keep its immediate and specific social program disengaged from its ideal of social righteousness. The immediate program is only the temporary instrument, which must be continually reformed and readjusted as a result of the experience gained by its experimental application. To return to our former analogy, it is the torch with which the nation gropes its way in the direction of the star. Dogmatic individualism and dogmatic socialism both conceive their specific programs, their immediate itineraries, as an adequate and a safe guide-book for the entire journey. Progressive democracy must abandon the illusion of any such assurance. No matter how firmly the progressive democrat may believe that his torch is radiating within the limits of its power the light of truth, no matter how confidently he may anticipate an acceleration of speed as a consequence of the increased power of the torch, he must still carefully distinguish between his itinerary and his goal. The goal is sacred. The program is fluid. The pilgrims can trust to the torch only in case they constantly alter and improve it, in order to meet the restless and exacting exigencies of the journey.

If the American people had been able from the beginning to distinguish their social ideal from their social program, they would have saved themselves many costly mistakes. They started on their national career with a serviceable

torch, labelled the bill of rights.   But instead of conceiving
it as a torch, they conceived it as a radiant sun of political
and social knowledge, which illuminated their whole national future.   In case they had acted on this conception,
they would not have had any national career.   A future
which is illuminated offers no attractions to the will.
But they neither abandoned this conception of the bill of
rights nor acted on it.   They talked as if their program
was the last word of political and social wisdom.   They
behaved as if it were a useful itinerary for a nation which
 was starting out on an exploring expedition.   They converted the bill of rights into a positive national economic
policy, and with this instrument began to open up some
new country.   For a while all went well.   The itinerary
predicted a green and bountiful valley, and lo ! there the
valley was — as green as young corn and as bountiful as a
tropical garden.   They waxed fat upon its bounty, but were
not content.   Their itinerary predicted an innumerable
succession of similar valleys, and the travellers pushed confidently on.   Instead they approached a much rougher and
more mountainous region, which was bristling with obstacles
and difficulties, of which their chart offered them no warning and suggested no practicable detour.   Of course, those
who had grown fat in the valley wished to return, and
abused their fellow-travellers, who had insisted on a continuation of the journey.   They pointed out that inasmuch
as the bill of rights constituted a radiant sun of political
wisdom, the whole journey was an absurdity.   But their
more ardent fellow-travellers would not turn back, even

if they could; and their first itinerary having failed them, they began to work out a new one, adapted to a rougher country and calling for more careful preparation and completer coöperation. The journey ceased to be a dress parade through a familiar and friendly country, and became frankly an exploring expedition — an expedition sustained by faith in the ultimate value of a clearly discerned goal, but ignorant of any authentic itinerary save that which can be worked out by means of a resolute and alert persistence on the road.

CHAPTER XI

POPULAR SOVEREIGNTY

THE emancipation of popular political power and responsibility from the overruling authority of the Law and the courts, which has been advocated in the preceding chapters, will appear to the majority of conservatives as a reckless and headstrong courting of national disintegration and disaster. Their apprehensions are based upon a conception of the nature of sovereignty in general and of popular sovereignty in particular, which tends to make the exercise of sovereign power, except under specific constitutional restrictions, necessarily inimical to individual liberty and public order. This conception of sovereignty has been inherited from the Fathers of the Republic, and before we can proceed any further, it must be subjected to a brief examination.

The traditional American conception of sovereignty was derived from the needs and methods of absolute monarchy. The essential attribute of sovereignty was its possession of the right to demand and the power to compel obedience. It became, consequently, the apotheosis of authoritative political coercion. The sovereign power was conceived as comprehensive and unlimited, and as sustained by the effective control of all the physical force necessary to make its commands effective. At the same time, this absolutism was not without the justification of a moral sanction, based upon the practical necessity for the existence of some source of effective political authority.

The foregoing conception of sovereignty was a natural outgrowth of the form of political organization with the help of which the European nations succeeded in getting under control the anarchy of the Middle Ages. Both the moral authority and the physical power of a highly centralized state had to be reënforced, to the end that the deeply rooted habits of domestic violence might be suppressed. The dominant political necessity was public order. The cost of domestic violence was so great that the power which could bestow and maintain order seemed to be divinely authorized and deserved the support of all patriotic citizens. The European monarchies, in spite of their absolutism, came, consequently, to be national in character. As the result of their services in suppressing domestic violence, they rested on an effective basis of popular support.

The nation in which this type of authoritative absolutism was most completely realized was, of course, Bourbon France. In none of the other European countries was so much pretension to moral authority reënforced by a formidable standing army and such a highly centralized administrative organization. But overwhelming as this combination of moral, military and civil authority appeared to be, it had acquired one fatal practical weakness. The French nobility had been so very unruly that their subordination had forced the monarchy to become over-ruly. The centralization of authority had been carried far enough to result in the impoverishment of the national life. The state was so organized and conducted as to be constantly under a strain. Its structure and policy implied the perpetual presence of a grave national emergency, which hindered the establishment of regular and reassuring rules and customs of national behavior. The aristocracy, after having been vanquished by the monarchy, took its revenge by improperly appropriating the new royal authority. When a marquis pleased to lock up a lackey in the Bastille, the same *raison d'état* was invoked in whose name insurrections were suppressed and war declared. A state of this particular type did seem to be an embodiment of human absolutism. It did seem to erect a barrier to the political and social development of mankind, unless it were deprived of its moral authority and subordinated to some code of righteous political behavior.

Later, when democracy became an effective political force, the conception of popular sovereignty was very much influenced by the foregoing conception of royal sovereignty. Technically the popular sovereignty seemed to need the same combination of moral authority and effective coercive powers as the national monarchies, but if that combination had in the case of monarchy exhibited the grave danger and weakness of a tendency to over-ruliness, a popular sovereign would be likely to exhibit an even greater similar danger. Royal sovereignty was indivisible and had made on the whole for public order. Popular sover-

eignty was similarly absolute in its claims, but it offered
no sufficient guarantee of a fundamentally unified political
authority.   Popular sovereignty had a tendency to disintegration. The physical authority of the state was handed
over to a majority.   The will of the majority might well be
expressed in a manner hostile to the national interest.   Discontent and revolution would follow, which could be suppressed only by the return to some kind of military dictatorship.   Thus a political system based on unrestricted
popular sovereignty resulted inevitably in an alternation
between mob rule and mob violence and martial law.

The foregoing conception of popular sovereignty forms
the major premise, upon which contemporary American
constitutional conservatism rests; but it does not deserve
either the apprehensions or the respectful attention which
it has aroused.   It is a mere political bogie, born of the
hallucinations of men who confuse the haunted castle of
feudalism and monarchism for the well-lighted mansion of
the American democracy.   Its formulas and fears are
divorced from the salient facts of American political life.
The behavior of the French Revolutionary democracy does,
of course, offer an apparent justification for installing the
bogie on a pedestal in the Hall of Political Wisdom, but the
French analogy has only a remote application.   In the
case of the French Revolution the new popular sovereign
did actually inherit an over-ruling power and an immediate
and exhausting responsibility, which was alien to the nature
and the orderly evolution of a democratic state.   It degen-
erated into a despotism, whose claim to respect consisted

in the fact that it did prevent foreign domination and restore some semblance of national integrity. The American democracy was never cursed with any such inheritance. Popular sovereignty as a living force in American politics was derived from a different parentage and was characterized by different merits and faults.

The effective political power which the American people took over from the Colonial governments and from the English Crown and Parliament was traditionally associated with orderly procedure, with a respect for legal forms, with a suspicion of the use of military power, and with the utmost administrative decentralization. Under the stimulus of popular political responsibility these traditional political methods and legal forms assumed a more rather than a less important place in the prevailing political system. The desire to find a rational and moral sanction for the new state resulted in the attempt both more precisely to define these traditions, and to place them, if possible, beyond the danger of harm. The new sovereign, although, as we have seen, it asserted the reality of its own power and responsibility, submitted obediently to a system of rules which tied its hands much more effectively than the hands of any other sovereign had ever been tied with its own consent. The American democracy recognized that popular sovereignty was necessarily associated with the reign of social righteousness, . and that it was wholly divorced from the old abstract and contradictory conception of authoritative political absolutism. It accepted the system of rules, because the rules were supposed to be the concrete embodiment of its social ideal.

Thus the American democracy was born into a world of law. It has always acted in its official capacity by means of orderly procedure. It has always instinctively shrunk from any concentration of executive or legislative power which would place one organ or function of government beyond control. It has, indeed, exhibited a pathetic and priggish confidence in the power of rules to determine reasonable and righteous political conduct — so much so that its freedom of movement and its ability to meet its own deeper responsibilities have been much hampered by its tenacious devotion to legalism. But whether or not this particular set of rules has the value attached to them by conservative publicists, the devotion of the American democracy to law in the sense of orderly procedure has been sufficiently proved. It would be strange, in case a democracy, after enjoying for four generations the benefits of regular methods of political action, should have acquired such a meagre attachment to the value of its own methods that it is over-willing to substitute for them some form of essentially violent and inconsiderate popular control.

The new assertion of popular political power and responsibility is not equivalent to the substitution of democratic absolutism for democratic constitutionalism. Constitutionalism necessarily remains; but the constitutions are intrusted frankly to the people instead of the people to the constitutions. Progressive democracy is not seeking to assume all the functions of government or to dispense with orderly procedure. It can afford to combine more democracy with more progressiveness than it has done in

Q

the past, partly because an attachment to legal methods has become deeply rooted in the national tradition. In no respect does it resemble the omnipotent and arbitrary mob which the constitutional conservatives 'profess to fear. Its development has been wholly emancipated from the rhythmic alternation of anarchy and despotism which is supposed to be the inevitable result of making the actual power of a democratic people commensurate with their nominal responsibilities. Even the French democracy seems as a result of four generations of education in the art of self-government to be liberating itself from bondage to any such law. The American democracy has never become entangled in it. With the exception of one brief period of Civil War, it has always been accustomed to orderly development. If it breaks with this custom in the future, the reign of orderly methods in government would seem to debilitate rather than to reënforce the national character.

Progressive democracy would cease to be progressive in case it departed for long from the use of essentially orderly methods; and excessive concentration of actual political power in the hands of the electorate might be as dangerous to order as would any similar concentration in the hands of the executive or the legislature. But while social justice depends upon order, order also depends upon the reign of social justice. To insist that loyalty to one kind of orderly procedure should stand in the way of a modification in the social policy of the American democracy would merely be to repeat the traditional conservative mistake. While its own necessities will compel democracy

to attach the utmost importance to the preservation of
legal forms and methods, it cannot allow its respect for
legal methods to outweigh its fidelity to its own needs and
purposes.   Orderly procedure must not only remain orderly,
but it must also remain or become procedural.   Any particular method of securing order, such as that prescribed
by the Constitution, must not be exalted from a method or
an instrument into a Higher Law.   It usually ceases to
make for order as soon as it ceases to serve contemporary
popular needs.   Unity is a matter of purpose rather than
of external conformity.   The Constitution provides much
more effectually for a desirable separation of the powers
than it does for an equally necessary coöperation of the
divided functions; and one of the great practical problems
of the American democracy has been to graft on the Constitution some regular method of giving back to the government sufficient integrity of organization and action.   In
the end this integrity must be derived not from constitutionalism, but from the ability of the people to achieve some
underlying unity of purpose.

Doubtless a dangerous ambiguity attaches to the use of
the word "people" as it was used in the preceding paragraph.   The "people" do not form a definite organized
agency of government.   The most popular organ of government consists in the legally qualified body of voters — the
electorate.   It would be absurd to attach the prerogatives
of sovereignty to the electorate, although the absurdity
of so doing does not prevent many progressives from doing
it.   The electorate is merely a fourth estate — a fourth

governmental power, which in the organization and operation of democracy has its special responsibilities and duties.
Its constitution and its procedure are determined by the
law. The electorate itself may have a good deal to say
about what such laws shall be and shall mean; but so have
the other departments of government. In any event the
electorate, quite as much as the legislative and the executive,
is subject to procedure, and cannot take any authoritative
action except in submission to established legal forms. In
the creation and confirmation of those established legal
forms other agencies of government besides the electorate
must coöperate; and by virtue of this coöperation popular
political action obtains a value and an authority which it
cannot obtain as a consequence merely of the exercise of
the voter's franchise.

A distinction must, consequently, be drawn between
the "electorate" and the "people." Numerically the active
electorate constitutes in different states between four and
fifteen per cent of the population. With the advent of
woman's suffrage and the improved political education
of the American people, this percentage will somewhat
increase even in states which now grant the vote to women.
But the electorate will always remain a small part of the
population. While it is not the "people," it is more nearly
coterminous with the people than any other representative
body. As the most sensitive agency of popular opinion,
it will necessarily be the final arbiter of political controversies; but such final arbitrament is not equivalent to
"popular sovereignty." It merely means that in a democ-

racy organized for action some agency must be provided to decide what immediate action is to be taken. The finality of any particular decision must not be taken too seriously. The decisions of an electorate are frankly tentative and revocable. It constitutes the court from which there is no appeal until the next election takes place, but when it does take place the court is not bound by previous decisions. The really effective sovereign power is to be found in public opinion, and public opinion is always in the making. It is always, that is, essentially active. Its sovereignty is wholesome in so far as its activity is determined by a sufficiency of information, the ability to understand and face the really pertinent facts, and real integrity of purpose.

Just as a monarchy was obliged to divide its enemies in order that it might rule, King Demos, the many-headed monarch, is similarly obliged to undergo subdivision. Popular sovereignty in its practical exercise brings with it a necessary distribution of power; but the power is distributed not for the purpose of its emasculation, but for the purpose of its moralization. An effective supplementary method of coördination is equally necessary. The old American democracy sought reunion in part by a literal worship of the law and the spirit of obedience. The democracy was to be nationalized by loyalty to its own rules and forms. As long as these rules and methods conformed to its practical needs, the spirit of literal obedience made for coördination without standing in the way of a large amount of unofficial disobedience and heresy. But the successful coördination must not be attributed merely to the obedient acceptance of the rules and devotion to them. The democracy became a nation, because the forms were useful instruments for the accomplishment of necessary purposes.

The way to continue the work of nationalization is not to continue to worship the forms, but to find, wherever necessary, new methods and forms better adapted to contemporary needs and a genuine formative ideal. Although the ideal of social justice with which constitutional government was associated has increased in authority, the program whereby that ideal was to be realized has been profoundly modified. If the new forms and methods are not supplied, the tendency towards disintegration, which is natural in a democratic state, will not be overcome by a really effective unity of purpose and spirit.

The traditional system possessed one specific form which, just as a matter of political mechanics, did more than anything else to convert a constitutional democracy into semi-democratic constitutionalism. This form consisted in the amending clause of the Constitution, which made the process of amendment almost insuperably difficult. That its excessive difficulty of amendment had some immediately desirable results during the early years of the Republic has already been asserted; but at the present time it is unquestionably the most formidable legal obstacle in the path of progressive democratic fulfilment. Professor Munroe Smith is justified in declaring "that the first article of any sincerely intended progressive program must be the amendment of the amending clause of the Constitution." In

practice the monarchy of the Law hangs suspended to the
nail of this particular bit of writing, and as long as it remains
intact the political destinies of the American people will
have to rest to an unnecessary and unwholesome extent
upon the dicta of a board of judicial trustees.

The new machinery of amendment ought to be very
much more easily worked than the old. It must make the
Constitution alterable at the demand and according to the
dictates of a preponderant prevailing public opinion. Instead of requiring the assent of two-thirds of Congress and
the legislatures of three-fourths of the states, the power of
revision should be possessed by a majority of the electorate.
The only limitations placed on this power should be a
method of procedure which allowed sufficient time for deliberation and a certain territorial distribution of the prevailing majority. The form proposed by Senator La Fol-
lette is probably the best which has been drafted. It
provides for the submission of amendments either by a
majority of both houses of Congress or by one-fourth of the
states, and their acceptance by a majority of all the voters
voting, provided that this majority is distributed throughout a majority of the states.

The necessity of any such revision of the amending clause
has been contested because two amendments to the Constitution have recently been proposed and ratified. The
successful adoption of these two amendments will have
the effect of making the revision of Article V seem less
necessary. It may well serve to delay the serious discussion
of the matter and to diminish for some time its practical

political importance. But in the long run progressive democracy cannot possibly submit to the abridgment of popular political responsibility which is implied by the present amending clause. It cannot wait until two-thirds of a Congress and the legislatures of three-fourths of the states are convinced of the desirability of any proposed modification. The existing method calls for amendment practically by unanimous consent. It removes proposals to revise the Constitution from the realm of partisan political controversy, and it necessitates the retention of means, similar to those which have been used in the past, to give the needed flexibility to the development of the Constitutional system — means which, as we have already seen, placed the political destinies of the American people under the immediate direction of a group of benevolent guardians.

A close connection has assuredly existed between the amount of discretionary authority actually exercised by the Supreme Court and the difficulty of amending the Constitution. No doubt a Federal system with an ambiguous dividing line between the central and state government required the aggrandizement of the courts for another purpose. No doubt, also, the logic of the whole system, based as it was on the supremacy of the Word rather than on that of a gradually educated and enlightened will; tended in the same direction. Nevertheless the supremacy of the Law and consequently the guardianship of the robe was based in practice upon the extreme difficulty of amending the Constitution. The nominal authority of King Demos was always admitted ; and this nominal authority did not become

effective, in part because it could not become effective by the
use of the regular legal machinery. As long as such intrac-
table machinery is preserved intact, a nation blessed with
political common-sense will be driven to adopt other and less
essentially democratic means of keeping its Law adapted
to its needs.

The other method which has been used most frequently
in the past was the assumption by the Supreme Court
of a constructive political responsibility. At present the
Court seeks to evade such a responsibility whenever it can
with any show of reason; but time was when it cordially
greeted the opportunity to pass essentially political judg-
ments. In order to find clear instances of this tendency,
it is not necessary to go as far back as the Dred Scott
decision. The period in which the Supreme Court exercised its powers with the largest latitude and with the most
complete conviction of the essentially political nature of
its duties occurred after the War. Again and again doubtful interpretations were imposed upon the Constitution by
the preference of one judge — interpretations which, if not
modified by the Court itself, required for their alteration the
express voluntary action of two-thirds of Congress and three-
quarters of the states. In the Slaughter-House cases it
did not hesitate by a vote of five to four to bestow a meaning on the Fourteenth Amendment which, in the opinion of
many commentators on the Constitution, was both arbitrary
and unwise. By a similar majority it altered the prevailing
reading of one provision of the Constitution and declared
invalid the income tax. In these and many similar cases

it welcomed the chance of writing the preference of a bare majority of the Court into the Supreme Law. That any such preference exhibited by five good lawyers embodied the majesty of reason, while an opposing opinion maintained by four equally good lawyers embodied palpable unreason could, one would think, hardly be maintained with a serious countenance. Yet it has been maintained, and the practice flourished for many years, in spite of the fact that it ignored the official theory supposed to determine the use of the judicial veto — the theory that laws should not be invalidated unless the violation of the Constitution was beyond reasonable doubt.

Of late years the Supreme Court has more and more avoided rather than welcomed political responsibility. The strong tendency towards social legislation, which set in at the very end of the nineteenth century, met with some resistance in the beginning from the Supreme Court; but as the movement grew in volume, the resistance diminished. The absurdity of the attempt by a small body of lawyers in a democracy to convert their political preferences into law under the cover of constitutional construction is being recognized. The judicial veto is being exercised by the Supreme Court only in the cases of manifest excesses and flagrant abuses of legislative authority. The tendency is, consequently, to throw the burden of political decisions on legislative bodies, which are supposed to be responsible immediately to public opinion. Instead of amplifying the scope of the individual rights guaranteed to American citizens by the Constitution and correspondingly restricting the exercise of the police power, they are allowing the police power to shelter an increasing array of interferences with individual liberties. The authority which the courts have exercised under the due process of law and equal rights clauses will gradually be pared down just as it was gradually built up, until finally the restraints put on the legislative power, both local and Federal, by the courts will become comparatively innocuous. A similar tendency was exhibited in recent decisions respecting the regulation by the states of railroad rates. The Court affirmed national control under certain conditions over intra-state rates, but left that control to be exercised by Congress. If this disposition continues and becomes even more emphatic, as it almost certainly will, the development of the American legal system will depend far more than it has in the past upon the will of the legislatures.

Any such shifting of the centre of gravity of the American political system would, however, count in favor of a revision of Article V rather than against it. Assuredly the exercise of a discretionary political power by a body of men directly representative of some phase of public opinion is preferable to its exercise by a body of men who technically are not at all responsible to public opinion. But the substitution of Congressional for judicial authority should not be pushed too far. Any tendency to Congressional omnipotence will have to face the opposition of deep and wholesome American political tradition — the tradition which distrusted the concentration of too much responsibility and power in any one department of the organized government. The courts were allowed to become the final regulators of the American political system, only because they were supposed to act, not from preference, interest or will, but in the light of a purely rational interpretation of a body of permanent political truth. But public opinion has never exhibited any intention of allowing essentially wilful political instruments, like Congress or the state legislatures, to become all-powerful within their respective jurisdictions. The relaxation of judicial control over legislative action will and should be accompanied by an increasing purpose to substitute some other kind of control.

The suspicion with which American public opinion has regarded the work of American legislatures has most assuredly been justified. Representative bodies which have exhibited such meagre powers of self-control can hardly be intrusted with complete legal authority over the lives and property of citizens and the policy of the state. The most important legislature in the United States has not in either of its branches succeeded in adopting a set of rules which combines the efficient transaction of public business with any sufficient freedom of discussion. Moreover, all American legislative bodies, Congress included, have proved wholly incapable of saving themselves from the enervating and disintegrating effect of excessive indulgence in special legislation. The causes of this ill-success of American legislatures are so numerous and raise so many doubtful matters of discussion that they cannot be considered in this connection; but whatever the cause, any early or complete bestowal of confidence by public opinion on Congress is neither to be expected nor desired. The more power Congress obtains at the expense of the judiciary, the greater will be the pressure to redress the balance by means of an increase of popular control — which can be accomplished only by the release of direct popular power over the Constitution.

Such is the one effective way in which the American people can obtain the legal direction of their own political destiny — the one effective way in which the Constitution can be made at once the instrument of democracy and a vitally educational influence on American national development. Then the social treasure of the American democracy will no longer be locked up in an inaccessible safe which cannot be opened except by conforming to a most complicated and difficult ritualistic combination. It will be placed directly in the custody of the people themselves, which will help the people to realize their own responsibility. It is a singular fact that in the past the American system was supposed to derive its democracy from what was in reality its least democratic aspect. It was democratic, not by virtue of the powers which the electorate were permitted to exercise through the agency of the government, but through the powers which the Law reserved to the people. But the powers which the Constitution reserved to the people were, as a consequence of the difficulty of amendment, even more effectually preserved from them. In so far as the Constitution was democratic, the amending clause converted its democracy into a golden hoard, to which access could be obtained only at rare intervals and after an heroic effort.

That a community which prided itself on being peculiarly democratic should have allowed effective popular political power in its legal form to be hoarded rather than put out at interest is a singular anomaly. It would be inexplicable, except in the light of the thoroughgoing individualism and particularism of the primitive American democrats. They were perfectly willing to see effective popular political power buried in a vault with triple bars, because effective popular political power meant effective national political power. The Constitution was the supreme law of the land. If it was difficult to amend, it would be correspondingly difficult to abridge the rights secured to the states and to individual citizens. If it was comparatively easy to amend, it would be correspondingly easy to impair those rights. Now democracy meant to these democrats the use of popular political power not for the benefit of a general national or social ideal, but for the protection of specific individual and local liberties. Their democracy was socially and nationally irresponsible. They were not interested in the people as a whole. They were interested in the people as divided into local groups and supposed individuals. On the other hand, the dominant purpose and effort of progressive democracy must be to bring into existence a genuine democratic community. It is the outcome of a far deeper sense of common responsibilities and policies, of the interdependence of individuals and local groups, of the necessity and fruitfulness of coöperation, and of the intimate relation between democracy and nationality. This sense of common responsibilities and purposes cannot be instructively and significantly realized, unless a dominant popular purpose can be expressed without unnecessary delay and without excessive effort.

The intimate association between popular and national control does not bring with it the substitution of a centralized for a federalized democracy. It implies, no doubt, that a stubborn majority of the American people could, if they would, unwholesomely centralize the American system of government, just as the Sixteenth Amendment probably enables Congress to tax out of existence, if it prefers to do so, the agencies of state political authority. But if a majority sought to do any such foolish thing and by so doing was squeezing the vitality out of the local centres of American life, it would surely mean that these local centres had not very much vitality left in them. After the amending clause had been altered, as has been proposed, the states might well be obliged to fight at times for the right to continue the exercise of certain functions; but if those functions had been or even could be properly exercised by the local authorities, the local opposition would have more than an even chance of being successful. In a democracy no part of the community is entitled to exercise any more power than public opinion, after a full hearing, will consent to bestow upon it. To place such powers beyond the control of a dominant element in public opinion is merely to invite their abuse. No more effective way of encouraging the improvement of state governments can be devised than that of relieving them from their merely legal safeguards. They will then be placed upon their good behavior and stimulated to find some means of adapting their local interests to those of the whole community. Progressive democracy will need and will value the state governments; but they will be needed and valued, not as independent and coördinate centres of authority, but as parts of an essentially national system.

American publicists have attached in the past the same sanctity to states rights as to individual rights; but in both instances they have weakened their case by an excessive literalism. They have attempted to sanctify a particular formulation of states rights and a particular formulation of individual rights. Progressive democracy must reject the finality of these specific formulations. Just as the amount of liberty which can be left to the individual without endangering the social interest will vary at different times, so the amount of authority which can be left with the state governments will also vary. In the past the theory has been that the states should have exclusive control over their own domestic affairs. But what are the domestic affairs of a state? Slavery was supposed to be a purely domestic institution, with which non-slave holding states had nothing to do ; yet the existence of this purely domestic institution almost wrecked the nation. The extent to which any particular economic and social activity is to be considered domestic or national in its incidence varies at different times. Business was once essentially a local activity and needed regulation, if at all, in the local interest; but business has become so nationalized, and intra-state business is so entangled with inter-state business, that its regulation has necessarily become a national responsibility.

The distinction between inter-state and intra-state commerce, which the Constitution makes of such huge legal importance, is of slight economic significance. In the same way the problem of public health, which under the conditions of a pioneer agricultural economy could be regulated so far as necessary by local authorities, is coming to involve the very future of the nation. In fact, the whole contemporary tendency is to convert social questions, which have been in the past considered to be exclusively within the jurisdiction of the state governments, into questions which cannot be effectively treated without some exercise of national authority.

If this tendency continues, it is bound to alter the balance and the character of the American Federal system. It is bound to convert the central government, as the representative of the collective interests of the American people, into a government whose activities and powers are not confined by rigid rules, but are commensurate with its responsibilities. I repeat that the nationalization of American democracy does not mean the abandonment of the federal principle, and the substitution for it of a lifeless centralization. Nationalization is not equivalent to centralization. It has frequently required administrative and legislative decentralization. France has long been a sufferer from administrative centralization. The republic has been unable to attack the evil directly, but it has begun an indirect attack by granting an increased freedom of association, which may in the course of time serve to loosen up and nationalize the French bureaucracy. The United

R

Kingdom is suffering from legislative centralization. Parliament has too much to do, and will be obliged to distribute some of its powers in the interest of genuine nationalization. In our own country the work of nationalization has usually demanded increasingly centralized control, but that was because the American nation had to be built up out of material supplied by local political and economic units. These units have usually clung to every particle of power to which they were legally entitled, and have tended to stake the whole cause of local political vitality upon the preservation of some particular distribution of state and central authority. But the problem is not one which can be advanced towards solution either by a dogmatic insistence upon any particular method of distribution or a dogmatic preference for central or local control. Other federal states, such as Canada, the German Empire and South Africa, have granted increased authority to the central government for the purpose of making the national power commensurate with the national responsibility; and they have succeeded in doing this without destroying the vitality of the local governments. A similar process is slowly taking place in the United States under the influence of inexorable practical needs.

The friends of an American national democracy should work not for the substitution of central for local control, but, wherever possible, for coöperation between the two. At first the spheres of the central and the state governments were supposed to be mutually exclusive, each being supreme within its own sphere. The Fourteenth Amendment subjected the state governments to negative supervision, but did nothing to promote coöperative action. Because of the lack of coöperation the administrative energy of the country is now being to a considerable extent dissipated and wasted. The one way for state authority to preserve its own proper sphere of action is not to make any attempt to exceed it. If the state authority will voluntarily restrict its legal activities within the limits necessarily imposed by a fair consideration for other states, by the desire for efficiency and by the general public interest, those powers can be gradually wrought into a genuine national legislative and administrative system. In certain cases such a system can be promoted by the use of the English device of grants-in-aid. Federal financial assistance will be offered to the states under conditions which tend to level local services up to a desirable national standard. But for the most part the desirable coöperation will be secured rather by pressure than by voluntary action and by bribes; and such pressure can be exerted in only one way. A prevailing public opinion, after the lapse of a sufficient time for deliberation, must obtain the power to accomplish any program demanded by the national interest. The revision of the amending clause of the Constitution is the indispensable effective method of giving to the American democracy a chance to be nationalized, and of giving American nationality a chance to be democratized.

Whether the American people will take full advantage of the method is another question. The increased opportunity to vote on constitutional amendments will of itself make them neither more national nor more democratic.

It all depends upon their will to use their increased control over their national policy in the interest of an ultimate social consolidation or of ultimate social disintegration. Critics of the plan will prejudge the issue. The proposed revision of the amending clause will be condemned as inevitably resulting in national dissolution. It will place the inestimable and costly gifts of individual and local liberty, as well as the general security of society, at the mercy of a capricious or headstrong majority. So it will. A free man can always commit suicide. But is there any better way of making majorities considerate and purposeful than by placing the immediate responsibility for the public welfare in their hands? And if a majority is inconsiderate and frivolous in its policy, how long will such a majority remain a majority? The issue hangs upon what and how much is demanded of and by democracy. A democratic community whose integrity is being gradually created by the active realization of a national policy instead of by obedience to rules, must depend upon popular majorities as the necessary vehicles of decisive action. It remains to be seen what kind of a democratic community the American people will choose to be.

CHAPTER XII

The Advent of Direct Government

THE Federal Constitution is in many other respects besides its amending clause a most unsatisfactory instrument for a courageous and thoroughgoing democracy. In the not very remote future it will have to be modified in certain essential matters — both by amendment and by interpretation. In the present connection, however, the discussion of the detailed character of these amendments need not detain us. As soon as public opinion is aroused to the plain fact that the amending clause is the most formidable legal obstacle to the democratizing of the American political system, that article of the Constitution will become the centre of attack. Conservatives of all classes will rally to its defence, and for a good many years the issue will dominate American politics and work havoc among existing partisan alignments. But until the fight is on and some of the intervening years have elapsed, it is scarcely worth while to discuss the specific use to which the democracy will put its newly won freedom of action. The controversy itself will help to develop a specific program of revision, the nature of which cannot be at the present time plausibly or profitably defined.

Very different, however, is the situation with respect to

the state constitutions and governments. They offer to the American people a unique and priceless opportunity for collective experimentation, which seeks to accomplish social purposes by means of democratic political agencies. Many American states are already using their legal powers with courage and with success in the interest of some kind of a social program. Almost as many have exhibited a similar intention to modify their political organizations according to what are considered to be thoroughly democratic political principles. In carrying out these social and political programs the people of the states are not hampered usually by the difficulty of amending their constitutions. A majority of the citizens voting at an election can, in a majority of the states, ratify constitutional amendments. They have used the machinery of amendment freely in the past. They are by way of using it at the present time more freely than ever. When using it, their action is generally dictated by the interest, or the supposed interest, of progressive democracy. The alterations which progressive democracy may or should make in state political organization become, consequently, a matter of immediately profitable political discussion.

The point of departure for any such discussion must be the record which the local democracies have left, of the previous use of their power of amending their constitutions. This record does not present a very encouraging superficial appearance. The state constitutions have, during the past four generations, been very much modified without being very much improved. In the beginning the typical state

political system was characterized by a consistency similar
to that of the Federal system. Its foundation was government by Law, but on this foundation was built a sufficiently
self-respecting system of semi-representative government.
It differed from the Federal system, in that the executive and
the courts were not usually as independent of the legislature
as were the Federal executive and courts. The tendency
was, however, to make the three powers more independent
one of another, and in general to modify the state constitutions so as to make them conform to the Federal model.

This tendency did not long endure. As soon as the local
democracies assumed power and gathered self-confidence,
the Federal Constitution ceased to have much formative
influence on the state constitutions. The power of comparatively easy amendment made the difference. The
lack of that power in the case of the Federal system resulted
in the erection of the Supreme Court into the regulator of
the whole political machine. The possession of that power
by most of the local democracies enabled them to keep
the regulation in their own hands. The Supreme Court
used its unique political opportunities and its wide discretionary authority for the purpose of preserving and improving the elaborate balance of the system. They added to
government by Law the kind of human service which was
necessary for its higher and completer development. The
local democracies were incapable of any similar feat of political construction. Their instinctive effort was not to develop but to democratize government by Law. They tried
to do so for one hundred years and they failed.

The general work of state political reorganization which was carried on during the first century of our national life has been described as that of imposing increasing limitations on the powers of the state legislatures. This formula emphasizes the most conspicuous aspect of the process, but does not define its essential nature. Essentially the process consisted of imposing every possible check on any and every positive function of state government. The legislative power suffered severer emasculation under these disciplinary measures than did the powers of the executive or the courts, but it was emasculated the more only because there was in the beginning more to emasculate. A similar process was going on throughout the whole governmental system. Although the executive and the courts did obtain in certain respects increased powers, their aggrandizement was only apparent. They had to be allowed some extension of authority, in order to serve as curbs on the legislature; but coincident with their aggrandizement as checks, they were being shorn of positive powers and responsibilities. The result was a system of government which was so completely checked that it lost all balance. It was comparable, not, as was the Federal system, to some elaborate masterpiece of artificial constructive genius, such as a Gothic cathedral, but rather to a bed of liquid clay. It became an indiscriminate mass of sticky matter, which merely clogged the movements of every living body entangled in its midst, and which exhibited a happy combination of uneasiness in its parts and immobility as a whole.

At the outset the legislatures were in theory and practice

the most powerful department of the government. It looked as if in the course of time the American political system might approximate to the English parliamentary system. But in spite of the initial prestige of the legislature among a people with the English legal tradition, in spite of its advantages as the most popular branch of the government, in spite of its intrinsic superiority as the law-making and money-appropriating power, it has pretty steadily declined both in the scope of its legal authority and in popular confidence. There was a moment, during the flourishing period of the Jacksonian Democracy, when the legislatures seemed to share in the increasing political authority which the people aspired to exercise; but it did not last. The local democracies soon became suspicious of all kinds of law and law-making power, except that which emanated directly from themselves. The people's law was embodied in the state constitutions, and these constitutions, rather than the legislatures, were considered to be the safest and the most effective agencies of the popular will. Much of the work formerly confided to legislatures began to be performed by constitutions. The latter waxed in size and abounded in detailed specification. In no matter did their provisions finally become more drastic than in their regulation of the body which was nominally supposed to be the source of all active regulation in the public interest. To a large extent the exercise of legitimate and necessary legislative discretion was checked and impaired. Inasmuch as the legislatures were unable to confine the power to pass special legislation within desirable limits, that power was so far as possible taken from them. They were not even allowed to determine their own procedure. Finally, they were in many instances forbidden to assemble too often or for too long a time. If ever any instrument of government was plainly and emphatically condemned by public opinion, such condemnation was visited upon the state legislatures.

The distrust of the state legislatures resulted in the strengthening of the executive veto, and in popular acquiescence to the gradual extension of judicial supervision over legislation. But in neither case was this strengthening of negative authority any evidence of general public confidence. The legislatures were not considered competent to govern themselves, but they were fully competent to prescribe most exactly and completely the behavior of the executive authority. Statutes passed by the legislatures usually went into the most exhaustive detail in order to prevent the erring administrator from going astray. Appropriation bills specified minutely the way in which the public money should be spent, the assumption being that if any discretion were left to the executive, it would be abused. Responsibility for the proper performance of an action must be fastened upon people who did not participate in the action. So far as the administration was concerned, this minute supervision by the law might be plausibly justified as a necessary consequence of the disintegration which executive power had suffered at the hands of democracy. The governor had been deprived of his natural function of appointing subordinate state officials, who were to a considerable extent elected by popular vote. Inasmuch as he had been deprived of any effective authority over his subordinates, he had ceased to be the responsible head of the administration. Yet his assistants had to be subjected to some species of control, and, as usual, the law was called in to perform the work which could not be intrusted to mere human beings.

Neither did the courts escape the effect of the prevailing effort to eliminate the personal equation from the operations of government. Judges who were considered wise and just enough to exercise the power, not granted to any European judges, of invalidating statutes, were usually considered incompetent to determine the procedure which ought to be used in their own court-rooms. When a judge was trying a case, he was generally supposed to be worthy of so little confidence that he was deprived of all effective authority over jury and counsel. Yet if the same judge were transferred to an appellate court, his authority became so magnified that he could on the most trivial grounds upset the findings of a trial court. In no part of the mechanism of state government could an official be found who escaped from this network of supervision and espionage.

Yet the net result of the multiplication of specific laws and of the absence of executive or legislative discretion was to convert the judges into the only effective public officials. The situation which prevailed fifteen years ago has been well described by Professor Roscoe Pound in a recent address before the Law Association of Philadelphia. "Law paralyzing administration was an every day spectacle. Almost every important measure of police and administration encountered an injunction. We relied on tax-payers' suits to prevent waste of public funds and misuse of the proceeds of taxation. In a number of states the courts would direct writs of mandamus to the governor where ministerial action was involved. Administration had become only a very subordinate agency in the whole process of government. Complete elimination of the personal equation in all matters affecting the life, liberty, property or fortune of the citizens seemed to have been attained. It was fundamental in our polity to confine administration to the inevitable minimum. Where some people went to extreme and were bureau-ridden, we went to the opposite extreme and were law-ridden."

Thus the American state governments carried government by law as far as it was humanly possible to carry it. They abandoned themselves to legalism as completely as a sail-boat abandons itself to the wind. Yet when abandoned to the wind the boat did not sail free without a man at the helm — it only drifted around. In spite of the ever increasing web of legal precautions woven about the unfortunate human beings who were trying to run this legalistic mechanism, there was no satisfaction with the result. In one way or another the public welfare was sedulously being sacrificed. The public moneys were misappropriated and misspent in spite of statutory specification and tax-payers' suits. Administrative officials could usually find shelter behind the law when things went wrong; but the law never helped to make things go right. Corruption

increased and abuses multiplied. Special privileges of all
kinds abounded. The equal protection of the laws, which
was guaranteed to all American citizens, was as remote as
possible from their equal administration. In practice the
equal protection of the laws meant the unequal opportunity
of bringing law-suits. In so far as government by law was
ineffective, it was government by corporations and political
bosses. In so far as it was effective, it was government by
litigation.

In point of fact, the local body politic had acquired a
chronic headache. When the pain had first appeared the
symptoms were treated as constituting the disease, and
powders were taken to cure the symptoms. More headaches were followed by further doses of powder until, finally,
a habit was established — the habit of having headaches
and of trying to alleviate them with powders. The malady
had become as closely associated with its supposed remedy
as it was with its original cause. If the headaches were to
be cured, not only must the disease be treated as something
different from its symptoms, but the powders must be
eschewed, even at the expense of a good deal of temporary
physical distress.

If the experience of the American state governments
proves anything, it proves that democracy and legalism are
incompatible. For over three generations the local democracies attempted most ingeniously and tenaciously to democratize government by Law — to make the Law the representative agent of democratic policy. They placed themselves completely in the hands of the lawyers; and the

lawyers legislated in the people's name on the assumption that the more specific the provisions of a law and the more comprehensive its responsibility, the more effective would be its supremacy. They built up a system of legal prescription which, in case it could have been enforced, would have been intolerable; but it could not be enforced. The democracy never intended that it should be enforced. Coincident with the system of legal prescription was built up a much more human system of partisan government, whose chief object soon became the circumvention of government by Law. In the actual government of the states the laws were obeyed or evaded or ignored, according as it suited the prevailing party leaders, — which could be done with impunity, because the power to administer or to enforce the law had been largely dissipated. The lawlessness of the extra-official democracy was merely the counterpoise of the legalism of the official democracy. The lawyer having been permitted to subordinate democracy to the Law, the Boss had to be called in to extricate the victim, which he did after a fashion and for a consideration.

Finally, in their distress at the predicament into which they had allowed themselves to get, the local democracies began to adopt a remedy which, whatever its ultimate value, looked in a new direction. Instead of continuing the attempt to make government by Law democratic, they are trying really to organize popular government and make it effective. They have fallen back on the power behind the Law. They are proposing to withdraw from Law the responsibility under which it has been suffering, and to exercise this responsibility themselves.   They are proposing to take the Law into their own hands.   Instead of embodying their program in a constitution which either accomplishes too much or not enough, they propose to retain the power to legislate and to prevent legislation from being adopted. The local democracies have suddenly decided or discovered that they themselves are free men worthy of confidence — even if their agents are not.   Instead of being governed by the Law, they intend to govern themselves, and thus to humanize the Law at its source.

This latest phase of local democratic experimentation has not been received with as much satisfaction by the legal profession as were its previous phases.   The class of lawyers, after having acquiesced in and assisted the slow inexorable process of converting every state official into a bond-servant of the Law, have suddenly discovered the value of human discretion as an agency of government. They object to direct legislation, because of its tendency to weaken the responsibility of the legislative body.   As if in the past they had not exhausted their ingenuity in devising expedients to check legislatures in the exercise of specific legislative functions!   They object to the recall of elected officials, because they fear that the threat of the recall will deprive governors or judges of that independence which is so necessary for the conscientious performance of administrative duties.   As if the system, for which they as a class are largely responsible, did not convert the judges, to whom was confided the actual administration of the civil and the criminal law, into perpetual suspects, who were regularly charged by counsel with dereliction and found guilty by a higher court! As if executive officials ever had any real independence under a legalistic mechanism of government which deprived them of every possible shred of discretion! Is it not somewhat late in the day for American legal conservatives to awaken to the value of government by men as a necessary supplement to government by Law?

Direct popular government may be fairly exposed to the kind of criticism which has been levelled against it by conservative publicists. I shall deal hereafter with the relation between direct and representative government. But before considering the nature and forms of a really democratic system of representation, we must try to understand the parentage and the probable effect of this new method of direct government. The relation between the old mechanism of democracy and the new is not as simple as either the friends or the opponents of the new democracy claim. When we consider the more obvious aspect of the instruments of direct government, they seem to make for the emancipation of democracy from the bondage to the Law. But from another and scarcely less obvious aspect the initiative, referendum and the recall seem merely to add one final comprehensive popular check to this network of personal and legal checks which has hampered the operation of the state political organization. Will the attempt of the democracy to exercise an ultimate discretion in the determination of public policy liberate the expression of the popular will or finally and effectually paralyze its expression ?

A consistent advocate of the second of these alternatives is President Butler of Columbia University. He considers the system of direct popular government to be reactionary, because its adoption would be comparable to the reversion from a higher to a lower organic type. It would mean the deliberate rejection of that specialization of structure and function which in the history of society, as in the history of organic life, has always been a symptom of progress. How can a sane body of political progressives propose to undermine further those specific organs of representative government which society labored so long and so hard to acquire ?

In urging this criticism so confidently is not President Butler being betrayed by his antipathies ? Was the system of state government which the instruments of the new democracy threaten to destroy — was it characterized by that specialization of structure and function which is the trademark of high forms of organic and social life ? Had not the legislature already been deprived of specifically legislative responsibility, and had it not already assumed many properly administrative duties ? Had not the executive already been deprived of specifically administrative responsibilities and been allowed to encroach upon the proper spheres of legislative and judicial action ? Had not the courts been weakened as expounders of the law and as purveyors of justice in order that they might be strengthened as law-makers ? The three powers which had been so carefully separated in theory were utterly confounded in practice. The old system contained no genuine specialization of structure and function which the machinery of the new democracy had a chance to destroy.

The peculiar merit of direct popular government consists precisely in its tendency to create that which President Butler declares it will destroy. It may introduce into American democratic political organization a long-needed and salutary adaptation of structure and feeling to function. The traditional legalism not only prevented the several departments of government from properly redeeming their specific responsibilities, but it paralyzed the electorate in the redemption of its final and comprehensive responsibility. The lack of specific adjustment of which President Butler complains was characteristic not only of the machinery of political action, but of the fundamental relationship between the responsibilities of democracy and its instruments. The foundation upon which government by Law rested was not the rock of faith, but the sands of apprehension. The suspicion with which the exercise of the executive, legislative and judicial powers was regarded was the natural consequence of the suspicion with which the exercise of popular political power itself was regarded. The popular will was divided by mechanical legalism from a confidential relation with its own necessary and desirable means of expression. No wonder that the structure erected on such a foundation proved unstable, and became more rather than less unstable as the network of espionage was extended. Such a system cannot obtain any real integrity until confidence in human nature is substituted for suspicion as its underlying impulse.

Thus the adoption of the machinery of direct popular government is not comparable to the substitution of a political amœba for a political vertebrate. It is comparable rather to the prescription of a draught of self-confidence to an invalid, who at least officially had been made sick with apprehension and remedial medicine. It corresponds, if you please, to the application of a faith cure to a patient the root of whose ailment had been an infirmity of will. It is a decisive and courageous step in the direction of a specifically democratic political organization. Its effect should be eventually to invigorate the whole political body. Of course even after the faith cure is applied, the patient will not be immediately transformed. He has many perverted ideas which can only be slowly eradicated. He has many frivolous and irresponsible habits which will seek their perpetuation under the very forms of the new faith. But the new faith certainly brings with it a new hope. While democracy may not realize the expectations of its advocates, the only chance it has of so doing is to build its structure on a foundation of self-confidence. Without departing from the ideal of orderly procedure which was so precious to the Fathers, it must still insist that government according to law shall derive its justification and its vitality from its conformity with the free decisions of the prevailing popular will.

The aspiration towards genuinely popular government has been struggling for expression throughout the political

history of our American states. It assumed a perverted
expression, because of the initial assumption that the necessary permanent program of democracy could be defined
in advance and would not need to be changed; but it was
insistent, if not self-conscious and clear-headed. In the
state bills of rights political liberties received the same kind
of consecration as civil liberties. The two were assumed to
be supplementary.   In the subsequent development of the
system popular political power was submerged under a
flood of legalism, but it was being submerged with its own
consent. The authority which had been invoked in order
to promote legalism was popular authority. During the
whole tedious and barren process of making constitutions
perform the work of legislatures and of making laws perform
the work of human beings, the power in the name of which
the Law had been aggrandized had itself undergone a similar
aggrandizement. The one positive element in the century
of state constitutional amendment had been the inexorable
expansion of the "People's Law" as embodied in the state
constitutions. The advent of direct government was the
necessary consummation of this process. The Law was not
serving the people any better than their legislatures and executives were supposed to serve them. The only remaining alternative was no longer to impose such huge responsibility upon it, and to depend upon the people for the
exercise of at least a part of this responsibility.

That the American democracy has consumed over one
hundred years in finding out that it cannot wholly delegate
the active exercise of its responsibilities is not surprising.

The preliminary attempts to create a democratic political system necessarily involve serious difficulties of adjustment with the varied and alien stock of living political institutions and traditions. These institutions originated during a period in which public opinion was sluggish, ignorant and incompetent, in which social development had frequently to be subordinated to social conservation, in which the popular will had no effective means of expression except in local riots, and in which the national will necessarily escaped popular control. Yet alien as they were to the policy and methods of a democracy, the prevailing political institutions were so deeply rooted in contemporary human nature that the new democratic system had to make use of them. A similar difficulty confronted the European democracies in an even more acute and difficult form. The contrivances which have been invented as instruments of democratic purposes and policy have varied widely in different countries; but they have all tended to have a common defect. They have all tended to impose upon certain traditional representative agencies duties which a thoroughgoing democracy needed, but was not sufficiently prepared, to accomplish for itself.

On the continent of Europe, for instance, where during the seventeenth and eighteenth centuries monarchy had become national without the assistance or check of a general representative body, the democracy, when it came, found it difficult either to get along without the monarchy or to get along with the monarchy. It was alternately too dependent on the executive and too suspicious of him. In

Great Britain the nation had become united under parliamentary rather than under royal leadership, and when democracy came, it confided its responsibility to Parliament and was for long apparently well satisfied with the result. But of late years the tendency has been to subordinate Parliament to the executive and for the executive to rest directly on popular public opinion. To an outsider it looks as if the necessary practical result of such a tendency would be an increase of direct popular control over the government. It is just beginning to be understood that representative government of any type becomes in actual practice a species of class government. It cannot succeed except by virtue of a ruling class, which has earned the privilege of leadership and which has deserved and retained popular support. But it does not work so well in the case of a nation like France, which has lost confidence in its hereditary leaders, without having altogether rid itself of the political characteristics with which that hereditary leadership was associated. Neither does it or would it work well in a country like the United States, which has and can have no ruling class, and which, from the beginning, has been feeling its way towards the development of some kind of leadership adapted to ultimate popular political responsibility. It remains to be seen whether a representative system can be wrought for the benefit of a people who seek wholly to dispense with class leadership, and who have exhibited a consistent desire to democratize all their institutions.

If economic, social, political and technical conditions

had remained very much as they were at the end of the eighteenth century, the purely democratic political aspirations might never have obtained the chance of expression. Some form of essentially representative government was at that time apparently the only dependable kind of liberal political organization. It was imposed by the physical and technical conditions under which government had to be conducted. Direct government did not seem to be possible outside of city or tribal states, whose population and area was sufficiently small to permit the actual assemblage of the body politic at some particular place, either at regular intervals or in case of an emergency. But in the case of states chiefly devoted to agriculture, whose free citizens were distributed over a wide area, and were, in any event, too numerous for actual assemblage in any one spot, it seemed necessary for the people to delegate to a body of representatives the power required not merely for public administration, but for the discussion of public questions, the adoption of public policies and the supervising of the administration itself. Some form of a responsible representative government, that is, was prescribed by fundamental economic and social conditions. The function was performed in the several states according to the method best adapted to local traditions and by the class which had proved itself capable of leadership.

In the twentieth century, however, these practical conditions of political association have again changed, and have changed in a manner which enables the mass of the people to assume some immediate control of their political destinies. While it is more impossible than ever for the citizens of a modern industrial and agricultural state actually to assemble after the manner of a New England town-meeting, it is no longer necessary for them so to assemble. They have abundant opportunities of communication and consultation without any actual meeting at one time and place. They are kept in constant touch with one another by means of the complicated agencies of publicity and intercourse which are afforded by the magazines, the press and the like. The active citizenship of the country meets every morning and evening and discusses the affairs of the nation with the newspaper as an impersonal interlocutor. Public opinion has a thousand methods of seeking information and obtaining definite and effective expression which it did not have four generations ago. The community is broken up into innumerable smaller communities, each of which is united by common interests and ideas and each of which is seeking to bring a larger number of people under the influence of its interests and ideas. Under such conditions the discussions which take place in a Congress or a Parliament no longer possess their former function. They no longer create and guide what public opinion there is. Their purpose rather is to provide a mirror for public opinion, to advertise and illuminate its constituent ideas and purposes, and to confront the advocates of those ideas with the discipline of effective resistance and, perhaps, with the responsibilities of power. Phases of public opinion form, develop, gather to a head, assert their power and find their place chiefly by the activity of other more popular unofficial agencies. Thus the democracy has at its disposal a mechanism of developing and exchanging opinions, and of reaching decisions, which is independent of representative assemblies, and which is, or may become, superior to that which it formerly obtained by virtue of occasional popular assemblages.

The adoption of the machinery of direct government is a legitimate expression of this change. After centuries of political development, in which certain forms of representation were imposed upon progressive nations by conditions of practical efficiency, and in which these representative forms grew continually in variety and complexity, underlying conditions have again shifted. Pure democracy has again become not merely possible, but natural and appropriate. The attempt to return to it is no more retrogressive than was the attempt to recover classic humanism after its eclipse during the Middle Ages. Society has been passing through a period of prodigious fertility, during which new social aspirations, purposes, instruments and activities have multiplied with unprecedented rapidity. If these new interests and activities are to be assimilated, they must be recognized and incorporated into the system of government. As a consequence of the attempt to incorporate them into the system of government, society may seem to be yielding to the power of disintegrating economic and social forces. This appears to be the beginning of a reverse process of denationalization which will be equivalent to dissolution. Those who place any such interpretation upon the facts of modern social development and the corresponding political changes fail to understand their meaning. Increasing direct popular political action is coming to have a function in the political organization of a modern society, because only in this way can the nation again become a master in its own house. Its very fecundity, and the enormous power which many of its offspring obtain, have compelled a democratic nation to adopt a more thoroughgoing method of promoting its integrity. As yet it is not making very much headway. It is distracted and disconcerted by its own fertility. It is terrified in particular by the capitalist and labor organizations to which it has given birth. But it will not continue to be disconcerted and terrified. It is adopting the very political instruments which are necessary for the purpose of keeping control of the increasingly numerous and increasingly powerful agencies of its own life. The attempt, far from being a reactionary reversion to an earlier political and social type, prepares the way, it may be hoped, for an advance towards a better and deeper social and political union, associated with direct popular political action and responsibility.

CHAPTER XIII

DIRECT *VERSUS* REPRESENTATIVE GOVERNMENT

IN the preceding chapter I have submitted some reasons for believing that direct government is not retrogressive merely because its methods exhibit certain analogies to those used in city and tribal states. Neither does the fact that the electorate in a directly governed state has certain positive functions to perform in relation to legislation place upon such a state the stigma of reaction. Direct government cannot be fairly condemned as reactionary unless the exercise of the broad general responsibilities which it imposes upon the electorate proves inimical to the delegation of sufficient and specific additional responsibilities to other departments of the government. This second aspect of the matter still remains to be discussed. Will the advent of direct democracy result in any increase of the confusion and disorganization which prevails in the mechanism of American state representation? Or will the draught of self-confidence, which our local democracies are by way of swallowing, be communicated to the behavior of the rest of the political mechanism and invigorate the whole system? Will direct popular government commit the same fatal mistake which, to a greater or smaller extent, has already been committed by the national monarchies, by parliamentary government and by democratic legalism? Will it seek to appropriate or emasculate legislative or administrative functions which need to be delegated to other human agencies?

The critics of direct democracy can hardly be blamed for considering doubtful the answers to the foregoing questions. The American experiment in direct democracy is still in its early youth. Its meaning and its tendencies cannot be demonstrated from experience. If the active political responsibilities which it grants to the electorate are redeemed in the negative and suspicious spirit which characterized the attitude of the American democracy towards its official organization during its long and barren alliance with legalism, direct democracy will merely become a source of additional confusion and disorganization. On the other hand, if, as a consequence of its rupture with legalism, the American democracy undergoes a change of spirit, if the attempt to discharge new and responsible activities in connection with its own government brings with it a positive inspiration and genuine social energy, the result may be to renovate American representative institutions and afford novel and desirable opportunities for effective political leadership. I prefer the second of these alternatives, but the preference can hardly be justified by a consideration of the results which have already been achieved in the directly governed states. It is born of an examination of the history, the needs and the ideals of the American local democracies.

The more dogmatic partisans of direct government do

not help us very much in making a decision between the
foregoing alternatives. In fact, they seem not to understand that any such alternatives exist. They usually
attach much the same automatic efficacy to the system of
direct government that the Fathers attached to constitutionalism and checks and balances. They have not,
indeed, any declared intention of substituting direct for
representative government. They admit verbally the
necessity in a pure democracy of some effective delegation
of specific governmental functions. But as a rule they
devote very little attention and thought to the problem of
a more powerful and efficient mechanism of legislation
and administration. They are preoccupied by the flagrant betrayal of the popular interest which took place
under the traditional system, and they seem to think that
the adoption of the initiative, referendum and the recall
will not merely protect the popular interest, but liberate
the popular will — even though the popular will lacks, as
much as it has lacked in the past, the impulse of positive
social purposes.

Such an attitude toward the instruments of direct government is merely another expression of the old superstitious belief in political mechanics against which progressive democracy is bound to protest. If the people in
the directly governed states consider the new instruments
of democracy as fundamentally a safeguard against abuse
and oppression, they may succeed in abolishing one kind
of abuse and oppression, but only at the price of its being
succeeded by other kinds. If they do not impose limits

on their use of the instruments of direct government, based
upon the conditions of their profitable service, it will prove
to be a barren and mischievous addition to the stock of
democratic political institutions.   The success of the new
instruments as negative safeguards will be commensurate
with their success as agencies for the realization of positive
popular political purposes.   Their serviceability as agencies
for the realization of popular political purposes will depend
upon the ability of democratic law-givers to associate with
them an efficient method of delegating popular political
authority.   Direct democracy, that is, has little meaning
except in a community which is resolutely pursuing a vigorous social program.   It must become one of a group
of political institutions, whose object is fundamentally to
invigorate and socialize the action of American public
opinion.

The salient reasons which make it necessary to associate
the advent of direct democracy with the attempt to realize
a positive social program have already been indicated.
They are derived from the profound alterations in the
balance of a political organization which is substituting a
positive for a negative social policy.   The abstract
legalistic individualism of the Jeffersonian democracy had
in theory no need of any machinery of direct popular control.   The activity of government was restricted, and its
organs were emasculated, in the interest of a specific formulation of individual rights.   Government was considered to be merely a form of temporary police supervision.
Such a political system was placed in irons by the Law

and lacked the power to do any harm.   It really needed to
operate somewhat independently of public opinion.   Fermentation of public opinion and active political and social
experimentation could not accomplish anything of real social
value.   The essential popular needs were already safeguarded in the Law, which deserved vigilant protection
and unquestioning obedience on the part of all good citizens.
Effective popular control of such a government was unnecessary.   Government was not intended to be the instrument of important popular social purposes.

In its actual historical development the government soon
became the instrument of important popular social purposes, and it was obliged to develop a corresponding method
of popular control.   But the popular social purposes
which the state and Federal governments formerly attempted to realize were derived from the old individualistic
social economy, and the control supposed to be exercised
by the partisan organizations was ineffective.   A wholly
new situation was created when the local democracies came
to need and possess a genuinely social policy, which threw
increased burdens upon the government, and commensu-
rately increased its power.   Under such conditions direct
popular control over the mechanism of government became
of essential importance.   A negative individualistic social
policy implies a weak and irresponsible government.   A positive comprehensive social policy implies a strong, efficient
and responsible government.   But a strong and efficient
government, which exercises a large part of the authority of
the state and which is not bound by the substantive pro-

visions of the fundamental Law, might well be dangerous not only to individual civil rights, but to popular political rights. Every precaution should be adopted to keep it in sensitive touch with public opinion. A lack of responsiveness to public opinion would tempt it to become domineering and oppressive, and would in the long run make its own work abortive as well as dangerous. A social policy is concerned in the most intimate and comprehensive way with the lives of the people. In order to be successful, it must rest on the basis of abundant and cordial popular support.

The mechanism of direct government has, consequently, an essential function to perform in the organization of a social democracy. The realization of a genuine social policy necessitates the aggrandizement of the administrative and legislative branches of the government. Progressive democracy recognizes the need of these instruments, but it recognizes the need of keeping control of them. A strong government with an affirmative policy and effective popular control are supplementary rather than hostile one to another. The realization of such a policy will in the long run demand both an efficient system of representation and an efficient method of direct popular supervision.

The friends of direct government do not usually advocate it, for the reasons indicated in the preceding paragraph. An exclusively representative government is to many of them a perfectly satisfactory form of democratic political organization. It is objectionable only because it has failed to be really representative. A recent convert to pure democracy, President Woodrow Wilson, has expressed in the following words the reasons for his conversion : "If we felt we had genuine representative government in our state legislatures, no one would propose the initiative and the referendum in the United States. Our most ardent and successful advocates regard them as a sobering means of obtaining genuine representative action on the part of legislative bodies. They do not mean to set anything aside. They mean to restore and to reinvigorate rather." And a much more radical critic of our traditional system, Professor J. Allen Smith, who also favors direct popular political action, asserts that "a government of the representative type, if responsive to public sentiment, would answer all the requirements of a democratic state."

The adoption of direct government may, it is true, end by reinvigorating representative government; but if so, the result will not be accomplished by refusing "to set anything aside." The first thing which must be set aside is the method of representation which has passed in this country under the name of representative government. Direct government will never reinvigorate our existing state of political institutions. What it may accomplish is to supply energy to a new and better method of delegating popular political authority.

A statesman whose dominant object was the reorganization of existing state representative government would be foolish to depend upon the initiative and the referendum for the accomplishment of his purpose. There are a score of ways in which American state government could be made more respresentative without any invocation of the instrument of direct government. The first condition of effective representation is the bestowal upon the representative body of some effective power and responsibility, which, as all admit, is precisely the condition which has been largely and increasingly absent from our so-called representative institutions. Direct government does not automatically satisfy this need. On the contrary, as the experience of the state of Oregon sufficiently proves, its merely external addition to the existing machinery of representation tends, if anything, to attenuate still further the meagre responsibilities officially conferred on our state representative agencies.

So far as these state representative agencies are concerned, a representative value cannot be restored to them, because they were never intended to be and never have been representative in any self-respecting meaning of the word. A thoroughly representative government is essentially government by men rather than by Law. The active exercise of effective political responsibility is confided to a body of the elect. They assume the same responsibility for the ultimate welfare of the state that the American system delegates to the Law and its official expounders. True, the legislative body may govern, just as the Law was permitted to govern, by virtue of an explicit or implied popular consent, but in a representative system popular power is exercised only to be delegated. For the time being, complete legal responsibility for the public weal is conferred upon the legislature. Quite obviously no such responsibility has been conferred by the American system either upon the legislature or upon the legislature and executive together; and, to my mind, it cannot be expected that any exclusively representative system will be even fairly successful on any other terms.

⌐ The Progressive Republicans, who are advocating an increase of executive power and a closer coöperation between the executive and the legislature as the most effective means of reinvigorating the representative system, can make a very strong argument in its favor.⌐ They can make a stronger argument than can those advocates of "pure" democracy who expect to develop a genuinely representative government by grafting the instruments of direct government on an essentially and fatally unrepresentative system. But they cannot make a strong enough argument. The coöperation between an executive and a legislature, each of which derives its authority directly from the people, cannot be made properly operative except by some method of referring disputes to the common master — which means a considerable measure of direct government. Moreover, an American electorate would not submit for long to the increased power of the organs of government which would result from their coöperative action, without the creation of some means of effective popular control. But even if ⌐ these difficulties could be overcome, it is doubtful how far any system can be considered really representative which does not bestow complete responsibility for the public welfare upon the government. The government must have the power to determine the Law instead of being circumscribed by the Law.⌐ Just in so far as its authority was curtailed, its sense of responsibility would be relaxed and its integrity would be undermined.

A purely representative system, such as that of the United Kingdom, seeks to accomplish the fundamental objects of government by a method opposed to that of the traditional American system. The former bestows complete legal responsibility for the welfare of the state and the course of its development upon the elect in the expectation that thereby society will obtain the boon of rational guidance. "Representation is not," says Guizot, who was one of its most ardent advocates, "an arithmetical means employed to count individual wills, but a natural process, whereby public reason, which alone has the right to govern modern society, may be extracted from the bosom of society itself." This account of the ultimate meaning of a purely representative system was accepted substantially by John Stuart Mill, although with certain significant modifications; and it manifestly constitutes the only justification for the enormous power and responsibility bestowed upon the legislative body. As the result of their deliberations the action of the representatives must embody a program based upon the enduring and the binding interests of the nation.

The American constitutional system did not need to create a powerful organ of government whose wise leadership would help to extract reason from the bosom of society. That desirable result had already been accomplished. Reason had been printed on the bosom of society in indelible ink by virtue of the embodiment in the Constitution of the great principles of legal morals. Its human purveyors were rather the judges than the legislature; and the business of the courts was not merely to declare the Word, but to keep the fire of political reason glowing in the political hearth. Under such a system executives and legislatures were not supposed, and did not need, to be particularly reasonable — which is certainly a proof of the wisdom of the Fathers of the Republic. They needed most of all to be obedient and self-restrained. For if any effective method exists of extracting reason from the bosom of society, the human purveyors of this rational extract certainly require some oracular writing for their guidance; and the more authoritative this oracle can be made, the better. So far as the object of political organization is to bring to the surface an already existing fund of reason, the method adopted by the founders of the American constitutional system may be preferred to the method characteristic of a purely representative system. The latter leaves the secretion and extraction of reason much more to the operation of a clumsy mechanism. As an edifice of political rationalism, the record of the discussion and action of the British Parliament during the past century cannot be compared to the constitutional decisions of the Supreme Court of the United States; and this is true notwithstanding the fact that even in the latter some traces may be occasionally discovered of the fallibility of that sovereign faculty.

Thus the difficulty with a purely representative government is similar to the difficulty which is involved in government by Law. The assumption made by the advocates of both of these systems is that society possesses at any one time a fund of social reason which, by virtue of its superiority to interested, inexperienced and perverse counsel, is entitled to determine social action. The state should be organized chiefly for the purpose of giving control to this fund of social reason. The means whereby this control is exercised differs radically in the two systems; but we need not bother about their respective advantages or disadvantages. Neither of them meets the needs of a progressive democratic society, because in a society of this kind no such fund of really authoritative social reason can be held to exist. There is a fund of social reason which should possess some authority; but it is so small compared to social aspirations and needs that a democratic society must be organized less to obey than to increase it. The work of extracting the stores of reason from the bosom of society must be subordinated to the more fundamental object of augmenting the supply of social reason and improving its distribution. Legalism and purely representative government are unsuited to the needs of a thoroughgoing democracy, because their method of organization depends on popular obedience rather than popular education. The promotion and the diffusion of social reason cannot be brought about without a reverence for orderly procedure and without the leadership of the elect; but the erection of legalism alone or of representation alone into a system is not sufficient to secure this most important of all political objects. The best chance of securing it opens up as a result a more thoroughly popular organization of the state. The electorate must be required as the result of its own actual experience and unavoidable responsibilities to develop those very qualities of intelligence, character, faith and sympathy which are necessary for the success of the democratic experiment.

Thus neither representative government nor government by law nor any combination between the two is competent to meet all the requirements of a democratic polity. A clear-sighted, self-confident and loyal democracy will keep in its own hands the active control of all the agents and instruments of its own fulfilment. The instinctive repugnance which the American democracy has always exhibited to the delegation of too much power to any one of the separate departments of government is explicable and justifiable. No plebiscite can bestow authenticity upon an ostensibly democratic political system which approximates in practice to the exercise of executive omnipotence. No intermittent appeals to the people for their approbation can wholly democratize a system which approximates in practice to the exercise of legislative omnipotence. No reverence for the law can guarantee political and social liberty to a body of democrats who confide their collective destiny to written formulas as expounded by a ruling body of lawyers. In practice each of these systems develops into a method of class government. The men to whom the enormous power is delegated will use it, in part at least, to perpetuate the system which is so beneficial to themselves. But even if they were as wise as Solomon and as gallant and disinterested as Sir Galahad, the systems for which they spoke and acted would still be evading rather than meeting the democratic problem. None of these systems make the people actively responsible for their own reasonableness and welfare. The people do not reap the advantages to which they are entitled, but if they did receive every possible advantage, they would not be earning it and could not keep what they received.

In all three of the principal departments of government, there are essential functions to be performed which must be delegated by a democracy to selected men under conditions which make for technical efficiency and individual independence and self-respect. The Fathers of the Republic were fully justified both in keeping the powers distinguished, and in seeking to balance one against the other. Their mistake consisted in the methods adopted for preserving or readjusting the balance. The preservation of a balance depends upon the harmonious development of several elements which enter into it; and as in the course of nature harmonious development is rare, the preservation of any such balance must usually be contrived by human insistence and intelligence. Only one part of a democratic system is entitled to exercise any such function — the electorate itself. The whole of a democratic political system is divided into three parts, not merely or primarily as a protection to individual and popular liberties, but rather to provide an essential positive function for the people to perform — the function of recreating the unity which is necessarily compromised by the no less necessary specialization of governmental function. Such is the part which the people, or the closest possible approximation to the people, have to play in the process of their own nationalization or socialization. They must divide in order to act, to think, to rule, to move on and to aspire; but they must not impose upon any one of the resulting classifications or subdivisions the responsibility of ultimate social cohesion. That responsibility rests with the whole people, and its fulfilment depends upon popular intelligence, sympathy and faith.

Many sincere social democrats in this country, as well as in England or France, regard any such dependence upon direct government with the utmost repugnance. The industrial and social program of a democracy can, in their opinion, be accomplished with less friction and delay through the agency of an authoritative representative body. They are probably right in expecting that in the near future direct popular government will increase the difficulty of securing the adoption of many items in a desirable social program. But reformers of this class, like the conservatives, attach too much importance to the accomplishment and maintenance of specific results, and too little to the permanent moral welfare of the democracy. They are willing to have the people imposed upon in the interest of what is or is intended to be the popular benefit. An authoritative representative government, particularly one which is associated with inherited leadership and a strong party system, carries with it an enormous prestige. It is frequently in a position either to ignore, to circumvent or to wear down popular opposition.

But a social program purchased at such a price is not worth what it costs. It makes no difference how benevolent the intention of the government may be or how wise its legislation. The program which is carried out by such means will do nothing to make the people worthy of their advantages. The result will either be popular servility or organized popular resistance or both. The country in which a benevolent government has succeeded in carrying out the most comprehensive social policy of modern times is the country in which a social democratic party, organized to overthrow the government, has succeeded in obtaining the support of a third of the electorate.

Social reformers must, consequently, be patient as well as eager and tenacious. A moderate program which is well understood and cordially supported by public opinion, and upon which the electorate has been in some measure specifically consulted, will be much more beneficial than a more extensive program which is not so well understood, and which does not represent a genuine popular affirmation. From the beginning of civilization the people have been constantly imposed upon by moral or social or physical force in the real or supposed interest of their own welfare. The process will doubtless have to continue in some measure; but if democracy means anything, it means popular liberation in precisely this respect. It means that social reformers must present their arguments primarily to the electorate, and welcome every good opportunity of allowing the electorate to pass judgment upon their proposals.

Our conclusion, then, is double-faced. Democracy im- |

plies and needs some method of representation which will
be efficient and responsible enough to carry out a social
policy, but which does not imply the delegation of its own
ultimate discretionary power to any body of men or body of
law. No such representative system can be found in the
provisions of existing state constitutions. An organization of the executive and legislative powers, which will
give increased energy to both of them and which is adjusted
to their coöperation both one with another and with a
sufficient measure of direct government, is what is needed
and must be contrived. The new organization will be
intended first, last and always to promote political education. It must be adapted to action, but the action must
merely be the decisive temporary result of widespread
popular fermentation. It must have the chance to be
efficient, but only for the purpose of being educational.
It must be able to educate, but primarily by the road of
efficient action. The new system can accomplish nothing
without human energy, intelligence, sacrifice and faith, but
if those qualities are present, it will make the best use of
them.

CHAPTER XIV

VISIONS OF A NEW STATE

IN the preceding chapter I discussed certain general phases of the relationship which ought to obtain between direct and representative government. The discussion tended to the conclusion that the two different methods of government were supplementary and mutually interdependent, but that their confidential association would serve to modify profoundly the character of each of them. Direct government has come to stay and is entitled to stay, but it cannot dispense with the use of representative agencies and it needs representative agencies of a special kind. One of the most critical problems which confronts the American democracy is the devising of a method of direct government which will articulate with a method of efficient representation.

The existing mechanism of direct government in the United States occupies an ambiguous relation to the existing method of representation. Its immediate effect is undoubtedly to weaken an already attenuated group of representative institutions, but a tendency also exists to substitute for them a different and a stronger mechanism of representation. In states like Oregon, which have taken the new instruments of popular legislation most seriously and used them most frequently, the effect has not been the reinvigoration of representative government but its increased debilitation. Since the process of reorganization began, the political life of Oregon has been freed from many abuses and much corruption. The new system is popular and may prove to be a valuable source of popular political experience and education. But in their use of it the people of Oregon have exhibited very slight respect for the residue of their former representative system. The tendency has been to make the legislature an increasingly negligible factor in the law-making power of the state. In the words of Mr. Allen H. Eaton, who has published the most careful and illuminating criticism of the operation in that state of the initiative and referendum, "There is a strong tendency on the part of the legislature to shift responsibility to the people, and there is an apparently widening gulf between the people and the legislature, for which the initiative and the referendum in the hands of men who abuse it seems to be largely responsible." The effect of the instruments of popular government on the administration is more equivocal, partly because the administrative problems of the state have remained comparatively simple, but the attitude of the Oregon electorate towards the administration is not precisely friendly. It is ready to concentrate large administrative responsibility in the hands of a railroad commission which exercises supervision over the most powerful corporate interests operating in the state, but, on the other hand, it is instinctively inimical to the creation of new administrative officials; and the one class of bill which it seems certain to reject is a bill increasing under any circumstances or for any purpose the salary of any state official.

When, however, the relationship between direct and representative government is considered in the light of more general prevailing conditions, the outlook is more encouraging. On the whole, a close connection can be traced between a tendency to strengthen state government and to enlarge its responsibilities and the tendency to increase popular control over the operations of government.

The best illustration of a form of government which is both stronger and more directly controlled by popular opinion is offered by the rapid spread of the practice of governing American municipalities by commission. The failure of the original type of American municipal government has been so long recognized and so flagrant, and the political life of our growing cities is so much more concentrated and sensitive than is that of the states, that the movement towards organic reconstruction has naturally accomplished most in the sphere of municipal government. In the East, the general tendency has been merely to add to the power and the responsibilities of the municipal administration and to diminish those of the municipal legislature without counteracting this increased power by any strengthening of direct popular control; but in the West a better balance has been preserved between the two aspects of the reorganization. While the governing commission is usually required both to determine the policy of the municipality and to manage its business, its members are individually subject to recall, many of its more important decisions may be suspended and referred to a popular vote and certain of its most important decisions must be submitted. Moreover, the electorate usually retains the power to initiate legislation and to adopt it without asking the consent of the administrative organ. Thus the commission form of government is a complete example of a simple and powerful mechanism of government, the success of which depends upon actual and continuous popular coöperation. In this instance the process of simplification may have been carried too far. The commission should not be made directly responsible both for the general policy of the city and for the details of its administration. Such a concentration of power may work well in small cities, whose administrative work does not require very much expert knowledge or experience; but in the case of large cities an elected official serving for a short term is not likely to possess the technical knowledge required for the efficient management of specific public services. On the whole, however, the popularity of the commission form of municipal government is the most encouraging expression of a desirable tendency to combine a simple, strong and efficient government with a thoroughly popular government.

In the case of state government no tendency of any similar importance, corresponding to the radical reconstruction which is taking place in municipal government, is as yet observable. Yet in this larger field of institutional experimentation the influence of analogous political ideas can be traced. During the long process of emasculating the active members of the state governments, some branches of the administration did not suffer as much as did the legislature. A certain tendency existed, even when the state governments were most corrupt and misrepresentative, to increase and to centralize state administrative authority. Although subordinate officials who had once been made elective were never restored to the list of appointees, and although the chief executive was still deprived of his essential responsibility for the execution of many of the state laws, still the new administrative officials created from time to time were often placed under executive control, the scope of the state administration was broadened and its organization somewhat concentrated. During the past twelve years, while so many of the western states have been adopting the mechanism of direct government, a similar tendency has gathered headway and volume. The need for the supervision of various phases of local industry has caused a considerable increase of state administration, which has been endowed by the legislatures or by the people with larger discretionary powers than was formerly the case. In California, for instance, the same general election which wrote the initiative, referendum and recall into the constitution of the state, created a group of commissions endowed with unprecedentedly comprehensive powers over the economic activities of its corporations and its people.

To a very considerable extent the tendency towards an increase of discretionary administrative power and towards the larger participation of the electorate in the work of government have originated independently one of the other and have not been connected in the popular mind by any essential bond. But of late years the leaders of the progressive democratic movement have begun to comprehend that the two phases of contemporary political reconstruction are united by something deeper than an accidental historical coincidence. Some of the men who have fought most stoutly for the adoption of the initiative, referendum and the recall have also been most emphatic in their advocacy not only of an increase in administrative authority, but of certain correlative changes in administrative organization. They have understood that the new responsibilities which have been imposed upon the administration will not be properly redeemed unless the administration is made very capable and very efficient. They have become earnest advocates, consequently, of a change in the ballot which will concentrate the attention of the electorate on the selection of a much smaller number of officials and so afford to the voters the opportunity of exercising more discrimination in their use of the franchise. The national platform of the Progressive party, for instance, grouped a declaration in favor of the initiative, referendum and the recall with a declaration in favor of a short ballot. A close association was implicitly declared between these two apparently different but really supplementary methods of making the popular will effective.

Many different methods are now being proposed to reorganize American state government in the interest of a combination of increasing administrative and legislative

U

power and increasing popular control. The problem of
effecting such a combination in a form which may prove
acceptable to local public opinion and adaptable to local
political traditions, is being earnestly studied in many different states both by political experts and by practical
politicians; but in no state is the study being conducted
with so much care and with so excellent a prospect of accomplishing useful practical results as in Wisconsin. Its
political leaders have cautiously approached the problem
from many different points of view. The administration
of the state has been reorganized, its powers largely increased and its efficiency so far promoted that the work of
the Wisconsin commissions has set the standard for similar
bodies throughout the country. The legislature has been
developed into an unusually useful organ, partly as a
consequence of an improvement in personnel and partly
by virtue of an improvement in the technique of preparing
legislation. In several ingenious ways attempts are being
made to coördinate the work of the different administrative
bodies and to establish a mutually helpful relation between
them and the legislature. Tentative plans are being considered for the establishment of some kind of a budgetary
system. At the same time the initiative and referendum
have been adopted — although in a modified form, which
seeks to prevent the legislature from being superseded as
the dominant source of legislation by the instruments of
direct government. Finally, proposals have also been discussed looking towards an increase in executive power over
legislation by bestowing the initiative upon the governor.

This series of separate and well-considered proposals towards state political reorganization constitutes the most interesting series of experiments which are being conducted in any state in the Union. Their object is to graft improvements upon the trunk of the present system without discarding anything of value in the existing institutions of the state and without seeking to bring about too many radical changes all at once. A reorganization brought about in this manner is likely to be enduring in its character and steadily fruitful in its results. Other American commonwealths would do well to follow such an excellent example. Nevertheless, in the following consideration of a specific plan of state political reorganization I shall look elsewhere for my illustration. In certain other states, such as Colorado, Kansas and Oregon, proposals are being made to supersede the existing system with a complete new outfit of state political institutions. The results of these wholesale experiments may well prove to be inferior to the more patient and cautious process of reconstruction which is being undertaken in Wisconsin; but they have one salient advantage for a writer who is discussing the general problem of state political reorganization. By presenting the various aspects of the new system in a sharp, consistent, impressive shape, they provide a better vehicle for the explanation and the emphasis of the more fundamental and momentous issues which are involved in an attempt to improve American state government.

Oregon, as we have already seen, is the state in which the instruments of direct popular government have entered most completely into the active political life of the people, while at the same time it is the state in which the system in its practical effect has done most harm to the essentials of representative government. It is the more significant, consequently, that in this same state of Oregon a movement has already made some headway, which seeks to erect on the basis of direct popular government a novel, responsible and powerful machinery of representation. The men who are behind this movement are, moreover, identical with the men who contributed most effectually to the introduction of the existing Oregon system. The proposed plan of state political reorganization has been prepared by the "People's Power League" of which Mr. W. S. U'Ren is secretary, and it has, in part, already been submitted to the electorate of the state with the indorsement of this organization. In spite, however, of such excellent backing it has not been received with favor. On two different occasions parts of the plan have been emphatically repudiated by the voters. It has consequently only a small apparent chance of being accepted at any time in the near future. Indeed it will probably never be adopted without a much more vigorous campaign of publicity in its favor than any which has yet been undertaken. The voters can hardly be expected to accept radical changes in their institutions without being prepared for them — either by the pressure of a critical situation or by systematic and lively public discussion. Unsuccessful, however, as has been the attempt to recommend this plan to the voters of the state, it is the most complete instrument of the kind which the increasing interest in this essential matter has as yet brought to light. It represents many years of hard work by a group of able men, whose disinterested preoccupation with the welfare of the American democracy has frequently been proved; and it is worth more respectful consideration from the students of American political institutions than it has received from the voters of the state.

Under this new Oregon plan the executive becomes the instrument to which is intrusted both the responsibility of carrying out the prevailing popular will and the power to redeem this responsibility. Effective political leadership of the state is concentrated in the executive, although the strengthening of the legislature is considered to be of no less importance, and means are proposed to accomplish that end. Both the governor and a legislature of one house are to be elected on the same day for the same term of four years, thus doing away with the meaningless and indefensible embarrassment of majority rule, which results from the constitution of two houses and an executive, each of which serves for different terms. In the governor is concentrated complete and exclusive executive power. He appoints not only his own cabinet and all state officials, but the local sheriffs and county attorneys. The one other state administrator elected by popular vote is the auditor, which is a harmless concession to a strong prevailing tradition. Among the official family of the governor is included a state business manager, who is to receive a comparatively liberal salary, and who does not have to be a resident of Oregon. Thus the plan embodies a thoroughgoing

application of the general principle of the short ballot. Integrity is conferred on the state administration. The attention of the voters is to be fastened on the election of practically one executive chief, who will possess full responsibility,
both for the management of state business and the enforcement of state laws. In making nominations for governor
the direct primary is abandoned as unnecessary. Candidates are nominated by petition and are elected by a system
of preferential voting which requires for the successful candidate the approval of an actual majority of the electorate.
The governor is, of course, subject to recall.

So far as yet described, the state governor does not
differ essentially in his functions from the President of the
United States — except that he may be recalled before
his term expires. But the Oregon democrats are not
content with strengthening him as the chief of the state
administration. He could not meet his responsibilities
as an administrator unless he were in a position to have a
positive influence on the legislation. The power merely
of recommending legislation, which he now possesses, is
increased by bestowing on him the right of sitting in the
legislative body, of casting a vote therein, of introducing
bills and of advocating them on the floor of the house.
He is deprived of the veto, because in any system of direct
government the veto belongs naturally to the electorate;
but he obtains the far more effective power of initiating
legislation and of urging its adoption by the legislature.
The veto in the hands of the governor becomes a mere
instrument of obstruction. It may prevent the enact-

ment of bad legislation, but it can rarely contribute to the enactment of useful legislation. The initiative is a much more powerful instrument and is a necessary part of the legal powers of an effective and responsible state political leader.

In the case of one particular class of bills the initiative of the governor is exclusive. All appropriation bills must be introduced by him. He and his cabinet prepare the state budget and submit it to the legislature very much as does the English Ministry. The legislature can reduce specific items in the appropriation bill, but it is not allowed to make any increases. The expectation is that by these means the financial business of the state will be very much more economically managed. The state administration can be held directly responsible by the legislature and by public opinion for any extravagance, while at the same time it will have a better chance of securing the money required for the carrying out of its policy. The heads of the departments will sit in the house, and can be made to answer questions, to explain in public how far they succeeded in their departmental work of the past year and what they propose to do during the coming year. They will be subject to much more effective control than they are at present, because they cannot avoid either full responsibility or close public scrutiny and criticism, but this control will not be of a kind which would hamper or prevent the carrying out of a definite administrative policy. The administration becomes, indeed, the government in the English sense of the word, whose duty it is to propose desirable measures of state policy and whose authority is sufficient to carry out its measures — as long as it retains public confidence.

Had the proposal been made ten years ago to bestow legislative initiative upon the state executive, it would have been deemed too fantastic for serious practical consideration; but during the intervening decade a remarkable change has taken place in the position which the executive occupies in the public mind. Wherever public opinion has been vigorously demanding the adoption of a progressive state policy, the agent to which it has turned for the carrying out of that policy has been a candidate for governor. Time after time governors have assumed an initiative not formally granted to them by the law, and have forced or attempted to force a program of reforming legislation upon a reluctant legislative body. These executives have usually been accused of usurpation of power, but the accusation has not apparently had any practical effect. At every new election the innovation becomes more popular. Candidates running on the ticket of both parties adopt it. Governors who reject it and who remain scrupulously loyal to the old theory of the separation of powers are considered weak and poor-spirited. At the present time a Democratic President and a Democratic Governor of the most populous American state are frankly assuming the political leadership of their respective constituencies without having incurred up to date any effective resistance or any particular obloquy.

The aggrandizement of executive power contained in

the Oregon plan merely authorizes executive leadership and provides it with its necessary machinery. At present it takes an exceptionally able and aggressive man, backed by an exceptionally conscious and resolute body of public opinion, to perform the work required of a gubernatorial boss. The man who undertakes it is hampered constantly by the inadequacy of his powers. If he is possessed of only ordinary energy and ability, he is usually incapable of meeting the demands of the situation. But if the executive were placed in a position which forced him to assume political leadership of the state and which provided him with all the necessary weapons and instruments of leadership, the adoption of progressive legislation would not depend so much upon the election of a very exceptional individual. A man of ordinary vigor and ability might be able to do the work demanded of him with sufficient success. When he announced his candidacy, he would have to seek the support of the electorate by making certain specific promises. He would come into office with his work cut out for him and with a yardstick of success or failure definitely established. The electorate would be intrusting the power not to a party, nor to a system, but to a man, yet it would not be granting to the man an unlimited franchise. He would be placed where he was to accomplish certain specific results. His achievement would be measured by the recollection of specific promises, and just in so far as he lost the confidence of his supporters, his power would automatically diminish.

Nevertheless, his legal powers, when reënforced by public

confidence, would give him an enormous advantage over any other specific branch of the government. Might not that advantage be so overwhelming as to degrade the legislature into an insignificant and unnecessary part of the governmental mechanism? Could not such a powerful administration easily arrange the convenience of a subservient legislative majority? Would not the result be to bestow upon the once omnipotent American legislature about as much power and dignity as had the legislative assembly during the early years of the second Napoleonic empire?

Such might very well be the result, provided the legislature of the regenerated American state continued to be elected from local constituencies; but the plan of the People's Power League reorganizes the state legislature as radically as it does the executive. The purpose of this reorganization is not merely to improve the quality of its membership and the vitality of its representative function, but also to erect it into an effective balance against the apparently overwhelming power of an executive acting in such close coöperation with the prevailing popular will.

The legislature consists of a single body of sixty members. The state is divided into a fixed number of districts of varying size, each district being entitled to a number of representatives proportionate to its population. The smallest of these districts elects two legislators. The largest, consisting of the county in which Portland is situated, elects eighteen. Each voter can select only one candidate and is allowed no second preference. A candidate must live in the district in which he is nominated, but a voter may cast his ballot for a candidate nominated in some other district. If any one-sixtieth of all the voters of the state select one person for representative, his election is insured. In a district entitled to two representatives the two candidates who shall severally receive the largest number of votes are elected. A corresponding rule applies to the larger districts. But every representative wields a voting power in the legislative assembly equal to the proportion of the total vote which contributed to his election. No bill can pass the Assembly unless it secures the approval of representatives who are proxy for an actual majority of the votes cast for legislative candidates. Defeated candidates for governor on any party ticket recognized by the laws of Oregon are *ex-officio* members of the legislative assembly and are proxy for the total number of electors in the state who voted for unsuccessful candidates of their parties for the legislature. Members of the assembly are subject to recall either by the state at large or by their own district.

The object of the foregoing organization of the legislature is, of course, to break away from the system of district representation and bring about the representation of salient minor phases of public opinion. The transition from the old system to the new is skilfully managed by means of the provision that a candidate must live in the district in which he is nominated; but the fact remains that any one-sixtieth of the voters resident in any part of the state could, by uniting, elect a preferred candidate. Minor phases of public opinion would have an opportunity of organizing and securing a representation proportional to their actual voting strength. If the labor unionists could command one-twelfth of the votes, they could elect one-twelfth of the assemblymen; if farmers constituted two-fifths of the population, they could, in case their interests were affected, command a corresponding minority in the assembly. So it would be with any other interest or phase of public opinion which was sufficiently self-willed or self-conscious to seek representation. Interests or opinions seeking representation in the assembly would vary at different times according to the vicissitudes of the political history of the state. The number and strength of the minorities would depend upon the political energy and power of cohesion which their membership could develop. While in general they would consist of the fundamental economic and social classes in the community, such as organized labor, business men, the learned professions and the like, any particular class might be very much under-represented, in case no issue arose which stimulated it to combine. But representation would not be confined to interests and classes. Agitators in favor of particular reforms would try to convert a sufficient number of adherents to obtain a voice in the legislature. If any particular agitation, such, for instance, as that in favor of the single tax on land values, gathered a numerous following, it might alter the whole balance of power in the state by forcing another powerful minority, such as the land-owners, into a league of self-protection. As any considerable minority increased in strength, it would seek to become a majority, but as it sought to become a majority either its purposes or its standing would gradually change. If its policy remained narrow and exclusive, it would alienate other interests and tend to create a combination among its enemies. But usually in order to obtain its majority it would have to conciliate other interests and to liberalize its own proposals. It would seek its majority in the electorate rather than in the legislature, and in either event the personality of some man would play a decisive part in the process. A majority could not easily be created and held together except by the powerful bond of individual leadership.

Such is the general outline of a state political system the express purpose of which is to combine efficient representative government with ultimate popular political responsibility. But the kind of representative government which it creates differs essentially from that which has been associated with a legalistic or with a parliamentary system. The representatives are not to represent districts or organized parties or the public reason or the leadership of any one class. They represent salient and significant phases of public opinion. The executive represents essentially the purposes of a prevailing majority in the political composition of the state. The legislature represents those minor phases of public opinion which have sufficient energy and conscience to demand some vehicle of expression. But after having thus divided the state up into powerful and significant groups, the electorate keeps in its own hands the power of ultimate control and ultimate adjustment.

Disputes among the groups must be referred to the voters; and they can always withdraw their confidence from an individual with whose behavior they are dissatisfied. The fundamental object of the plan is to create a representative system which will act and react upon an energetic and responsible classification of popular opinion.

Although the plan remains at present merely a project, yet the probability is that it or some similar plan will be tried in certain American states. It brings into a coherent combination a number of ideas upon which many progressives are agreed, and a number of tendencies in state government which have had a powerful influence without receiving an official expression. Its relation to real phases of contemporary opinion is sufficiently close to entitle its provisions and purposes to detailed discussion. Its most superficial critic would anticipate that its adoption would work grave changes in American state government; but probably not even its advocates fully understand how far-reaching those changes might be. Popular political consciousness would be stirred to its depths. The unconscious habits as well as the conscious purposes of the state political body might well be profoundly altered. Some attempt should, consequently, be made to indicate the nature of these changes and what relation they would bear to the fundamental objects of political association.

CHAPTER XV

MAJORITY RULE AND PUBLIC OPINION

THE type of state political system sketched in the preceding chapter has been described as the organization of executive leadership. It imposes functions upon the executive very different from those required by the traditional system. He would, indeed, remain, or rather he would for the first time become, really responsible for the execution of the laws and for the efficient transaction of the public business; but he would be equally responsible for the passing of such new legislation as was demanded by the prevailing popular opinion of the state. Thus his functions would be more representative than administrative. He would have obtained office by virtue of the support of a specific body of popular opinion for the purpose of accomplishing a definite program of legislation. This body of public opinion would constitute him as the political leader of the state with full power to carry out its will.

Advocates of direct government may claim that executive leadership of this class would be both dangerous and useless as long as the electorate could make its will prevail by means of the initiative and referendum. Why concentrate so much power in the hands of any one individual? In answer to this question we shall have to consider carefully how much and what kind of results can be accomplished for popular public opinion by the delegation of power. If the electorate actually could make its will prevail by means of the initiative and referendum in their ordinary form, the organization of executive leadership might be useless, if not dangerous; but the point is that the organization of executive leadership provides popular opinion with an able and indispensable instrument of formulation and of collective action. The advocates of direct government often assume that at any particular time a perfectly mature and definite popular public opinion exists upon the various questions of state policy, and that such an opinion can be automatically registered by means of the instruments of direct government. Such is not the case. Public opinion requires to be aroused, elicited, informed, developed, concentrated and brought to an understanding of its own dominant purposes. The value of executive leadership consists in its peculiar serviceability not merely as the agent of a prevailing public opinion, but also as the invigorator and concentrator of such opinion.

Progressive democracy needs executive leadership, because it accomplishes so effectively one very important object of democratic political organization. Better than any exclusively parliamentary system, any legalistic system or any system of pure democracy, it organizes and vitalizes the rule of the majority. As a consequence of bestowing the leadership of the state upon one man who represents the dominant phase of public opinion, it develops and consolidates majority rule as it has never yet been developed and consolidated in the history of democracy;

and precisely because it gives power and meaning to majority rule, it will make a desirable contribution to the art of democratic government.

In the history of democratic political institutions there has never been any serious attempt made to contrive for the rule of the majority an efficient organization. Most of our so-called democratic instruments of governments originated during a period when democratic political institutions were considered to be both undesirable and impossible. Existing agencies of class government have gradually been adjusted to the more pressing needs of a democracy, but the adjustment has never been complete or satisfactory. Its incompleteness has been at least partly due to the persistent desire rather to avoid than expressly to recognize and to organize the rule of the majority. In the history of municipal democracies the domination of majorities had been almost universally factious and destructive of the integrity of the body politic. Democrats themselves have usually been apologetic about it, or else have associated it with some fatalistic conception of its necessary righteousness and efficiency. In neither case has it been considered in a disinterested spirit as an indispensable instrument of democracy which should be operative only within certain limits, but which within those limits has a particular function to perform of exceptional importance. In a mature democracy majority rule ought not to be feared nor avoided nor worshipped. What democrats should try to do is to create it — to give to it an appropriate form, sufficient power and an effective counterpoise.

None but an idolater could believe for one moment that
the initiative and referendum in the forms which they
have ordinarily assumed are instruments of majority rule.
They depend on popular action, but the proportion of the
people who act and in particular cases rule is never a majority. They are instruments of minority rule and usually
of the rule of a very small minority.

The ordinary mechanism of the initiative operates so as to
give to a small percentage of the voters the right to force
the electorate either to accept or reject a specific legislative
measure. This is an extremely valuable privilege, because
the right to force a vote on specific legislative projects,
which cannot be discussed in detail or amended, but which
must be approved or disapproved as a whole, places an
enormous power in the hands of a skilful and persistent
minority. The initiators might frequently be able to wear
down or circumvent the opposition of a less able and tenacious majority. The privilege, valuable as it is, should be
granted, so that the electorate may have certain reserves
which are not stationed on the political frontier, and which
can be called up in times of need. But it should be granted
only at the bidding of a carefully validated petition signed
by a comparatively large number of voters, and whether
granted or not it still leaves the problem of majority rule
unsolved. It confides the leadership in legislation to small
minorities, and allows to the majority only the negative
function of submitting to the imposition or rejecting it.
In any event the great weakness of the initiative in its
ordinary form consists in its failure to work sufficiently in

favor of the popular political education. Measures submitted by this method to popular vote cannot in the very nature of the case receive that thorough ventilation and discussion which tends to inform and illuminate popular opinion. The general issue raised by the proposed law, upon which an ordinary voter may have formed an intelligent judgment, will be obscured behind specific provisions in which the average voter has little interest. The questions on which the voters are called upon to vote should be questions of general policy which are presented to them under conditions which will stimulate public attention.

The machinery of direct government not only confides the leadership in legislation to minorities, but in its actual operation it validates the adoption of legislation by minorities. It is, of course, notorious that when measures even of great importance are submitted to the electorate, they are not voted upon by anything like as large a proportion of the electorate as are the candidates for governor. At its highest the vote on a proposed law is rarely over eighty per cent, not of the registered vote, but of the vote for governor, while it frequently falls below twenty-five per cent. The average is about sixty per cent. Hence the provision which has sometimes been used, that a proposed law shall not be considered adopted unless it receives a majority of all the votes cast at the election, makes the whole system practically inoperative and is vigorously opposed by the advocates of the initiative and the referendum.

The friends of direct government do not pay enough attention to the fact that their proposed instruments of democracy entirely break down as agencies of majority rule. No doubt the minorities which do legislate under the existing Oregon system are better qualified for the task than is the more inert majority. No doubt the system operates to confer on alert and energetic voters much more influence on legislation than was formerly the case. But surely when a sincere democrat offers arguments such as these to justify the operation of supposedly democratic instruments, he is comparable to a man who is sawing off the limb of a tree on the outer end of which he himself is sitting. Democracy is not government by peculiarly qualified people or by a peculiarly qualified part of the people. It is or it should be government in which the largest possible proportion of the adult citizenship of the country effectively participate. The fact that in this instance the failure of the majority to participate is its own fault makes no essential difference. A democracy should not be organized so that the alert and vigorous minority can easily make its will prevail over their less vigorous fellow-citizens. It should be organized so as to stimulate the liveliest possible political interest over the widest practicable political area. Such agencies of minority rule as the initiative and referendum in their ordinary form fail absolutely to contribute to the accomplishment of this necessary democratic purpose. Their real value is that of negative safeguards, the existence of which may help to reconcile popular opinion to the more powerful organization of the fighting forces of a democratic state.

The several kinds of representative government do not,

of course, pretend to be agencies of majority rule. The particular function of representation by law in the traditional American system was to tie the hands of the majority and reduce it to insignificance in the management of public affairs. Representative assemblies, on the other hand, were supposed to embody not the will of any definite fraction of the community, but the dim religious light of public reason. Second chambers were universally constituted so as to check the power of a possible majority in any one legislative assembly. In practice, however, parliaments were never very successful as radiant centres of public reason. Their first business was to govern. They could not govern by unanimous consent or, like the Supreme Court of the United States, by the power of the Word. They had to govern through the agency of a majority, so that the essential aspect of parliamentary government came to be the creation and maintenance of a majority. But the mere fact that parliament, like the electorate, was a many-headed body made the creation and the maintenance of a majority a matter of great difficulty. A majority for what purpose? If all the members of a parliament took the trouble to form convictions of their own on all public questions and insisted on voting according to their convictions, the majority would be an unstable quantity and would be composed of different ingredients on different questions of public policy. Yet if a parliament was to live up to its professional part as the incarnation of public reason, it was surely the duty of each representative to make up his mind about all public questions and to vote according to his convictions. As the effective government of the country a parliament needed to be organized primarily for definite and effective action; but its composition adapted it very much better to the work of deliberation and discussion.

The only solution of the difficulty was to build up a majority which would act together, no matter what its individual members thought. The result was the organization of national parties which placed loyalty to the party above individual conviction. Parties of this kind have never been organized in continental parliamentary bodies, partly because Frenchmen and Italians took their individual convictions more seriously than did Englishmen, and partly because the administrative system of continental countries was independent of the legislative assembly and gave in any event a certain strength to the government. But in Great Britain the administration was the creature of Parliament. Parliament had to be able to act decisively and efficiently. A majority had to be organized for that purpose. The necessary instrument for organizing and maintaining an effective majority was a partisan bond and machinery. A similar necessity existed in the legalistic government of the United States. In both cases strong national parties were built up for the purpose of democratizing essentially undemocratic institutions. The function of organizing efficient majorities was turned over to extra-official partisan organizations. These organizations were strong, because partisan loyalty was deliberately cultivated as the most effective means of binding citizens together for the promotion of the public interest. They became the real government of the country.

The two-party system is the most effective method which has yet been devised for the organization of majority rule. But it has serious and, to my mind, fatal drawbacks. It can never get away from the initial vice of being no more than an attempt to democratize a group of undemocratic political institutions. Just in so far as a group of really democratic political institutions are created, the foundations of the two-party system are undermined. The two parties seek to accomplish for a democratic electorate certain purposes which such an electorate ought to accomplish for itself. The system results in the organization of one artificial majority and one artificial minority, bound together by partisan traditions, personal loyalties, community of interest, and to a minor extent by common ideas of public policy. The individual citizen can be politically effective only in so far as he becomes a member of one or the other of these parties; and as a member of one or the other of these parties he is committed to the sacrifice of his personal and of his class convictions for the sake of partisan harmony. In this respect the system costs too much. Of course a citizen can never enter into any effective political association except by sacrificing the attainment of less important public purposes to the attainment of more important public purposes. In the case of the two-party system, however, the cost for a man of definite convictions outweighs the compensation. The object of the system is to organize public opinion in the interest of action, which is a desirable and necessary object; but in a genuine democracy it should be associated with a method of stimulating significant differences in public opinion. The development of such significant differences of public opinion is precisely what the two-party system seeks most to avoid. It organizes a majority so effectually that a voter cannot count politically unless he belongs to an organized party, and unless the maintenance of that party becomes his dominant political object.

Executive leadership provides, at least so far as the states are concerned, an alternative official method of organizing a majority for purposes of government. Very much as the cabinet with the prime minister at its head acts as official leader of the British Parliament, so the governor becomes the official leader of the people of the state. He acts for them or for as large a majority of them as he can gather together under his banner. · He will himself have in some measure created this majority. He will have won the support of a sufficiently large proportion of the population of the state by submitting to them a program which appeals to them and by convincing them of his personal good faith. His power will depend not upon the support of a machine, which must be paid for getting out the vote, but on his ability to secure and to hold the attention of public opinion. He becomes not the popular ruler, but a temporary popular leader, whose business it is to present a program which will obtain the approval of a majority; and this majority will be tied together also by some measure of personal loyalty for him. A majority cannot itself initiate legislation. It must act through an agent, and the best agent for the purpose is an individual endowed with the leadership and with the ordinary authority of an executive.

This temporary individual leadership can never take the place of a relatively permanent political association. As we shall see later, it must be built upon a foundation of more permanently organized social and political groups. But it may take the place of permanent partisan associations, whose object is not to express class interests or class and individual convictions, but merely to subordinate significant expressions of public opinion to the formation of an artificial voting majority. By grouping a majority around a man it associates majority rule with human interests and loyalties, just as the bipartisan system has always been associated with human loyalties and interests. Strong individual leadership supplies popular opinion with a needed mental and moral tonic. A vague popular aspiration or a crude and groping popular interest often requires incarnation in a single man, in order to reach a preliminary understanding of its own meaning and purposes. His exhortation and explanations and his proposals to convert such aspirations and interests into action bring them to a head and start them on a career of adjustment to the general social interest. Even the most sophisticated societies are rarely able to feel much enthusiasm about a principle or a program until it becomes incarnated in a vivid personality and is enhanced as a result of the incarnation. In the case of less sophisticated people, such as compose the majority of a modern democracy, no program is likely to be politically effective unless it is temporarily associated with an effective personality.

The success of any form of government in which the electorate has positive and active functions to perform depends upon its ability to create a popular interest in its operations and purposes, deeper, more general and more discriminating than that which is invoked by a bipartisan legalistic or representative system. Executive initiative and leadership, acting on behalf of a prevailing majority, will create such a popular interest, not merely because it personifies a program and brings with it an unusually large numerical popular support, but because a state organized primarily for positive action tends by its very nature to arouse and concentrate public opinion. The new state, if it ever comes into existence, will act as a result of the declared purposes of the majority. It will awaken the interest of people who want programs accomplished, and who are eager to fight for or against specific proposals. The present system is supposed to embody reason, and is intended to subordinate the collective will to rules which will prevent it from going astray. In practice its reasonableness is tantamount to automatic operation in the interest of existing property owners. It arouses lukewarm interest in its behavior, except on the part of those who benefit from its operation. Politics is a game in which the players are allowed to risk only small stakes by the benevolent management of the bank. The bank takes its reward for ruling against excessively high play by appropriating a regular percentage of the smaller returns. The new system, on the other hand, becomes the organized embodi. ment of a will — not a blind will, but one charged with a definite program. Politics under such a system ceases to be a game and becomes identified with the realities of life. The state is seeking under concentrated collective leadership really to accomplish something. Its proposed action may have momentous consequences for all individuals and classes, and will correspondingly compel their attention. The organization of majority rule will give unprecedented intensity and meaning to the political life of the state.

Assuming that executive leadership will constitute an effective organization of the rule of the majority, the criticism will naturally follow that the states will gain nothing by the new system except a new master. The unofficial partisan boss will be succeeded by a far more powerful official boss who will be the actual and inevitable ruler of the state rather than merely its leader. Some such result might eventually take place — provided executive leadership were merely added to the present system. But in the plan of political reorganization sketched in the preceding chapter, the other departments of the state political system are modified in a similarly radical manner. Both the legislature and the electorate will have the ability to make an effective resistance to any attempt by the executive to convert his leadership into an irresponsible executive despotism.

A legislative assembly, as described in the preceding

chapter, would constitute a natural and effective balance to the power of the executive. Just as the executive represents the dominant phase of popular opinion — popular opinion in so far as it could be consolidated and organized in favor of an immediate program — so the legislature would represent a frankly divided popular opinion. It would represent the salient, conscious, wilful, well-organized minorities which helped to make up the community. It would, consequently, lay bare public opinion at a different angle — public opinion separated into its ingredients — public opinion in its fragmentary, fermenting, striving and growing aspects. Minor phases of opinion would not merely be expressed, but they would be stimulated. The provision made for their official expression would encourage their formation and their activity. Leadership would be developed. The individual representative would bear the same relation to a special phase of opinion that the temporary executive leader would to his more general and more numerous constituency. The special body of opinion would become articulate in him and in his associates. He would, wherever possible, advance its purposes by his vote; but he would be, for the most part, a speaker rather than a voter. The primary function of the representatives of the minorities would be to popularize the convictions and the purposes of their constituencies.

Public opinion in its divided minor aspects, like public opinion in its dominant aspect, has been gradually obtaining by extra-official means an increasingly effective representation. A large number of voluntary associations have sprung up during the past twenty years, devoted to the propagation of special economic interests or special political and social ideas. Very often the primary object of these associations has not been political. Labor unions, farmers' associations and chambers of commerce were organized for social or business reasons, and have mixed in politics only incidentally and on special occasions. But just in proportion as the legislation of the state was determined by a social ideal, the special interests of these classes have become more and more affected by political action, and they have themselves been forced to participate in politics. They will be forced hereafter into still more active participation. The associations of business men, of farmers and of wage-earners will increase in numbers, in influence and in political responsibilities and opportunities. Just in proportion as they become politically active and responsible, they will seek some more effective method of political representation than that which they can obtain through the existing bipartisan district system.

These significant minor phases of public opinion are not, however, based exclusively on economic classes. The voters are also being grouped in relation to their convictions upon special phases of political economic and social reform. The number of civic societies, voters' leagues, ballot associations, woman's suffrage unions, single-tax clubs and the like are increasing steadily and are exercising more and more influence upon the political action of their members. All these associations are competing both with one another

and with the traditional political parties for the allegiance
of a certain proportion of the electorate. They are becoming the most effective formative elements in American public
opinion, and more than anything else they justify an
increase of direct popular political power and the creation
of a system of direct representation. In the course of time
they are certain to demand some official vehicle of expression — some better method of presenting their claims for
general consideration. As soon as their existence is encouraged rather than discouraged by our representative system,
they will increase still more rapidly in numbers, in self-
consciousness, and in aggressive vitality.

In a representative system which depended for its
vitality upon partisan organization the encouragement of
minority representation would be attended with grave
drawbacks. It would help to undermine partisan discipline and consequently the efficiency of the government,
which is the creature of partisan discipline. But under the
proposed plan majority representation by means of executive leadership has already been officially constituted, so
that the legislature can become without any loss of efficiency the proper agency for giving energy, self-conscious-
ness and experience to the agitation of the salient minorities. Public opinion in all its vital phases would be aroused
and would obtain appropriate means of expression. Instead of pressing the varied aspects of popular conviction
and interest into two artificial moulds, as does the two-
party system, every significant idea or interest could earn
official recognition and expression, but without depriving

the government of the concentration necessary for efficient and responsible action.

The legislative assembly would become a parliament in the old sense of the word — a talking body, a battle-ground of opinion. The government would introduce its program of legislation. If it was a strong government and represented a substantial consensus of public opinion, its proposed legislation would probably obtain the support of enough of the legislators to be assured of final passage. If it was a weak government and represented a bare majority, the legislature might very well reject its proposals and force an appeal to the people at the following election. But whether the program of the administration was accepted or rejected by the legislature, it would be sure to arouse the opposition of a certain proportion of the delegates. The special minorities would probably be represented by their abler spokesmen, who would give vigorous expression to their reasons for opposing the official legislation proposals. The supporters of the program, both in the cabinet and in the legislature, would be stimulated to make an equally vigorous statement of their reasons for supporting it. The course of the discussion would be followed with lively interest throughout the state, because voters would realize that it reflected and developed the clash of their own vital interests and convictions. Probably the record of it would be sufficiently circulated by voluntary agencies; but if it were not, it should be circulated at the expense of the state. Thus every proposal to carry out a definite public policy would have its

wholesome reaction on public opinion. If the bill were
finally rejected and had to be referred to popular vote, the
electorate would have had every chance of forming a decisive and intelligent judgment.

The peculiar value of effective minority representation
is that it demands of all significant phases of popular opinion a frank statement of their case. They must come out
into the open and present their claims for consideration
under trying and testing conditions. As a consequence of
this exposure they may become socialized. The raw material of the social fabric consists of special interests and
special centres of association of all degrees of popularity,
force, maturity, flexibility and worth. They play the
same part in society as do particular desires and purposes
in the life of the individual. They are dangerous, not in
case they are allowed to obtain a normal development in
coöperation with other special interests, but in case they are
either allowed to overgrow or are unnecessarily suppressed.
The best way to prevent either overgrowth or undergrowth
is to make them public — to make them depend for their
effective relative influence less upon legal safeguards than
upon their ability to convince public opinion of their value.
Instead of proposing, as did certain reformers a few years
ago, to drive special interests out of politics, the object of
a really educational political organization should be to
drive them out from behind the law or away from illegal or
antisocial conspiracy into politics. Just in so far as they
are made to argue their case in public and to prove their
social value by reasons which will appeal to other special

groups of interest and opinion, just to that extent they may tend to become a useful part of the social organization.

The vitality of the resulting discussion would, of course, be increased by the fact that the state would be organized for action as well as consultation. Political ideas would obtain an increasing reality, because of their close relation to political action. A minority would be fighting not merely for verbal expression, but for the opportunity of legislating. Any minority with a good case and a sufficient program would have a chance of becoming part of a ruling majority. As soon as it entered into a majority it would be subjected to the supreme test of active political responsibility. In that event the exposure would become complete and the penalty of failure severe. Thus every phase of public opinion, whether minor or major, would be involved in a welcome struggle for existence. It might obtain temporary protection from such a struggle by the incorporation of its program into the relatively permanent political social heritage of the community; but even so it might at any time be hailed into court and asked to prove its social value.

Under the operation of the proposed plan the words "majority" and "minority" would assume a somewhat different meaning from that which is attached to them in ordinary political discussion. A majority is usually assumed to be a permanent collection of voters, organized for the purpose of keeping their representatives in power. Inasmuch as it can depend to a considerable extent upon the support of its individual members, no matter what its behavior

may be, it will have a natural tendency to act oppressively
and tyrannically towards the minority. Under a representative system which depends upon parties to organize the
effective government of the country, or in a country in
which any one class was socially dominant, some justification might exist for attaching such a meaning to the
word majority; but the kind of majority which would be
created by a system of executive leadership would assume
a different character. It would not be an organized collection of voters, tied together by a partisan discipline and
patriotism, but a temporary grouping which could be
easily and rapidly disintegrated. Instead of dominating
and superseding the official government, as does a partisan
organization, and instead of surviving the failure or displace-
ment of such a government, it would fall apart as soon as
its opportunities for action vanished.

In a modern state, with its complicated and varied
economic interests, its numerous and diversified classes,
its nice balance of economic and social forces, its heritage
of authentic traditions, knowledge and ideas, and its sensitive machinery for gathering and expressing public
opinion — in such a state the will of a prevailing majority
is beset by those of a cohort of possible majorities. Any
miscalculation of strength on the part of the government,
any unwarranted exercise of power, any error of judgment
in preparing or advocating its program, any access of
knowledge or resolution on the part of a certain proportion
of the electorate, would easily displace an existing government and substitute a different combination of interests,

classes, associations or individuals. No prevailing majority could travel too fast or too far along the road of special legislation, whether in the interest of a locality, a class, or an economic reform, without losing many of its marginal adherents, and consequently the security of its hold upon power. Majority rule under such conditions would be salutary, precisely because it would be fluid and adjustable. Every important minority would be an incipient or part of an incipient majority. Majorities and minorities instead of being essentially hostile elements in public opinion would become supplementary. They would interpenetrate one with another, and would be fighting or coöperating according to the character of the existing government, the nature of its program and the support to which it was entitled. The government would not be confided to any one majority, but to a succession of majorities. Although no one of them would represent the people as a whole, the result of their successive domination would be to give all the vital opinions and interests of the electorate the opportunity to exercise influence upon the political policy of the state. The ensuing government would be more than that of a party or of two parties or of a group of special interests and classes. It would tend to be a government in which the ideas and the preferences of a great majority of the people would at some time or another be put to the test, and which would become a government of the whole people just in so far as the obstacles to social unity were gradually eradicated and an effective desire for a genuinely social consummation came into being.

Notwithstanding the important functions bestowed on the executive, and the attempt to create a legislature which would constitute an effective check upon executive domination, the essential political responsibility in such a plan of government falls upon the electorate. The voters are not confiding to the executive the unlimited discretion which the French voters confided to Napoleon III. Neither are they confiding any discretion to the legislative assembly similar to that which is confided to the British Parliament. These representative agencies obtain a special, not a general, license. They have made specific promises and incurred specific obligations to their constituencies. Of course, inasmuch as all the exigencies of government cannot be foreseen, a certain amount of general discretion must be granted to any representative; but neither executive nor legislator can travel very far on an unpopular course. The electorate reserves for itself an effective immediate or proximate control. At present the powers reserved to the people are accessible only at long intervals and under rare conditions. According to the proposed plan, these powers would always remain in a state of incipient activity. They would be comparable not to a fleet which required four years to build, but to a fleet-in-being, which could strike with a little more coal in its bunkers and a few hands in the forecastle. A democracy would be merely foolhardy to grant the great powers necessitated by efficient administration to any man or group of men without providing for the possibility of a serious mistake. Every part of this machinery of representation, but particularly the executive, would have continuously to seek and to earn the confidence of a sufficient constituency, just as the British cabinet is obliged to keep the confidence of a majority of the House of Commons.   The people would have the means to revoke their trust not merely at stated intervals, but at any time when in their opinion it was in danger of betrayal.   The reservation of such a power does not bring with it any guarantee that a majority of the electorate would not be duped or bribed into the support of an unworthy man or an unsocial policy.   No people can be guaranteed against the consequence of their own unintelligence, selfishness or lack of public spirit.   But most assuredly the voters could not be betrayed except with their own explicit and continuous consent; and if a serious mistake were made, they would have every opportunity of discovering the error and every inducement to repair it.

The value of the recall as an instrument of genuinely democratic government has not been sufficiently appreciated.   It provides the ultimate safeguard against betrayal, which may and should induce a democracy to bestow strength and efficiency upon its organs of government. In the absence of the recall a democracy can scarcely be blamed for reducing the length of official terms, and for using one department to check another.   If the choice had to be made between a relatively inefficient but entirely popular government, and one which was highly efficient but alien to popular sentiment, any convinced democrat would select the first alternative.   Above all else a democratic government must be kept closely in touch with public opinion. The recall makes it more possible to keep an administration closely in touch with public opinion without any necessary sacrifice of efficiency. Once possessed of this effective and fundamental safeguard a democracy has no longer any reason to apprehend serious consequences from its own mistakes. It can afford to do away with minor safeguards. It can elect its officials for a number of years and bestow on them as much power and responsibility as is demanded by high standards of practical efficiency.

The recall is supposed to turn all officials elected subject to its operation into cowards — to deprive them of independence of conviction and purpose. If it produces any such effect, the ultimate failure of democratic government is tolerably well assured. No doubt the recall would prevent an executive from using his official power to impose upon a majority of the electorate a policy with which they disagreed; but in so far as the executive had any such power the government would be autocratic rather than democratic. A man of independent but unpopular convictions has every right and should be afforded full opportunity to convert his fellow-countrymen; but he has no right to force them to accept the consequences of his convictions or those of any other individual or minority. Independence is a trait which every popular representative should possess; but he should be allowed to exercise it only on condition that it has been earned. An elected official, endowed with a long term and with effective powers, yet subject to the recall, would have a far better chance of being independent than an official who had an indefeasible title to an impoverished office for a comparatively limited term.   The fact that he would constantly be threatened with the loss of popular confidence would act upon a man of independence of conviction as a stimulus to personal initiative.   He would possess an extraordinary opportunity of recommending his own opinions to the public.   He could make himself independent just in so far as he was capable of maintaining his leadership of public opinion; and only to that extent would he as a representative official be entitled to independence.   Whenever under such conditions he ceased to be independent, the fault would be his own.   It would mean that his leadership had failed, that he had lost his following and that he would do well temporarily to retire. Doubtless the very conditions which might afford a strong and a shrewd man an opportunity of guiding public opinion would convert a weak and unscrupulous man into a mere demagog; but such a danger is inseparable from any system of organized popular political leadership.   The very condition which offered the demagog his opportunity would expose him, in case he sought to use it, to the severest of all tests.

The reader must not misinterpret the purpose with which I have entered into the foregoing analysis of a new state political system.   My object has not been to recommend a particular plan of state political organization as the only plan which will meet the needs of a progressive democracy.   What I have tried to do has been to explain the needs and requirements of a genuinely popular system

of representative government; and the plan of the People's
Power League of Oregon has been used as a peg upon which
to hang this discussion. The particular method of state
political reorganization may or may not be adopted, but
whatever its fate, its underlying principles have a permanent value. A sincere progressive democracy must, in my
opinion, ultimately consider them. The fundamental political responsibilities of a democracy should not be delegated to any body of law, to any representative individual
or assembly or to any extra-official bipartisan political
machinery. Yet a democracy, like any other active and
progressive community, must have organs for the consideration and the realization of its policy. If it seeks to convert
the ballot-box into the chief instrument of democratic
action, it will most assuredly disintegrate. It needs an
efficient method of representation, but its agents should not
represent districts or parties or an elusive and remote
public reason. They should represent, first, the essential
function of determinate action; secondly, the various vital
popular interests and classes; and, finally, the effective
popular ideals and aspirations. A system of this kind would
enable a democracy at once to act, to deliberate and, most
of all, to learn.

With a society, as with an individual, fertility and growth
depends upon the attainment of a mutually helpful relation
between the will and the intelligence. The traditional
American political system did not establish such a relation.
By subordinating the community's power of action to specific rules derived from past political experience, it not only

enfeebled the power of collective action, and forced the democracy to create an unofficial method of accomplishing its necessary purposes, but it also enfeebled its power of thought. The American democracy could not think candidly, sincerely and vigorously, because its thinking, like its action, was circumscribed by the supposed authority of a system of rules. The emancipation of its power of collective action will bring with it the emancipation of its power of thought. The community will deliberate more earnestly and more fruitfully, because it has obtained freedom of action. The control of public opinion will be more effective under the new system than under the old, because the public will have to think as well as to act for itself. Publicity is not merely a matter of the advertising and communicating of opinion. An insincere and hypocritical opinion could be placed on the headlines of every newspaper in the country and shouted from every house-top without really becoming public. Really public opinion must be candid and consistent, and must be expressed in words which can be harmonized with other words and with actions. Public opinion could not be really public under the traditional political system, because it was concealing from itself the incompatibility between government by law and popular government. Public opinion under a genuinely popular representative system can become public and consequently effective, because it is no longer condemned to a necessary equivocation. The American democracy will become more considerate, because it will be obliged to think for itself.

CHAPTER XVI

EXECUTIVE *VERSUS* PARTISAN RESPONSIBILITY

DURING the preceding discussion of state political reorganization the two-party system has been incidentally
condemned as unsuited to the needs of a progressive democracy. Can any such condemnation be sustained? Certain eminent political publicists would agree that the two-
party system had worked badly when applied both to
municipal and state government, and that the relaxation
of partisan discipline was necessary to any radical improvement of the state political systems. But they would vigorously assert that the two-party system was indispensable
in the successful practical operation of the Federal government; and their assertion could undoubtedly be supported by a very formidable array of arguments. The
two-party system has an extraordinary record of achievement in both of the countries which have, in their own
opinion, been most successful in practising the art of popular
self-government. It has proved to be the one practically
effective method of organizing majority rule and of adapting
the exigencies of a complicated and responsible political
system to the realities and frailties of human nature. For
better or worse the great majority of American citizens
are still, politically speaking, as much as anything else

Republican or Democrat. If progressive democracy comes
to prevail, can they continue to remain as much as anything
else either Republican or Democratic?

The answer to the foregoing question will depend chiefly
upon one's general opinion of the nature and importance of
progressive democracy. As we all know, there is a progressive Democracy as well as a progressive Republicanism,
both of which are supposed not only to be compatible with
progressive democracy, but to be identical with it. On the
other hand, there is another brand of partisan Progressivism,
which is neither Democratic nor Republican, but which,
none the less, considers itself to be more progressively democratic than its older partisan competitors. For the present
many millions of the American people are, in their own
opinion, both progressive and either Democratic or Republican. If the matter were put to an immediate vote, they
would declare by an overwhelming majority that the advent of progressive democracy need not disturb their traditional partisan allegiance. Are they likely in the future
to associate progressivism with either Democracy or Republicanism? And if so, will such an association help or
hinder the possible future triumph of progressive democracy?

A convinced opponent of the system of partisan government will do well to recognize one preliminary fact of decisive immediate importance. Although the bipartisan
system may have outlived whatever usefulness it has had in
relation to state governments, it remains, to a certain extent,
an indispensable agency for the government of the nation.

The national political system is, no doubt, beginning to feel the effects of the trend towards direct democracy, which is doing so much to modify the state political systems; but the acid is working much more slowly in one case than in the other.   There is every reason why it should work more slowly.   The central government has been far more successful than the state governments.   It has never exhibited the same uneasiness, the same constant need of internal readjustment.   It has been modified, of course, at once by amendment, by judicial construction, by the aggrandizement of one or the other of its departments and by extra-official additions; but up to date its development has not tended either to disintegrate the traditional system or to substitute for it a more frankly democratic system.   It has retained throughout the four generations of our national political history a tenacious integrity, and it has exhibited an equally stubborn power of resistance to external attack. Its persistent vitality is a sufficient indication of its service-ability and its future endurance.

The one way in which this government by Law can be democratized is, as has already been pointed out, to amend the amending clause of the Constitution.   But it will be many years before this result can be accomplished.   The friends of the "gateway amendment" are still scarce in Congress.   Even after they have become numerous they will be obliged to overcome a strong and obstinate resistance which may well be proof against all assaults, until some crisis in our national affairs necessitates the calling of a constitutional convention.   In the meantime the prevailing system will persist with only minor modifications. The prevailing system is not workable without being supplemented by an extra-official system of partisan organization. But if an extra-official system of partisan government is necessary for an indefinite period, it must be made effective; and the effective method of partisan government is a two-party system.

A conviction of the persistent practical importance of the party system was an influential consideration with many progressives who contributed to the formation of a Progressive party in the summer of 1912. Their argument ran as follows: The future of progressivism as an idea demands the formation of a party exclusively devoted to the interests of that idea. Neither the Democratic nor the Republican parties can be depended upon to be sincerely and radically progressive. .They both contain a large number of adherents who are essentially conservative. Even if these conservatives do not constitute a majority of either party, they form a strong and able minority. As long as progressives remain associated with conservatives in a partisan organization, progressivism will be hampered by unnecessary and demoralizing compromises. If partisan loyalty and partisan patriotism mean anything, they mean that progressive Republicans or Democrats should be willing at times to abandon or to postpone their own political purposes in the interest of party harmony. Admitting that all effective practical political association demands some such sacrifices, do not the sacrifices which a progressive is obliged to make as the price of his alliance with conservatives cost too much? Why remain in political association with a group of men when your points of difference with them are more fundamental than your points of agreement? A progressive who remains politically affiliated with conservative Republicans and conservative Democrats is acting as if Republicanism and Democracy were of greater value to the American people than is progressivism.

Thus the formation of a Progressive party made a strong appeal to many radicals, to whom progressivism meant more than did Democracy or Republicanism, and who appreciated the importance of partisan organizations in the operation of the national political system. The progressive democratic program was considered to be indispensable to the welfare of the American people. It demanded the organization of a party united fundamentally by their devotion to that program. The whole history of political and social reform in the United States could be cited as a proof of the way in which the partisan organizations adopted reforms only for the purpose of neutralizing them. Ballot reform, civil service reform, primary reform and the like had been taken up by the party organizations in response to public opinion and had been made the subject of legislation; but this legislation was not framed in good faith by sincere men who were determined to make it successful. It went just far enough to placate public opinion, but it always stopped short of seeking to accomplish effective results. If progressivism was not constantly to be betrayed by its ostensible friends, it needed a partisan organization whose dominant purpose was the advancement of progressive policies.

A Progressive party was organized, and polled for its presidential candidate a larger vote than that received by his Republican competitor. Whatever the future history of this party, it has in one respect lived up to the expectations of its organizers. It has done more to make the progressive idea count at its proper value in American public opinion, and to make possible the realization of a certain portion of the progressive program, than has any other agency of progressive expression.

Its weakness in the state and national legislative bodies has prevented it from having any direct effect on legislation; but the fact that it holds the balance between the two older political parties has given to the program of those parties a stronger progressive tendency and has strengthened the hands of their more progressive members. President Wilson owes his nomination and probably his election to the creation of a third party. His ability to exercise an effective influence over his Democratic associates is partly due to the necessity which a governing minority is under to stick together and submit to discipline. If the Progressive party were to disintegrate, the President's situation with respect to his party would be altered very much for the worse. The Democrats would be less in need of emphatically progressive leadership, to which they are obliged to submit in order to keep the sincere progressives in their own party true to their partisan allegiance, and would not be placed so very much on their good behavior. In the

same way the Republicans are obliged to wear a mask
of progressivism in order to win back the progressive
seceders.   The conservative element in both parties would
be very much strengthened as soon as a living partisan
progressive alternative ceased to exist.

The resulting situation is curiously paradoxical.   The
future of the Progressive party depends on its ability to
convince the American people that progressivism is so
novel and important a political idea and so jealous a master
that it is incompatible with traditional Democracy and
traditional Republicanism.   Both the Democrats and the
Republicans repudiate any such aggrandizement of progressivism in theory; but they are both becoming as progressive as they know how to be in practice in order to keep
their own members out of the Progressive party.   Republican and Democratic progressives, that is, are struggling
to make a Progressive party unnecessary, and in so far as
they succeed, their own influence in their own parties will
be considerably diminished.   On the other hand, if the
Progressive party should be right in its contention that
the realization of the progressive program cannot be intrusted to half-hearted friends or covert enemies, and if it
gradually wins the support of the social and political radicals of both parties, it will be confronted by the almost
hopeless task of reconciling loyalty to the progressive ideal
with loyalty to a particular partisan organization.   The
logic of the progressive democratic principle will count
against it.   Just in so far as a progressive political program
is carried out, progressive social democracy will cease to
need a national political party as an instrument.

For the present, however, the machinery of the Federal government can be operated only by national parties which are bound together by common memories and traditions as well as common ideas, and whose members are under obligation to sacrifice their convictions of what the public welfare requires for the sake of partisan harmony. President Wilson is making a most significant, intelligent and gallant attempt to give renewed vitality to partisan government and to convert it into an agency of what he understands by progressivism. He has frankly assumed the leadership of his partisan associates, and by virtue of that leadership has conferred upon his party unprecedented powers of effective action. Discipline is enforced and opposition stamped out by the constant use of the caucus; but no dangerous ill-feeling seems to result. The Democrats in Congress accept his leadership at least as willingly as their forbears accepted that of Jefferson and Jackson. They are so surprised and delighted with their own partisan efficiency and with the privileges, emoluments and prestige of office that they are glad to pay the market rate for these boons. Up to date they have had few individual convictions which they were not entirely ready to sacrifice at the bidding of the President and of the caucus. Under Mr. Wilson's leadership they have passed the only tariff bill of the last seventy years which represented an honest attempt to subordinate special interests to the national economic welfare. Their currency legislation was an intelligent, a painstaking and, on the whole, a fair compromise between the local and the national financial needs. Consid-

ering the tendency which the Democratic party in the past
has exhibited towards dubious financial doctrine, their passage of this bill was a most notable and reassuring event.
For the first time in their history the Democrats placed on
the statute book a piece of really constructive legislation.
No wonder they are willing to accept the leadership of a
man who can convert the party into a positively useful
and purposeful political organization.

President Wilson has done more than to help the Democratic party to become a united, self-confident and efficient
political association. He has tried to persuade the American people that the Democracy is peculiarly entitled to be
the instrument of progressivism. In his "New Freedom"
he has placed an interpretation on progressivism which
associates it with a revival of the old Jeffersonian individualism and expressly distinguishes it from a social democracy. The object of the "New Freedom" as a program is
to remove the impediments which have hampered the individual in the exercise of his political and economic rights.
The emancipation is to be accomplished chiefly by negative
means — that is, by destroying excesses of political and
economic power in private hands and by imposing restraints
which will prevent the reappearance of any such undesirable
company. The legislative program of the party has only
in part conformed to the theories of its leader. In practice
the "New Freedom" has approximated in certain respects
to the "New Nationalism." But the Democratic party
has never been very much interested in squaring its
behavior with its theories. President Wilson's "New

Freedom" has served its purpose in enabling his party to believe for a few years in the existence of a friendly relation between traditional Democracy and the legislative needs of a modern democratic progressivism.

The attempt which President Wilson is making with so much ability and tenacity to prevent progressivism from escaping from the confines of the old party system is fraught with weighty consequences. If he succeeds for a sufficiently long time in keeping the leadership of the Democratic progressives without breaking with the Democratic conservatives, he will make the position of the Progressive party extremely precarious. It may fall to pieces and its membership be divided among the Democrats, the Republicans and the Socialists. He seems to have, moreover, a certain chance of success — chiefly because of the peculiar nature of Democratic conservatism. It is a conservatism of local interest rather than definite economic and political conviction. Its habitation is for the most part in the southern states. As long as their dominant local interest is safeguarded, the southern conservatives will make any sacrifice of less important matters for the sake of partisan harmony. They will accept progressive leadership, partly because they are enjoying so many of the fruits of partisan success, but chiefly because they have no political alternative outside of the Democratic party. No doubt they have had small reason to protest against any progressive legislation which has been hitherto enacted. The tariff, currency and trust bills were aimed chiefly at northern rather than southern conservative interests. But they will dutifully accept a far larger dose of repugnant progressive legislation than any they have been obliged to accept without raising any irreconcilable opposition to it. They cannot afford to permit a split in the Democratic party, because the consequences of such a split would be fatal to their own political influence. They could not ally themselves with a northern and western conservative party, which would consist for the most part of former Republicans; and if they formed a separate sectional organization, they would always remain in a hopeless minority. In so far as their Democracy is inevitable, the persistence of the old dual partisan system is essential for them.

The inability of southern Democratic conservatives to make any effective protest against northern Democratic progressivism will artificially prolong the efficiency of the two-party system. President Wilson and his immediate advisers will be able to dictate the policy of the party. They will not be obliged to compromise with their conservative partisan associates to at all the same extent as would Republican progressives. Of course, the progressive Democrats will go through the form of consulting their conservative associates. They will have to use tact, forbearance and even conciliation; but when it comes to an important difference of opinion, they will rarely have to yield. They can depend upon the southern Democratic votes just as Bryan always could — in spite of the fact that the southerners were never very much interested in Bryanism. This gives them an enormous advantage over progressive Republicans. If progressive Democrats can live up to this opportunity, it should enable them to keep the upper hand in a continuation of the duel with their traditional opponents. Their eventual failure, if and when it takes place, will be due chiefly to the poverty of their own progressivism ideal, and to their inability to make their program conform to the demands of a genuinely progressive democracy.

The enforced partisan loyalty of southern conservative Democrats may well enable progressive Democrats to prevent progressivism from undermining Democracy. But the old two-party system will merely be prolonged rather than really resurrected. Associated as it is with representation by law, it cannot survive the advent of an official representative system based upon direct popular government. The two-party system, like other forms of representative democracy, proposes to accomplish for the people a fundamental political task which they ought to accomplish for themselves. It seeks to interpose two authoritative partisan organizations between the people and their government. It demands of them that they act and think in politics not under the influence of their natural class or personal convictions, but according to the necessities of an artificial partisan classification. In this way it demands and obtains for a party an amount of loyal service and personal sacrifice which a public-spirited democrat should lavish only on the state. The unity of purpose and the effective power of joint action which results from the action of partisan discipline and patriotism should accrue to the benefit not of Republicanism or Democracy, but to that of the nation and of the really significant social ingredients which enter into the national composition.

The two-party system is a semi-democratic device which was intended to democratize an undemocratic political organization. For a couple of generations it was an effective agency of American national democracy. That it has ceased to be an agency of democracy is sufficiently proved by the means which are now being taken to reform it. The parties which were organized for the purpose of making an undemocratic government responsive to the popular will are now being reorganized by the law for the purpose of democratizing the supposed instruments of democracy. The reorganization is mechanical and is merely following the lines of the least resistance. It recognizes the peculiar importance of partisan allegiance in American practical politics, converts parties from unofficial into official instruments of popular government and seeks to democratize them by forcing their members to select their regular candidates by popular vote. Direct primaries have resulted in making the domination of the machine in defiance of partisan public opinion much more difficult; but by popularizing the mechanism of partisan government the state has thrust a sword into the vitals of its former master. Under the influence of direct primaries national parties will no longer continue to be an effective method for organizing the rule of the majority.

A party is essentially a voluntary association for the promotion of certain common political and economic objects. It presupposes a substantial agreement of opinion and interest among the members of the party, and a sufficient amount of mutual confidence. If they differ vitally in interest and opinion, and have little or no confidence in one another, the association should not be regulated; it should to that extent be dissolved.   By regulating it and by forcing it to select its leaders in a certain way, the state is sacrificing the valuable substance of partisan loyalty and allegiance to the mere mechanism of partisan association.   Direct primaries will necessarily undermine partisan discipline and loyalty.   They will make it more necessary for every voter to belong nominally to either one of the two dominant parties; but the increasing importance of a formal allegiance will be accompanied by diminished community of spirit and purpose.   Such is the absurd and contradictory result of legalizing and regularizing a system of partisan government.   If the two-party system is breaking down as an agency for democratizing an undemocratic government, the remedy is not to democratize the party which was organized to democratize the government, but to democratize the government itself.   Just in proportion as the official political organization becomes genuinely democratic, it can dispense with the services of national parties.

The state governments are, as we have seen, by way of being reorganized into more effective and representative instruments of popular rule.   In the case of the central government, the corresponding process has not been carried very far; but it is being carried far enough to indicate the gradual devitalizing of the partisan system.   In spite of the praiseworthy record which the Democrats are now making of partisan efficiency, the prediction may be confidently ventured that it will not be continued.   Partisan government at Washington will remain necessary for a long time; but it will become increasingly less effective. The system of direct presidential primaries will result in intense and bitter contests for the nomination, and in the consequent undermining of party cohesion. The party, instead of being organized in order to enable its members to consult one another and reach an agreement upon differences of opinion, will be organized chiefly as an official machinery of naming candidates. The candidate, after having been named by a majority of the voting members of his party, becomes comparatively independent of its other leaders. He has the power to write his own platform and practically to repudiate the official platform of his party. He becomes the leader, almost the dictator, of his party, as no President has been between Andrew Jackson and Woodrow Wilson. A wise, firm, yet conciliatory man like President Wilson can so exercise his enormous power as to make his party a more rather than a less effective instrument of government, just as a monarchy may become, in the hands of an exceptionally able, independent, energetic and humane administrator, a temporarily beneficent form of government. But a Woodrow Wilson is not born of every election, and when he is born the benevolent domination which he exercises over his party is a source, in the long run, of weakness rather than of strength. As a consequence of direct primaries, a party ceases to be a representative democracy. It obtains and retains its cohesion only as the result of a benevolent dictatorship.

Under the conditions defined in the preceding chapters

official executive leadership, in the name of a temporary majority of the electorate, may be an essential and fruitful instrument of democracy; but in order to be fruitful it needs to be accompanied by some method of minority representation and by the recall. In any event it is incompatible with a really vital partisan system. If the other party leaders are men of conviction who take their joint partisan responsibility to the electorate seriously, they will not submit to a method of leadership which is necessarily dictatorial. If they are not men of conviction and are united chiefly for the attainment of local or personal ends, they will submit; but they will submit to the official dictation of the President just as they formerly submitted to the unofficial dictation of the boss. They are accustomed to take orders; and when orders are lacking, they flounder hopelessly around. The old system cannot be galvanized into any real life by virtue of executive leadership. The necessity of such leadership is itself an evidence of the decrepitude of the two-party system.

President Wilson's success is making it difficult to convince people of the truth of this indictment. His manner is so conciliatory and so deferential, he claims so elaborately to be speaking and acting in the name of his party, that people are deceived as to the real nature and effect of his influence upon Democratic policy. In the case at once of the tariff, the currency, the canal and the trust legislation, he did not, as he has claimed, speak for his party. He spoke to them at a time when they were going astray and told them what to do. He can, of course, hide behind the fiction of partisan responsibility, whenever he wants to avoid speaking to his party about a legislative proposal upon which he is likely to encounter serious resistance; but no suavity of manner and no amount of wise self-restraint in the employment of his power can obscure the real facts of the situation. At the final test the responsibility is his rather than that of his party. The party which submits to such a dictatorship, however benevolent, cannot play its own proper part in a system of partisan government. It will either cease to have any independent life or its independence will eventually assume the form of a revolt. The same alternative may be stated from Mr. Wilson's point of view. The President himself, in spite of the "New Freedom," cannot permanently reconcile progressivism with Democracy. He has had the advantage hitherto of dealing with questions upon which public opinion had been informed by a long process of agitation and upon which his own party was not fundamentally divided. But unless he retires at the end of his first term, he will be obliged eventually to come out more into the open and either abandon his progressive leadership or else carry his point, as he did in the case of the canal tolls and as governor of New Jersey, by high-handed methods. The question of woman's suffrage is one among many on which the South may not be subservient, but which demands the assumption of a definite position by a progressive party leader.

In another respect, also, are the irresistible trend and needs of progressive democracy undermining the two-party system. Progressive democracy demands not merely an increasing employment of the legislative power under representative executive leadership, but it also particularly needs an increase of administrative authority and efficiency. When the system of partisan responsibility was organized in order to make government by law operative, the pioneer Democracy sought in this way to accomplish two purposes. It proposed to get both the making of the law and its administration under control. In fact, the American Democracy really did not care so much who made the laws, provided they were administered by good Democrats in conformity with individual and local interests. Thus the partisan system bestowed upon the divided Federal government a certain unity of control, while at the same time it prevented the increased efficiency of the Federal system from being obnoxious to local interests. The power of congressman and senators over the local Federal administrative officials was constantly strengthened. These officials were far more responsible to the local party organization than they were to the law or to their administrative superiors. The Republicans, in spite of their need of a stronger administration of the law, followed in this respect the example of the Democrats. The consequent weakening of administrative authority has persisted until the present day and still remains an essential aspect of the two-party system. Under American conditions a strong responsible and efficient administration of the law and of the public business would be fatal to partisan responsibility.

During the past twelve years an improvement of administrative standards has unquestionably been taking place. Presidents Roosevelt, Taft and Wilson, each in his own way and along essentially different lines, have contributed to this improvement. Increased administrative authority and efficiency is as necessary to any system of executive leadership as it is fatal to Congressional government by parties. But it has been unable to make more than a slight occasional dent in the pernicious traditional system. What with the Tenure of Office Act, senatorial courtesy, and the lack on the part of the executive of any alternative machinery of selecting appointees, the local party leaders dispose of appointments much as they please; and the appointed officials are naturally more solicitous to please their real than their technical superiors. The executive has not the power to make an effective fight against the system, because public opinion, on which he depends for his weapons, still fails to understand its real importance. In cleaving to it, party leaders in Congress are cleaving to the strongest and most necessary prop of the party system; but by so doing they are making the destruction of that system an indispensable condition of the success of progressive democracy.

CHAPTER XVII

THE ADMINISTRATION AS AN AGENT OF DEMOCRACY

THE preceding chapter closed with an assertion which, if true, is important. The overthrow of the two-party system was declared to be indispensable to the success of progressive democracy, because, under American conditions, the vitality of the two-party system had been purchased and must continue to be purchased at the expense of administrative independence and efficiency. Party government has interfered with genuine popular government both by a mischievous, artificial and irresponsible method of representation, and by an enfeeblement of the administration in the interest of partisan subsistence. We have considered certain plans of political reorganization which will substitute a flexible, natural and stimulating method of representation for the two-party system. But the very fluidity of the proposed methods of representation necessarily imposes an increased burden on the administrative department of the government. In this and in many other respects progressive democracy seems to bring with it administrative aggrandizement. The necessity for such aggrandizement has been foreshadowed in early chapters of this discussion; but the idea has never been pushed home. The time has now come to consider the proper function of administrative agencies in the realization of a progressive democratic policy.

The grant of any considerable responsibility and power to administrative officials has been repugnant to the American political tradition both in its legalistic and democratic aspects. The common law subordinated executive officials to the law as interpreted by the courts; and Parliament had confined administrative discretion to within very narrow limits. In our own country a still higher estimate was placed on the ability of the law-maker to provide in advance against every contingency involved in the administration of the law. Government by Law was developed so far that nearly every administrative act of importance encountered an injunction and had to be validated by a law-suit. The old democracy acquiesced cordially in this annihilation of administrative independence, because it did not want a faithful or an independent enforcement of the laws. It sought to exercise the same kind and amount of control over appointed that it did over elected officials; and this object was accomplished by converting these officials into temporary agents of partisan policy instead of permanent agents of the accepted policy of the state. The injunctions and the law-suits became merely part of the game. However effective they were in undermining administrative independence and efficiency, they could not prevent the partisan democracy from getting what it wanted — which was the emoluments and opportunities of office.

Yet in spite of the opposition of the old-fashioned Democrats, the politicians and many of the lawyers, the administration has been steadily aggrandized at the expense both of the legislature and of the courts. Legislatures have been compelled to delegate to administrative officials functions which two decades ago would have been considered essentially legislative, and which under the prevailing interpretation of the state constitutions could not have been legally delegated. The courts themselves, and particularly the Supreme Court, are continually broadening the scope of the valid exercise of administrative discretion, and consequently curtailing their own power of subsequent interference. These changes are manifestly the result of the large volume of progressive social legislation, the carrying out of which is being left increasingly in the hands of administrative commissions. Administrative aggrandizement has been carried so far that some of its earlier friends are becoming alarmed and are insisting upon more circumspection. For this and for other reasons the purpose and the necessity of the administrative as an agent of progressive democracy must be carefully considered.

The repugnance which men who inherit the Anglo-Saxon political tradition feel towards government by administrative officials has had much apparent justification. If the political experience of mankind has established anything, it has established the undesirability of ordinary bureaucratic government. Officialism may sometimes be redeemed by an ideal of public service; but an ideal of public service very rarely survives the steady occupation under the old conditions of an administrative office. The professional official tends to become one or both of two things. He becomes either a slave to routine, who assumes no responsibility, who avoids all initiative and who protects all his acts with an order or a rule, or he becomes obsessed with his own official importance and attaches a kind of infallibility to the exercise of his own judgment — in which case he likes to use his authority in an arbitrary and sometimes an insolent manner. As a matter of fact, many officials succeed both in being the victims of routine and of acting on occasions most arbitrarily, for the two states of mind are by no means incompatible. The traditional official finds it difficult to escape the illusion that he belongs to a specially favored and enlightened class, whose orders cannot be protested without a kind of political impiety.

Englishmen and Americans, however, have not suffered seriously from this particular class of bureaucratic officialism. The nearest approach to it in our own national experience is to be found in the behavior not of bureaucrats, but of certain state judges during the last two decades of the nineteenth century. It has flourished chiefly in certain European countries whose national unity had been built up by the action of a powerful executive. In such countries a highly centralized administration was considered necessary both to internal order and as a protection against foreign attack. A group of officials on whom such an onerous responsibility was imposed would tend to consider themselves a specially favored and enlightened class, and would naturally become arbitrary in their decisions and overbearing in their behavior. They would in their own opinion represent a permanent and momentous social interest, which would give them the right to interfere much as they pleased with the behavior of individuals, associations and localities. The exercise of their function was intimately connected with public order and public security, and justified a certain amount of arbitrary action on the ground of its necessary finality. Such behavior was sanctioned by the ominous rule that the safety of the state constituted the Supreme Law. The administration was the human machinery for making the *raison d'état* effective.

Thus the particular kind of arbitrary administrative action which Americans fear was the product of an essentially coercive conception of sovereignty. In so far as the exercise of popular political power in a democratic state is dissociated from the exercise of merely coercive methods, and derives its authority from the consent of public opinion, administrative action cannot very well become an agency of oppression. Its aggrandizement will necessarily be confined within certain limits, determined by the more fundamental necessity of keeping public opinion alert and acquiescent. To be sure, a democratic administrator, like a judge or legislator, may become obsessed with his own official importance, and may abuse the limited discretion granted to him by the law, but he cannot carry his excesses very far. The democratic administrator will derive his legal powers and his reason for existence from a political and social situation wholly different from that of a continental bureaucrat. Any merely vexatious, any essentially co-

2 A

ercive exercise of his authority would, in the long run, be suicidal. He is more of a probation officer than a policeman. He is more of a counsellor and instructor than a probation officer. He is the agent not of a merely disciplinary policy, but one of social enlightenment and upbuilding. He must seek, above all, to use the authority of the state and its material and scientific resources for the encouragement of voluntary socializing tendencies and purposes. Whenever individuals, classes or local groups cannot or will not bring to the work of social formation an effective spirit and measure of coöperation, the ultimate alternative is not coercive regulation by administrative agents. Even though coercion may be tried for a while, the final method of meeting such a situation in a progressive democracy is either to refrain from interference or to assume exclusive control of the rebellious economic activity.

In order to understand the function which the administration ought to perform in a social democracy a sharp distinction must be drawn between the administration and the executive. Americans have usually tended to undervalue this distinction, because, according to the theory of the separation of the powers, the executive was conceived as almost exclusively an agency for enforcing the law. But such has not been its traditional function. It has always been an initiator of public policy, and it has always exercised a decisive influence on legislation. European executives have consistently done as much, both where they were immediately responsible to a legislative body, as in Great Britain, or where, as in Germany, they are not responsible to the legislature.   Under both of these systems the executive is, more than anything else, an agency for leading and focussing public opinion and thus preparing it for decisive action.   In spite of our theories as to the proper limits of executive action, American executives have frequently assumed a similar function; but until recently it was considered bad form for them to do so, and their example did not impress the popular imagination or modify the traditional view of proper executive behavior.

In the plan of state government which I have sketched in a previous chapter the executive has become essentially a representative agency.   His primary business is that of organizing a temporary majority of the electorate, and of carrying its will into legal effect.   He becomes primarily a law-giver and only secondarily an agency for carrying out existing laws.   Yet he is none the less at the head of the administration; and the great majority of the progressives want him to be more responsible than he is now for administrative efficiency.   They want him, that is, to have the power of appointment and dismissal over the upper grades of the civil service in very much the same way that the owner of a private business would have over his employees, and they want to liberate the power of appointment from the partisan abuses which have resulted from the custom of confirmation by a senate.   But they propose to grant this power to the executive in the interest not of frequent changes in administrative personnel, but in that of a relatively prolonged official tenure.   The more clear-sighted progressives almost unanimously believe in a body of expert administrative officials, which shall not be removed with every alteration in the executive, but which shall be placed and continued in office in order to devise means for carrying out the official policy of the state, no matter what that policy may be.

Such is, of course, the situation in European countries. The executive changes more or less frequently in nations governed by a Parliament, but the administration remains. The executive is willing to have it remain, because a new group of cabinet officers cannot pretend properly to administer the business of the country without the assistance of a permanent body of officials who bring experience, training and expert knowledge to the job. These officials do not in theory exert any influence upon the policy of the government. They are professional servants, whose business it is to contrive the means necessary to execute existing laws and to carry out any policy which has been decided upon by a departmental chief or by the cabinet. An American executive who is placed in power for the purpose of realizing the will of a temporary majority of the electorate, will also need the assistance of a body of permanent officials to assist him in converting his program into well-framed and well-administered laws and to carry on the business of the state in an efficient manner. It is essential that such an executive shall have the power to dismiss or to transfer presumably permanent sub-heads of department, but that he shall refrain from exercising it — unless in his opinion, and that of his personal cabinet, he were unable to get loyal and efficient service from his higher administrative assistants.

There is no way of guaranteeing that executives who have the power to undermine administrative efficiency by dismissing or transferring officials from motives other than the good of the service, would not misuse it. The expectation that the system would result in the building up of a permanent body of expert officials is founded on the probable action of ordinary human motives. Assuming that an executive is elected who is responsible both for the successful business administration and for the successful enactment of a legislative program, and assuming that the legislative program is aimed primarily at accomplishing some policy of social amelioration, such an executive would need trustworthy expert assistance. If he did not use it in so far as it was already furnished by the state, or seek it out in so far as it was lacking, he would be courting failure and exposing himself to merited and relentless criticism. The need of the assistance of expert officials as necessarily follows from the practical situation of such a leader as did the fear of it from the situation of an irresponsible partisan executive. The irresponsible partisan executive did not want expert officials, because his success in office did not depend upon the carrying out of an administrative or legislative policy. It depended on his ability to satisfy his partisan superiors and associates without an excessively flagrant betrayal of the public service. The presence of experts in the public offices was under such circumstances as superfluous or as inconvenient as it would be convenient and useful to an executive who was really responsible to an alert and self-conscious constituency.

The need, however, of a permanent expert administration in a progressive democratic community depends upon more fundamental facts than the motives of individual leaders. In a state such as I have been sketching and such as seems to be demanded by prevailing political and economic conditions and ideals, a strong permanent administration is necessary as an agency of political continuity and stability. In the past our American states have derived their stability and continuity from a presumably permanent body of constitutional law, which was not supposed to enter into practical partisan political controversy and become subject to ordinary legislative and administrative vicissitudes. In the future there will probably be substituted for this permanent body of law a social program which will not make any corresponding pretensions to finality. Part of the program will have been embodied in law, and will be entitled to be considered as the prevailing policy of the state. Other aspects of it will still remain in a much more experimental condition, and will be a matter of active political controversy. But the really permanent element in the life of the community will be derived not from the accepted aspects of the program, but from the progressive democratic faith and ideal. The community will be united not by any specific formulation of the law, but by the sincerity and the extent of its devotion to a liberal and humane purpose.

The legislative and executive departments of the government will be occupied chiefly with the more fluid and experimental aspects of the social program. They must be adapted to the work of arousing, formulating and focussing public opinion rather than to the task of giving expression to its achieved decisions. They have no more authority than they can earn from one election to another; and it is essential that they should remain in this somewhat precarious condition. An intelligent democracy would not care to bestow so much power on a government whose membership and policy could not be readily changed. The proposed organization of majority rule escapes being dangerous only by being essentially fluid. Its strength would depend upon the size of the majority and the reasonableness of its policy. No majority could expect long to survive the active stimulation of minority opinion which would be constantly taking place, — unless one economic class occupied a numerically preponderant position in the state.

A government of this kind, however, might escape one danger only to be involved in another. Its career might degenerate into a succession of meaningless and unprofitable experiments, which would not get enough continuity either to accomplish stable results or to teach significant lessons. This danger would not be serious in the case of an intelligent and purposive democracy. The sincere intention of such a democracy to promote individual and social welfare would give continuity to its policy and enable profitable lessons to be drawn from its experiments; but if any such result is to be accomplished, it must provide an appropriate agency for the work. The only agency which could be organized and equipped for its accomplishment would be a permanent body of experts in social administration.

Just as the executive and the legislature would be concerned primarily with the more tentative and experimental part of the social program, so the administration would be concerned primarily with its comparatively permanent aspects. A certain part of the social program would be embodied in achieved legislation, upon the desirability of which public opinion was, for the time being, sufficiently agreed, and which was actually accomplishing or was failing to accomplish the desired results. Such is the case, for instance, with the workmen's compensation acts which have been passed in so many American states, and with the new and more stringent laws regulating public service corporations and manufacturing industries. Legislation of this kind has been passed in response to a relatively permanent and widespread popular demand. It is less than formerly a matter of active political controversy, but at the same time it is far from having passed wholly out of the experimental stage. In almost every case it depends for its success upon the ability and the disinterestedness with which the law is administered. Blundering and ignorant administration would condemn any of these laws to futility and unpopularity. They all of them confer large discretionary powers on administrative officials, and being experimental, they will require subsequently to be modified or supplemented in the light of the experience gained in their actual operation.

Thus the experts charged with the administration of these laws would become the official custodians of a certain part of the accepted social program. They would have better means of knowing than any one else how well the existing law was serving its purpose; and they would exercise indirectly a good deal of influence upon any modification of the law which might be recommended by the executive and discussed and accepted by the legislature. Their work in enforcing the law, in watching its operation and in advising its amendment or supplementation would be dignified by an element of independent authority. Representing, as they would, the knowledge gained by the attempt to realize an accepted social policy, they would be lifted out of the realm of partisan and factious political controversy and obtain the standing of authentic social experts. The conscientious and competent administrator of an official social program would need and be entitled to the same kind of independence and authority in respect to public opinion as that which has been traditionally granted to a common law judge.

Although the kind of administrator that I am describing must obtain the standing of an expert, he must also be something more than an expert. He is the custodian not merely of a particular law, but of a social purpose of which the law is only a fragmentary expression. As the custodian of a certain part of the social program, he must share the faith upon which the program depends for its impulse; and he must accept the scientific method upon which the faith depends for its realization. Thus with all his independence he is a promoter and propagandist. As long as he remains in the government service, he should not carry his propagandism further than the official social program justifies him in carrying it; but he should carry it as far as he can. He qualifies for his work as an administrator quite as much by his general good faith as by his specific competence.

As the amount of social legislation has increased, the tendency has been more and more to make its success depend upon the good faith and competence of its administration. The scope of discretionary administrative authority has been enlarged. In the past the administration of the civil law, except through the agency of the courts, was of small importance, because the law was supposed merely to recognize and interpret customary ways of economic and social behavior. But when the chief object of legislation is to carry into effect an experimental social program, the administration of the law has a different and more responsible function. Legislation is being used as a means of modifying social behavior, not social behavior as an excuse for formulating legislation. The legislator has become an innovator. He is dealing with an extremely complex and elusive material, and it is most difficult for him to define in advance how the objects of the law are best to be realized. The difficulty of the job has not prevented him from very frequently trying it out; but he has learned something from his failures. He is learning that an extremely detailed and comprehensive statute is usually ineffective, because of the impossibility of anticipating all the conditions which affect the operation of a specific rule. Social legislation is coming more and more to demand results rather than prescribe means. Statutes are being passed in the interest of the safety of employees in factories, which merely define safety as such freedom from danger to life and health as the nature of the employment will reasonably permit. The duty of drawing up a set of regulations which will provide sufficient safeguards for the life and health of the operatives is intrusted to a commission. All that the legislature does is to declare that industrial employment shall be reasonably safeguarded. The commission makes a comprehensive investigation of the conditions upon which the health and safety of the industrial employees depend; and it issues orders based on the result of its investigations. These orders can be attacked in the courts, but in adjudicating the case the courts have to accept as final the commission's record of the facts.

Legislation of this kind fits in very well with a system of direct government. The general question of policy involved in the attempt to protect the life and health of industrial employees is precisely one of those questions which can, if necessary, be submitted to popular vote with the reasonable assurance of getting a sound expression of popular opinion. If the bill contained a group of specific regulations intended to accomplish the desired result, popular attention could be diverted from the acceptability of the general policy to that of the efficiency of the proposed means. Public opinion would have two verdicts to pronounce instead of one; and none but an extremely well informed voter could feel any valid assurance as to the efficiency of the specific provisions of the law. But a bill which merely declared that the state wanted its industrial operatives to work under safe and wholesome conditions, and gave to certain specially equipped men full power to create safe and wholesome conditions, would be unequivocal in both respects. It says what it means; and, unlike so many American statutes, it means what it says. Instead of imposing a set of rigid regulations on factory operation, and of converting the administrator of the law into a policeman, it provides for the possibility of flexible and articulate human adjustments. The state, in the person of its industrial commissioners, will attempt to work with the manufacturers and their employees, and, after a full hearing and most assiduous consultation, to frame a reasonable and effective group of regulations.

A commission which gives a specific expression to the general policy of the state has been called a fourth department of the government. It does not fit into the traditional classification of governmental powers. It exercises an authority which is in part executive, in part legislative, and in part judicial, and which must be sharply distinguished from administration in its conventional sense. Such is undoubtedly the case, but even though it does not fit into traditional classifications, neither does it supersede them. It legislates, but without being or dispensing with a legislature. It administers, but without being or dispensing with an executive. It adjudicates, but without any power of attaching final construction to the law. It is simply a convenient means of consolidating the divided activities of the government for certain practical social purposes. Government has been divided up into parts, be-

'cause no one man or group of men can be safely intrusted with the exercise of comprehensive governmental functions; but within the limits of a necessary and desirable separation of powers a partial reunion may be permissible and useful. It does not involve the same danger of usurpation as would result from the grant of legislative power to the executive, of executive power to a legislature, or of either or of both to the courts. The administrative commissions are really free only to do right. Just as soon as they go astray the bonds tighten upon them. They derive their authority from their serviceability, from their knowledge, and from their peculiar relation to public opinion. They constitute a tentative instrument for the accomplishment of a positive popular social program. They will disappear in case public opinion cannot unite upon a program, or in case they prove to be a defective instrument. There must preëxist as the condition of their success an honest popular aspiration for social improvement, a sufficient popular confidence in the ability of enlightened and trained individuals to find the means of accomplishment, and the actual existence for their use of a body of sufficiently authentic social knowledge.

The authority granted to the fourth department is criticised because its social justice is supposed to be a justice without law — a justice which lacks the relative certainty and impartiality which can be obtained only from judgment according to accepted rules. I cannot understand the force of this criticism. The specific orders, issued by a commission after full investigation of the facts, will have the same value as a precedent for future administrative action as would a rule declared by a court. The only difference is that the order of the commission would be adjusted and readjusted whenever the commission found, upon investigation, that it was confronted by different facts. Courts are tempted to modify their own precedents in the interest of justice, whenever the adjudication of a novel case demands such modification; but they are loath to do so, because they do not like to abandon the secure footing of an accepted and tested rule. They are obliged to accept any groups of facts certified to them in the record, and they cannot be sure of being confronted by the real facts or all the facts. But an administrative body which has been commissioned by the legislature to prevent practices injurious to the health of factory employees has received a general mandate to promote a desirable social result. It must accomplish its work by means of definite orders which will be as much a matter of public record as the ruling of a court, but its rules, like all rules, are to be applied only in so far as they actually accomplish the result of promoting health. In modifying or supplementing these rules, as new or different conditions may demand, the commission will be able to discover by investigation and to place on the record all the relevant facts. It can, consequently, keep its rules in much more reasonable and effective operation than can a court; but it does not for that reason either dispense summary justice or dispense with rules. An administrative court is merely provided with a different procedure and with different instruments adapted to the more positive and formative character of its work.

Underlying the contention that an administrative court can only dispense a kind of improved oriental justice is the general idea that justice derives its reasonableness from rules. Justice cannot be reasonable without being embodied temporarily in rules, but the rules are not reasonable in themselves: they are made reasonable by the way in which they are specifically applied. The reasonable application does not result automatically from the application of the rule to a particular case. It depends upon the insight of the judge into the meaning of the rule and into the facts of the particular case and upon his good-will. An administrative court has in this respect as fair a chance of laying down a valid rule and of giving to it a reasonable application as has a regular court. An administrative court represents, it is true, an organization of the collective will for the accomplishment of a social program; and in this respect it is not impartial in the sense that a regular court is supposed to be impartial. But reasonableness is not necessarily associated with impartiality. It all depends upon the validity of the social program and of its vitalizing social ideal. If the social program is necessary to social welfare, the bias which it gives to the judgment of an administrative court may prevent it from being impartial, but it will not prevent it from being reasonable. On the contrary, administrative bodies, by uniting action in the interest of a binding and fruitful social policy with the acquisition of the knowledge needed for still more discriminating future action along the same lines, are tending to accomplish what representative government has been supposed to accomplish: they are becoming an effective agency for extracting from the bosom of society the immediately available supply of social reason.

Administrative and regular courts should be kept separate and be allowed to fight out their comparative claims on the consideration of liberal public opinion. The administrative court represents a social policy based upon a collective social ideal. The common-law judge represents a social policy founded on the protection of individual rights. A judge whose essential function is the application of legal rules impartially to specific cases, and who is obliged to accept the facts as recorded by interested litigants or as determined by juries, cannot become a satisfactory or a sufficient servant of a genuinely social policy. The peculiar importance attached to the exercise of his functions was fully justified in so far as social justice was considered to be the inevitable consequence of the protection of individuals in their traditional rights; and doubtless for an indefinite future the protection of the individual in his rights will continue to be an essential phase of social justice. As long as such protection is necessary, the orders of an administrative court will remain subject to the review of the regular courts; but even if it is subject to supervision, the administrative court has the more inspiring work to do. Its duty is not to prevent injustice to individuals and, consequently, to society, but to discover and define better methods of social behavior and to secure coöperation in the use of such methods by individuals and classes. It is, as we have seen, a social promoter, and its whole work is one of circumspect but intrepid social enterprise.

In the past, common-law justice has been appropriately symbolized as a statuesque lady with a bandage over her eyes and a scale in her fair hands. The figurative representation of social justice would be a different kind of woman equipped with a different collection of instruments. Instead of having her eyes blindfolded, she would wear perched upon her nose a most searching and forbidding pair of spectacles, one which combined the vision of a microscope, a telescope, and a photographic camera. Instead of holding scales in her hand, she might perhaps be figured as possessing a much more homely and serviceable set of tools. She would have a hoe with which to cultivate the social garden, a watering-pot with which to refresh it, a barometer with which to measure the pressure of the social air, and the indispensable typewriter and filing cabinet with which to record the behavior of society; and be assured that our lady would be very much happier in the possession of her new tools and duties than in the possession of the old. For having within her the heart of a mother and the passion for taking sides, she has disliked the inhuman and mechanical task of holding a balance between verbal weights and measures, the real and full value of which she was not permitted to investigate.

Whether or not a class of expert administrators can successfully accomplish the work which is being imposed upon them remains to be seen. Their ability to accomplish it depends finally upon the increase of authentic social

2 B

knowledge. Administrators could not beneficially assume this onerous work in the past, because the necessary social knowledge was not available. Until recently the cohesive element in society was supplied by traditions and customs — which in the case of a country like Great Britain could be administered by the courts, but which in the case of continental countries had to be confided in larger part to executive officials. But the cohesive element in the more complex, the more fluid, and the more highly energized, equipped and differentiated society of to-day necessarily consists in a more conscious social ideal, which requires for its realization the completest possible social record. An adequate and systematic attempt must be made to perfect this record; and an organization must be gradually provided for the purpose. Such an organization cannot perform its work unless its record is the official translation of a much larger amount of desultory voluntary investigation and inquiry by individuals. But it can bring to the work of creating the social record the power to elicit facts, a continuity of purpose and an abundance of resources which no individual or group of individuals can possess. It is the instrument which society must gradually forge and improve for using social knowledge in the interest of valid social purposes.

Thus the administration, in the sense which is now being fastened to the word, must provide a general staff for a modern progressive democratic state. It is created for action. It is the instrument of a clear, conscious, resolute and inclusive purpose. But it is also organized for the acquisition of knowledge. It plans as far ahead as conditions permit or dictate. It changes its plans as often as conditions demand. It seeks above all to test its own plans, so as to discover whether they will accomplish the desired result. It cannot continue to plan without having some opportunity to act, because as the instrument of a social program it must have a hand in creating the social experience which it is also recording; but it will have a much better opportunity of testing its plans than has the general staff of an army. A social program is in the course of being realized in all modern countries. The difficulty is not the lack of facts, but the ability to accumulate, to compare and to digest them. The planning department of a progressive democratic state will have much more to do than the general staff of an army. It will always be planning, and it will, in a sense, always be fighting chiefly to convert its enemies, but it will be planning not for the sake of fighting, but for the sake of learning and building.

The most doubtful and difficult question connected with the administrative organization of a progressive democracy concerns its ability to obtain and to keep popular confidence. Democracies have almost uniformly distrusted administrative officials who tend to escape direct popular control. The American people have had more than their fair share of this distrust. The Jacksonian Democracy arranged for the periodic redistribution of the non-elective offices, because it wanted to popularize the administration. It was right in wanting to popularize the administration, but it was egregiously wrong in expecting to do so by substituting the professional political office-holder for the professional administrator. The question remains: How is an expert administration to be popularized? Democracies rarely seem to be satisfied with the control which they can exercise either by means of elected official superiors or by means of laws. They realize that the permanent official tends to escape control of this kind, and that just so far as he is an expert, he is commissioned to exercise discretionary authority with independence and resolution. The administrator must manage to be representative without being elective, and yet one of the salient characteristics of advanced social and labor democracies all over the world is their repudiation of the really representative quality of expert administration. They are as much opposed to any tendency to bureaucratic government as were the Jacksonian Democrats.

It has been suggested that the administration can be popularized by submitting the administrators to direct popular control. Professor John R. Commons, for instance, has recommended that the expert administrators be subject to the recall, in case they incur popular displeasure. In my opinion the adoption of any such device in the interest of administrative popularity would in the long run fatally injure the value of administrative agencies to a progressive democracy. The recall is a useful device for preventing officials who are elected for long terms and endowed with large powers from misrepresenting their constituents; but its application to administrative experts, whose authority depends upon their ability to devise adequate means of carrying out the declared policy of the state, would be disconcerting and mischievous. The administrator has no control over controverted policies, except in so far as he can exert personal influence on elected officials or public opinion. His authority, in so far as it exists, is essentially scientific. Whenever he is incompetent or faithless he must be removed, but he must not be removed for reasons that would undermine his independence as an expert. The successful performance of his work depends upon a condition of indifference to political opinion. He has received his orders from the state, and until those orders are changed he must be preoccupied by the task of carrying them out with the utmost efficiency.

An administration which is to be representative without being elective must be kept articulate with the democracy, not by voting expedients, but by its own essential nature. The administration itself must be democratized at once by its organization, its method of recruitment, its behavior, its sympathies and its ideals. The popular suspicion which it incurs is based in part upon class differences, and in part upon an essentially undemocratic internal economy. The want of democracy in administrative organization is almost as harmful to its specific efficiency as it is to the confidence which it inspires in the ordinary voter; and if the administration is to play the part which it is supposed to play in the progressive democratic state, it must be radically reorganized both in its own constitution and in its relation to society.

The administration, hke the other departments of the government, has been inherited from an undemocratic system, and has been taken over by a democratic state without sufficient modification and criticism. No sufficient attention has yet been paid to the way in which it is to be modified. A prolonged period of investigation and experiment will be necessary before a satisfactory reorganization can be carried out. The results of such an investigation cannot profitably be anticipated; but certain suggestions may be made as to the nature and direction of the more fundamental changes.

If administrative officers are not only to conduct the business of the government, but within the limits prescribed by public opinion to plan its constructive activities, the administration will have to borrow from the army the organization as well as the idea of a general staff. A general staff does not consist of a group of generals who occupy permanently the same offices at the headquarters of the army. A constant series of changes is taking place between the staff and the line. Officers are detailed for staff duty during a certain number of years and are then returned to the command of companies, battalions or regiments. Thus the staff officers are prevented from hardening into bureaucrats and are kept in touch with the actual condition of the army, its needs and opinions. The same man helps for a few years to do the thinking for the army, only in the end to take his place among his fellows as an active working officer. In the majority of cases he is a better staff officer because of his service in the line; and he is a better line officer because of his experience on the staff. A certain sacrifice of efficiency may sometimes result, because particular individuals may have a gift for planning and administration, and may be far more serviceable at headquarters than with their regiments; but any loss of efficiency which may follow from the sacrifice of gifted individuals will be more than made up by the general good effects of the system. The army and its leaders will have mutual confidence one in the other; and its leaders will have the training and experience of all-around men.

A similar system can be adapted to administrative work. Its salient feature would be the systematic interchange between the men who are working in the offices and those who are working in the field; and such an interchange should take place so far as practicable in the low as well as in the high grades of the service. The organization and the distribution of the duties should be adapted to the making of men rather than of office-holders; and a certain variety of experience is essential to the building up of a man. It is a mischievous idea that the expert is merely the specialist. The ability to deal with men, to meet practical emergencies, to adapt a rule to a situation, to coöperate with non-office-holders rather than merely to order them about, to envisage a program or a law in its actual operations among men and women — abilities of this kind are more necessary to an administrator than to any one else. He cannot cultivate them at a desk; and until he does cultivate them administration can hardly command sufficient popular confidence. The pioneer democracy was right in placing a high value upon the all-around man and upon a sympathetic and accommodating disposition. It was wrong in believing an all-around man was necessarily condemned to being an uncritical amateur and an indiscriminate individualist. The administration of a progressive democracy will need and must foreshadow a completer kind of democratic manhood.

Another condition must also be satisfied before an expert administration can expect to obtain popular confidence. Its authority will depend, as we have seen, on its ability to apply scientific knowledge to the realization of social purposes; and if a social science is unattainable or does not command popular respect, popular opinion will be reluctant to grant to the administration its necessary independent authority. Now in what way can a body of social knowledge be made to command popular respect? In the long run, doubtless, by the increasing demonstration that social knowledge is the fruit of a binding and formative social ideal and that it is really serviceable for the accomplishment of a social program. But is such a demonstration sufficient? Is there not another and equally necessary method of increasing popular confidence in the expert — the method of giving a much larger number of people the chance of acquiring a better intellectual training? Is it fair to ask millions of democrats to have a profound. respect for scientific accomplishments whose possession is denied to them by the prevailing social and educational organization? It can hardly be claimed that the greater proportion of the millions who are insufficiently educated are not just as capable of being better educated as the thousands to whom science comes to have a real meaning. Society has merely deprived them of the opportunity. There may be certain good reasons for this negligence on the part of society; but as long as it exists, it must be recognized as in itself a good reason for the unpopularity of experts. The best way to popularize scientific administration, and to enable the democracy to consider highly educated officials as representative, is to popularize the higher education. An expert administration cannot be sufficiently representative until it comes to represent a better educated constituency.

CHAPTER XVIII

INDUSTRIAL DEMOCRACY

THE type of democratic political organization which has been roughly sketched in the preceding chapters has been characterized as fundamentally educational. Although it is designed to attain a certain administrative efficiency, its organization for efficiency is subordinated to the gathering of an educational popular political experience. Indeed it is organized for efficiency chiefly because in the absence of efficiency no genuinely formative popular political experience can be expected to accrue. It assumes an intrepid and inexhaustible faith in the value to humanity of an ideal of individual and social fulfilment. It assumes the ability of the human will, both in its individual and its collective aspects, to make an effective contribution to the work of fulfilment. It assumes the ability of the human intelligence to frame temporary programs which will provide a sufficient foundation for significant and fruitful action. It anticipates that as the result of such action a progressive democracy will gradually learn how to be progressively democratic. But the result of its education will not be the attainment of its ideal of individual and social fulfilment. It will only be at best the conquest of a more liberal life by a larger number of living men and women.

If the organization of political democracy for educational purposes is of so much importance, the educational organization of democracy in its economic aspect is certainly of no less importance. The creation of an industrial organization which will serve to make individual workers enlightened, competent and loyal citizens of an industrial commonwealth, is most assuredly a task just as essential as the creation of a loyal and enlightened body of voters. I do not believe, as do many social democrats, that a more democratic industrial organization will bring with it necessarily a more enlightened democratic political organization. But neither do I believe that the creation of an industrial democratic citizenship will take care of itself, provided we can obtain a more satisfactory democratic political organization. Effective measures of an essentially non-political character must be taken for the creation of an industrial democratic citizenship.

The traditional American democracy expected to create industrial citizens as an incidental result of its consummate legal and political system. For a couple of generations the attempt was rewarded with a sufficient measure of success. The American pioneer or territorial democrats were, according to their own lights, freemen both in the economic and political sense. They had organized successfully for the purpose of controlling that part of the national political policy in which they were most interested; and possessed as they were of their freeholds, they had every promise of ultimate economic independence. If the supply of freeholds contained in the public domain had been inexhaust-

ible, and if the commercial and industrial organization of
the country could have remained local and particularist,
the early success of this system might have continued;
but, as we have seen, the increasingly complete appropriation of the public domain rapidly converted the American
people from a freeholding into a wage-earning democracy.
To be sure, industrial development brought with it many
large and small personal property owners; but the number
of wage-earners increased more rapidly than did the
number of property owners of all classes. The wage-
earners have not as yet attained the same numerical preponderance that they have in England and to a less extent
in Germany; but eventually they will constitute a considerable majority of American voting populations. How can
the wage-earners obtain an amount or a degree of economic
independence analogous to that upon which the pioneer
democrat could count?

A large part of the ordinary social program of progressives all over the world is intended to promote the economic
independence of the wage-earner. Whenever he forfeits
his assumed independence, it is usually because periods of
idleness and sickness lower his standard of living and force
him to accept inferior kinds of employment. Or in other
cases his wages are not sufficient at best to enable him to
sustain a decent standard of living and to emancipate him
from apprehension and deprivation. Progressives propose, consequently, to insure him against unemployment,
sickness and old age, to guarantee to him wholesome conditions of work, and to make it impossible for a faithful

worker to be paid less than a fair minimum wage. They expect to enable the wage-earner to keep his head above water and to prevent him from being submerged by the vicissitudes of his health and work.

Special legislation of this class is criticised by conservatives on various grounds. They do not entirely reject it, but they fear that its general tendency will be not to promote the independence and character of the wage-earning class, but its sense of dependence. Wage-earners obtain a benefit from the state which they have not been economically strong enough to extort; and increasing burdens are placed on industry without any attempt to provide a corresponding increase of industrial output. The criticism has a great deal of force. This kind of social legislation seeks only to diminish acknowledged evils. It may enable an independent and self-respecting wage-earner to maintain what independence he has; but it certainly does tend to create a class of industrial citizens who are free in the same sense that the pioneer democrat was free.

The conservative urges the foregoing criticism with the intention of proving that the wage-earner can secure independence only by becoming a property owner. He will be independent, in case he saves enough money to enable him to get over a period of hard times and to bargain on something like equal terms with his employer. His character will be exhibited and strengthened by his ability to deny to himself and his family immediate gratifications for the sake of ultimate security and freedom. It is difficult to treat this argument with patience and courtesy. The wage-earner, who in the majority of cases earns only enough to keep himself and his family in the necessities of life, is asked to deny such necessities to himself and to his dependents; and unless he makes these sacrifices, he is to be considered a weak, dependent individual and to be deprived of industrial citizenship. His citizenship is to be based upon asceticism, upon the denial to himself and his family of the opportunities of a genial and expansive life, such as all well-to-do people cherish as their birthright. Industrial citizenship for the poor is to be founded on cruel and ruthless deprivation. The enlargement of the bank account is to be accompanied by the vital impoverishment of men, women and children. No doubt wage-earners spend enough money in foolish ways, which, if it were saved, would do a great deal to make them independent; but under their circumstances it is more human to waste than it would be to save. To spend money on liquor which ought to be spent on better food, warmer clothing, or proper instruction for children, is deplorable, but it is far more deplorable to ask a man deliberately to bring about the vital impoverishment of himself and his family for the sake of economic emancipation. It is fortunate, indeed, that the great majority of wage-earners are lacking in that kind of "character."

The truth is that the wage-system in its existing form creates a class of essential economic dependents. Even if they attain some measure of emancipation as small property owners, they remain dependent as wage-earners. Their economic situation is determined in part by forces over which they as individuals can exercise but little control, and in part by the good or ill will and the good or bad management of their employers. Their employer is literally their master. He supplies the opportunity of work, determines its conditions to a large extent, and is responsible for its success or failure. They are often free to change their employer, but a new employer is only a new master. In a multitude of individual cases the autocratic control is benevolently exercised. Fidelity and competence are rewarded, and the deserving wage-earner comes to occupy a privileged position as compared to his fellow-workers. But he has no assurance of any such reward. The number of people who graduate from the wage-earning class without the assistance of some kind of favoritism, is small compared to the total number of wage-earners. By the very necessities of the case the vast majority of wage-earners are condemned to a Hobson's choice among masters.

Ordinary progressive special legislation is intended to improve the operation of the system without touching its essential defect. But if plans of social insurance and minimum-wage boards have any tendency to undermine the independence of the wage-earner, that tendency results from the system itself, not from the attempts to improve it. The social legislative program cannot give real independence to people whose relation to their employers is one of dependence. In undertaking such a program the state is merely assuming a responsibility towards wage-earners whose fulfilment is necessary to social conservation. This responsibility should already have been

assumed by employers capable of recognizing the righteous
claims which their employees had upon them as the result
of the employment. But no matter who assumes the
responsibility, the relation of dependence remains; and the
wage-earner has to choose between two grim alternatives as
a means of possible emancipation. He may seek independence either by becoming a favored worker or by becoming himself a property owner. The first of these alternatives is denied by the very necessities of the case to the
vast majority of wage-earners. The second costs more
in human satisfaction than it is worth as a discipline of
independence. Both of them divide the interest of the
individual worker from that of the mass of his fellow-
workers.

The creation of industrial citizens out of wage-earners,
if it is to be brought about at all, will demand the adoption of different methods. The wage-system itself will
have to be transformed in the interest of an industrial self-
governing democracy. Progressives must come to recognize two fundamental facts. Modern civilization in dealing with the class of wage-earners is dealing with an ultimate economic condition, the undesirable aspects of which
cannot be evaded by promoting one wage-earner out of
every thousand into a semi-capitalist or a semi-employer.
If wage-earners are to become free men, the condition of
freedom must somehow be introduced in the wage-system
itself. The wage-earner must have the same opportunity
of being consulted about the nature and circumstances of
his employment that the voter has about the organization

and policy of the government. The work of getting this opportunity for the wage-earner is the most important single task of modern democratic social organization.

Although the evils involved by the wage-system in its existing form are cruel, progressive democrats should welcome the opportunity of dealing with them. There are many grounds for encouragement in the assertion that wage-earning, as distinct from property-owning, has become an ultimate fact which modern democratic civilization is obliged to face. The democratic ideal has a better chance of being sincerely accepted among people whose property consists in their work than among people whose outlook is largely determined by the possession of accumulated property. A democracy of essential workers can be more quickly and thoroughly socialized than a democracy of essential property owners, because property owners can be emancipated without being socialized as a consequence of their emancipation.

The emancipation of the wage-earner demands that the same legal security and dignity and the same comparative control over his own destiny shall be attached to his position as to that of the property owner. As soon as such legal security is granted, the good worker will no longer be offered a strong inducement to separate himself from his fellows by becoming a property owner. His work will be his fortune, and will depend for its productivity upon effective coöperation. The wage-earner whose greatest stimulus to work is assumed to be the ultimate chance of becoming a property owner, may be a hard worker, but he

2 C

will rarely be a good worker or a desirable citizen in an industrial democracy. As a worker his eye will be fixed rather on the goal than on the job. As a property owner he will be afraid of being unable to keep his property. In both aspects his motives will be interested and self-involved rather than disinterested and social.

Hitherto, however, neither the conscience nor the intelligence of modern industrial society has recognized the impolicy and the injustice of asking workers to seek economic independence by taking their eye off their work, by impoverishing their own lives and by practically deserting their associates. The wage-earners have been obliged to seek on their own hook an inferior kind of emancipation by means of an inferior kind of associated action. They have borne witness to the necessary fellowship of workers by organizing trades-unions; and these trade associations have had to make the economic emancipation of the individual depend on the emancipation of the whole class. The individual wage-earner has been compelled to forego whatever chance he has of obtaining a better position for himself by agreeing to accept nothing which is not shared with his fellows. The fight for associated independence requires of the individual worker great sacrifices, of which the greatest sacrifice of all is an obligation to take his eye off his work. Society is responsible for this sacrifice by refusing to him the security and dignity appertaining to his calling.

The attitude of the employing class has forced trades-unions to become for the most part fighting organizations.

Workers have been obliged to fight primarily for an in-creased share of the necessaries of life and for the recogni-tion of their unions. In the case of certain skilled trades they have compelled their employers to recognize the unions, to pay a comparatively liberal rate of wages and to submit to conditions in the conduct of the business which tended to restrict the output. They have not used the power which they have obtained in the interest of industrial productivity; but why should they do so? Both the economic and the legal systems with which they are dealing force them to seek primarily their own class inter-ests, and refuse to grant to them as workers an appropriate dignity and security. They naturally take their social ethics from their opponents and regard their work as a kind of property, which has to be saved for the benefit of a private interest rather than expended in the public interest. They have their eye fastened not on the work, but upon the goal.

Many employers have been obliged to yield to these demands, but they have not yielded willingly. The average employer considers a business for which he has found the capital and most of the brains as exclusively *his own* business, in spite of the fact that it depends for its success upon securing the coöperation of the energy and brains of other human beings. When these other human beings get together and insist upon securing better terms of employment collectively than they can individually, and do so without any regard for his convenience, he com-plains of oppressive interference with *his* business. At the same time he expects his employees to take as much interest in *his* business as if it were theirs. But much as he dislikes and resents the older trades-unions, which work by means of collective bargains, and which are to a certain extent an offshoot of an essentially capitalist control of business, he dislikes and resents with much greater vehemence the newer unionism, which has a much more radical program than the old. The newer unionism, instead of seeking gradually to force employers to grant better terms to wage-earners, roundly declares that business belongs by right to the people whose work contributes to its success; and they propose to capture and take away the industries of the country from their present owners by essentially violent and revolutionary means. Whenever this newer unionism shows its head, it is ruthlessly and often violently suppressed.

A man who repudiates with abhorrence the proposed revolutionary methods of syndicalism may still believe that it is infusing into unionism a necessary ferment and into modern economic civilization a necessary ideal. The older unionism was driven into the proclamation of a restricted and interested program, which converted work into a kind of class property, and which proposed to exchange a minimum of work for a maximum of cash. Economists rightly regarded a labor policy of this kind as dangerous to the welfare of economic civilization; but very few of them understood that wage-earners, in adopting such a policy, were merely borrowing their economic standards from a system of moral values determined by the

possession of property. It was a distinct gain when syndicalism demanded of the old craft unionism that it cease to
be a parasite upon a perverted economic system, and that
it should fight and plan for the creation of a new system,
based upon the dignity, the responsibility and the moral
value of human work. The fact that the advocates of the
new system propose to establish it by methods which
might be fatal to civilization must not be allowed to obscure the essential nobleness and humanity of their underlying purpose. They are proposing to secure to the
laborers of all kinds the opportunity and responsibility
of operating the business mechanism of modern life ; and in
so far as they succeed, work will cease to be convertible
merely into property, and the worker will gain every inducement to keep his eye upon his work. The attempt to establish such a system may fail, but assuredly it is a profoundly
practicable system, born of the will to enhance the essential
human values involved in the process of economic civilization.

A deplorable result may well occur, in case the conscience and the intelligence of the American democracy
fail to recognize the peculiar promise and nobleness of the
syndicalist ideal. Syndicalism has adopted a revolutionary program, because for impatient spirits there seemed
to be no way of imposing such a radical change of attitude
upon modern economic society save by the use of organized
violence. Civilization may well perish in the resulting
conflict. The best chance of avoiding such a consummation is the recognition that the new unionism does cherish

an ideal whose realization is necessary to democratic fulfilment. Once such recognition has become sufficiently widespread, the new unionism may be encouraged to abandon its revolutionary program, and to seek a substitute for it along a more practicable, a more humane and instructive route.

The alternative consists in the deliberate education of the wage-earners for the position, which they must eventually assume, of being responsible as a group of self-governing communities for the proper organization and execution of the productive work of society. The attempt immediately to impose such a responsibility on the workers as a class would fail, as the various experiments which have already been made in self-governing workshops have sufficiently proved. The wage-earners must be gradually trained in industrial self-government and in that ability to keep their eye on their work, upon which industrial self-government must in the long run depend for its success.

The process of industrial education, like the process of political education, does not, however, consist primarily in going to school. It consists primarily in active effort on behalf of an increasing measure of self-government; and the only form which such active effort can take is that of fighting for its attainment. The independence of the wage-earners as a class would not amount to much, in case it was handed down to them by the state or by employers' associations. They must earn it in the same way that every modern nation has earned or protected its independence — that is, by warfare appropriate for the purpose.

Their "Constitution of Freedom" must be gradually extorted from their employers by a series of conflicts in which the ground is skilfully chosen and permanent defeat is never admitted. In that way only can the wage-earning class win effective power, the devotion of its own members and the respect of its opponents. It requires for the purpose of this warfare a much more general and intense feeling of class consciousness and responsibility than it has at present, and a much more tenacious and enlightened class policy. Practically all of the wage-earners as a group should be unionized as the result of this warfare; and they should be unionized because of the substantial benefits which the unions were able to confer on their members.

This warfare, in so far as it was successfully conducted, would be educational in several different ways. The wage-earners would become actually less dependent on their employers and would have earned their independence. Their independence would be bound to assume a definite legal form. They would obtain as the result of collective bargaining effective control over some of the conditions under which they worked. Their observation of the working of these agreements would give to them an increasing knowledge of the business and of the problems and difficulties of its management. Finally, their sense of fellowship with their classmates would be very much enhanced. They would learn the necessity of standing together, and of not allowing any differences in grades of employment to divide them one from another. All this would still be very far from a really democratic industrial system; but in so far as it was represented in definite agreements, it would assume the form of an industrial constitutionalism. The unions would gradually appropriate the function of criticising and vetoing any action of the management of the business which vitally affected the welfare of employees either individually or as a whole.

In order, however, that either the winning or the operation of a system of industrial constitutionalism should be educational in the larger social meaning of the word as well as in a more limited class meaning, it would need the impulse of something more than a class ideal. Neither the workers nor society itself will ever be educated up to the necessary standards of industrial democracy merely as the result of a class struggle. The class struggle must be fertilized by an increasingly general understanding of the practical economic and moral value of democratizing industry, and of enabling the workers within limits to organize their work and determine its conditions and costs. A genuinely democratic industrial system, that is, must in part be born of the will to realize in industry a better ideal of human amelioration — of a conscious attempt to convert internally remunerative work into a source both of individual and social fulfilment. This ideal must be freely accepted and patiently worked out by clear-sighted and resolute progressive democrats of all classes. Those who believe in it must take risks on its behalf. They must seek to put it into successful practice just as they would seek to introduce an approved labor-saving device into their business or an improved anæsthetic into surgical operations.

For although the methods by which democracy is to be incorporated into the economic system are experimental, the ideal of humanizing industry by means of an increasing measure of industrial self-government is as authentic as the process of civilization itself. The necessity of reorganizing modern industry for the purpose of liberating the workers, of making them responsible for the success of their work, and of securing and earning their loyalty, is a manifest inference from the very nature of social democracy.

Self-government can hardly be introduced into industry without the effective participation of certain enlightened and wilful employers. Organized society can do a great deal to accelerate the work and to establish its results. It can enact legislation in favor of union labor, which will strengthen and conciliate unionism without establishing any demoralizing discrimination in its favor. In so far as the state is itself an employer, it can offer a good example to its fellow-employers. But the essential work must be done by responsible business men, who are not afraid to reorganize their own industries in the interest of a constitutional system. They must be prepared to risk the prosperity of an established business for the sake of making the operation of that business conducive to the increasing independence, responsibility and loyalty of its workers. They must be able to carry on this process of reorganization while still holding their own in competition with employers who are making no such experiments. They must not depend upon external supports to pull them through the experimental period. If they cannot maintain their position without favor against less enlightened competitors, they will be failing to accomplish their appointed task. A constitutional industrial system, as the first step towards industrial democracy, must be able to prove from the start its practical superiority to an autocratic industrial system.

The only help which such enlightened employers would be entitled to get would be at most the coöperation of the unions and of the wage-earners immediately affected by the experiment. An employer who was doing as much as he could to introduce a constitutional system into his business should not have to suffer the same persistent hostility from the unions as would an ordinary employer. They should recognize that he is helping them to accomplish their work. They should not for that reason abandon to him their own special part of the job. They should insist upon the maintenance of their associated independence, and of an organization which, whenever necessary, would be strong enough to declare war. They might well seek immediate representation in the actual management of the business so that they would be in a position to know with how much intelligence, resolution and good faith the work of reorganization was being undertaken. But while preserving necessary safeguards, they should understand that a contribution of this kind by enlightened employers is essential to a practical transition from industrial autocracy to industrial democracy. The employer who will risk the stability of his business in such experiments is a brand plucked from the burning. He is as necessary to the education of his fellow-employers and to the discovery and testing of sound methods of industrial constitutionalism as the unionizing of labor is to the social education of the wage-earner. Whenever they feel assured that such an employer is acting with intelligence and good faith, the unions should discriminate in his favor and try to work with him.

However liberating and enlightening the education would be which democratic citizens might derive from the actual exercise of political responsibilities, they would derive very much more from the exercise of industrial or business responsibility. The phrase "industrial education" usually means the prevailing system of technical instruction; and the importance of the best methods in a complete system of industrial education can scarcely be exaggerated; but behind any sound technical instruction there must be taking place a process of educating workers to get and keep a fruitful moral and mental attitude towards their work. To industrial education of this kind the installation first of constitutional and then of democratic government in industry is indispensable. As soon as a business becomes in certain respects the business of all the participating workers, the latter will undergo a change of attitude towards their work. The dignity and the serviceability of their calling and of their occupation will be recognized in the economic organization. Presumably they are being rewarded, not perhaps according to the value or cost of the work (if that were possible), but at least with as much liberality as the productivity of the business will permit. The further improvement of their position does not depend upon their acquisition of property. It depends upon the increasing productivity of the industry; and increasing production will depend upon the increasing excellence of individual work, upon the equally meritorious work of the coöperators, upon skilful and economical management, and, finally, upon the general increase in industrial and social efficiency. Thus the wage-earners will have won a kind of independence, in which devotion to work will individualize their lives without dividing them from their fellow-workers. The democracy will derive its education, both morally and socially, from the liberalizing, leavening and humanizing effect of its working activity and of the resulting responsibilities and discipline.

In one respect at least the older economists were right. The opportunity for the enjoyment of a more liberal life by the great majority of the wage-earners depends ultimately on the increasing productivity of human labor. The workers may be justified in not taking this statement very seriously, as long as the economic organization permits the private appropriation in the form of rent, profits and interest of such a large share of the social income; but even if it were practicable and equitable to distribute the existing fund of rent, profits and interest among the workers, the democracy would still be lacking in the necessary economic basis of a liberal life. A more socialized economic system would benefit from a reduction in the waste involved by existing methods of organizing industry and luxurious class standards of consumption, but its expenses would in many respects be enormously increased.

It would have to supply to all its citizens a far larger amount of leisure, a far longer preliminary educational discipline, and far greater opportunities for recreation and diversion. Consider the increased bill for telephoning, in case the telephone became part of the equipment of every residence. Consider the increased bill for travelling, in case everybody enjoyed in some measure the opportunity of visiting other countries, now enjoyed only by a small minority. In these and in many other ways, a society, the great majority of whose inhabitants were leading liberal lives, would require a huge increase in both production and consumption — which can be obtained only by a corresponding increase in the productive efficiency of human work.

The necessary increase in efficiency can ultimately be derived from only one source — from the more comprehensive and more successful application to industry of scientific methods and of the results of essentially scientific research. The use of scientific methods and results in industry is the natural and inevitable accompaniment of its reorganization in the interest of democratic fulfilment. Industrial democracy will never accomplish its purpose, unless science can be brought increasingly to its assistance; and the needed assistance will have to be rendered in a most liberal measure.

Modern industrial civilization is, of course, based upon the achievements of science and the more effective control of man over nature. The surplus economic value on which the hope of human liberation depends is the product of the inventor, the machine, and ultimately of the scientific investigator. But the existing economic system has not, until recently, been able to make any sufficient use of scientific methods, and the capitalistic machine has been indifferent and even alien to the scientific spirit. Science is patient, deliberate, critical, organic and disinterested. The organization and methods of business have been impatient and amateurish, and its purposes have been selfish and hidebound. The hero of the industrial revolution is the flexible and energetic promoter, who divined the opportunity of establishing new enterprises, and who could command the necessary capital and ability, but who was himself essentially a pioneer, a sportsman and a man who lived upon the country. Economic development in its earlier phases owes an enormous debt to these adventurers, but the permanent occupation of the country which they invaded has required a different group of methods, qualities and, finally, of motives. It is better to depend on a well-equipped general staff, which will obey the orders of society and carry out an approved policy, than upon Napoleons, who convert the national economic resources into an instrument of personal aggrandizement.

Although the day and the value of the industrial pioneer are by no means entirely over, he is being gradually superseded. The Napoleons of business are being succeeded by the Von Moltkes. Business men are depending less upon crude energy, insistent innovation and speculative adventures, and more upon the patient and careful preparation both of business methods and programs. They are aiming less at indiscriminate and costly expansion and more on the intensive farming of their existing territory. Business policy is being analyzed, criticised and continuously developed. Business operations are being recorded and their results exhaustively compared. Business problems are being studied with as much tenacity, patience and method as are purely scientific problems. Large business organizations are coming to have planning departments, which not only determine the methods used in the shop and record the achievements of the plant and of the employees, but which are responsible for working out the lines of future expansion. In many cases these planning departments include laboratories, in which large resources are placed at the service of groups of scientific investigators, who spend all their time in the coöperative discovery of needed technical improvements. Thus the work of invention itself, which has been supposed to be peculiarly the fruit of happy accident and individual genius, is being, in part, socialized and reduced to method. The heavy expense of these planning departments is willingly incurred, because the resulting systematization of the work brings with it a substantial increase of output and, in some cases, an astonishing diminution of unit costs. Scientific management, in the largest sense of that word, is coming to be the great critical and regenerative influence in business organization.

The discerning reader will not have failed to remark certain similarities between the function of scientific management in the operation of a private business and the function of a general administrative staff in the operation of public business. The parallelism is, as a matter of fact, extremely close. The successful conduct of both public and private business is becoming more and more a matter of expert administration, which demands the use of similar methods and is confronted by the solution of similar problems. Both are coming to meet on the same plane of scientific method and social responsibility. Private business of all kinds is becoming affected with a public function, and must be equipped for an increase in efficiency and for an increase in human responsibility. The demand for increasing efficiency in the transaction of public business is equally peremptory and general, and it is accompanied by a kindred demand for the recognition of the individual interests involved in public work. The public employee is as much in need of self-government as the employee of private business. He is rarely overworked or underpaid; but like other wage-earners he remains a dependent. As the state becomes more of an employer, it will be confronted by the same necessity of emancipating its workers and dignifying their work as are the private employers. Any improvement in public administration should have a wholesome reactive effect on private business, and any successes of scientific management in private industry should stimulate the permanent administrative official to obtain correspondingly excellent results. Just in so far as the staffs of the two armies are alert and inquisitive, they experiment for each other's benefit and will willingly teach what they have learned and learn what the other has to teach.

A serious difficulty, however, remains. Although the

application of scientific methods to public and private business constitutes a decisive and a life-giving contribution to the creation of a civilized economic system, its future development is endangered by one powerful enemy. It meets with the stubborn opposition of the unions. They resent its effect upon their work and lives. They are afraid that it will undermine the increasing solidarity of the wage-earners by inducing them to prefer their individual interests to the common interests of all the workers. They resent it also because it imposes upon the wage-earner an unprecedented severity of shop discipline. He must obey more orders more scrupulously than he has ever yet been obliged to obey. He is apprehensive, consequently, of becoming still more completely entangled in the coils of an inhuman industrial system. His enmity to scientific management is deeply rooted and is often fierce. If it continues, it will check, if not entirely prevent, the spread of scientific methods in business.

Those who believe in the strengthening of the unions as a necessary step in the direction of industrial democracy, and who also believe in the regeneration of industry by the application of scientific methods, are apparently confronted by a disastrous contradiction. The alliance between business and science, from which business may be expected to derive some of the fearless, critical, candid and disinterested scientific spirit, and a technical efficiency which is indispensable to a generally higher standard of living, has incurred the enmity of the practical living agency of a future industrial democracy.

2 D

This opposition between scientific management and the labor unions is often supposed to be due to misunderstanding, which will disappear as soon as the purposes and effects of the new spirit and methods are fully understood by the union workers. I doubt whether it can be done away with so easily. Scientific management is an exacting master. The workers are required to submit to an amount and degree of regimentation not dissimilar to that required of an army. Such severe discipline cannot be imposed upon free men by a merely external authority or for any exclusively self-regarding purpose. The one chance of securing acquiescence by the wage-earners in discipline of this kind lies in a wholly different direction. They must be free to accept or reject it. Its rigorism must be authorized by their own choice. Scientific management must bring with it as a condition of its acceptance the self-governing work-shop. The workers must have the sense that they are imposing the discipline on themselves for the good of the service. They must explicitly acquiesce in the policy and have confidence in the staff wherefrom the discipline is being derived. A free man can obey the most rigorous and exacting orders without any loss of self-respect, but only in case the orders concern methods and are necessary to the realization of a policy that have been submitted to him and are approved by him. The opposition which the unions have been displaying towards the application of scientific methods to industrial operations can hardly fail to continue as long as wage-earners occupy the position of dependents, whose only hope of independence consists in the strength of their trade associations. Scientific management without effective unionism increases the burden of their dependence, while at the same time it seeks to reconcile them to it by a system of bonuses. In proportion as they gain their independence and are made jointly responsible instead of jointly irresponsible for the success of their work, they may be converted to scientific management.

In asserting that industrial democracy may reconcile the workers to the discipline required by industrial efficiency, I am not merely allowing the wish to be father to the thought. The adjustment between the two will not be automatic and general. But it will take place in certain instances as the result either of enlightened planning by employers or enlightened leadership among the workers; and wherever it takes place, it should quickly and decisively prove its superiority. The mutual dependence between democracy in business and science in business will be established in practice. Scientific management can never reach its highest efficiency in a community of apprehensive and self-regarding dependent wage-earners. It requires for its better operation alert, intelligent and interested workers and cordial and insistent coöperation among them. The morale of the scientifically managed shops, which are also self-governing communities, will be superior to that of the business autocracies, just as the morale of an army of patriots, who are fighting on behalf of a genuinely national cause, is superior to that of an army of merely mercenary or drafted soldiers. The severer the

discipline which men are required to undergo, the more
they need the inspiration of a disinterested personal motive
and complete acquiescence in the purpose for the benefit
of which the discipline has been contrived. Scientific
management will need the self-governing workshop quite
as much as industrial democracy will need the application
of scientific methods to business.

The practical dependence of scientific industry upon
industrial democracy is the indication of an underlying
fellowship of spirit. The subordination of nature to human
purposes is associated with the determination of social
forms and conditions by human ideals. Both involve
victorious assertion of the human will and the faithful and
imaginative exercise of the human intelligence. Without
the help of science the human race would have remained
forever the victim of vicissitudes in its supply of food.
Without the advent of democracy science would have become merely an engine of class oppression and would have
been demoralized by its service. Both expand in an atmosphere of candor, publicity, mutual good faith and fearless
criticism. Both shrivel up in a secretive, suspicious, timid
and self-regarding atmosphere. Democracy can never permit science to determine its fundamental purpose, because
the integrity of that purpose depends finally upon a consecration of the will, but at the same time democracy on its
spiritual side would be impoverished and fruitless without
science. The fulfilment of democratic purposes depends
upon the existence of relatively authentic knowledge, the
authority of which a free man may accept without any com-

promise of his freedom. The acceptance of such authority becomes a binding and cohesive influence. Its representatives can within limits serve the purposes of a democratic community without the friction or the irrelevance of an election. Yet just because science is coming to exercise so much authority and be capable of such considerable achievements, a completer measure of industrial and political democracy becomes not merely natural, but necessary. The enormous powers for good and evil which science is bringing into existence cannot be intrusted to the goodwill of any one class of rulers in the community. The community as a whole will not derive full benefit from scientific achievements unless the increased power is widely distributed and until all of the members share in its responsibilities and opportunities. All along the line science is going to demand of faithful and enlightened men an amount of self-subordination which would be intolerable and tyrannical in any but a self-governing community.

CHAPTER XIX

Social Education

THE difficulty, which was uncovered in the foregoing discussion, of the relation between scientific business and an economic democracy is general rather than special in its scope and meaning. In every region of practical activity an increase of discipline is coming to be demanded in the interest of efficiency and, consequently, of individual and social amelioration. The need of imposing more exacting standards of behavior upon the citizens of an industrial democratic state applies to the citizen as citizen no less than to the citizen as worker. Democracy has assumed an express responsibility for the achievement of the stupendous task of making this world into a place in which more human beings will lead better lives than they have hitherto had an opportunity of doing. It will never succeed in making better men and women, unless an unprecedentedly large number of democrats seek to be better men and women. The being of better men and women will involve, as it always has involved, the subordination, to a very considerable extent, of individual interests and desires to the requirements of social welfare. In so far as the democracy succeeds in its intention of enabling society to do very much more for the individual, it will necessarily ask the individual to do very much more for society.

In spite, however, of the apparent necessity that increasing social discipline must needs accompany increasing social achievement, modern democracy in certain of its impulses and aspects threatens to be more than usually reluctant to accept discipline of any kind. It has its manifestly destructive and disintegrating tendencies. It is attacking many traditions and conventions which have in the past served to hold society together. It is proposing to modify profoundly the institution of property, the function of law and the whole basis of social authority. It is proposing not only to emancipate the workers from dependence upon the property owners, but it is proposing to emancipate women from economic dependence on men. An increasing proportion of the wage-earning democracy is seeking to accomplish its class purposes by frankly revolutionary means. The syndicalists are expecting that the union workers will take over, as the result of organized violence, the machinery of modern industrialism and operate it without the benefit of any preliminary period of experimental training. The fighting program seems wholly impracticable; but it cannot be dismissed on that account. The temper of the wage-earning class is far more rebellious than it used to be; and, notwithstanding an undertone of social aspiration, it frequently derives its ethical standards from its interests rather than from its ideals. For these and other similar reasons many serious students of society are doubtful whether existing social bonds will be strong enough to survive the strain. They fear that social cohesion is really imperilled, and that at best modern industrial civilization will have to confront and survive a period of acute and prolonged social disorder.

Thoughtful conservatives and thoughtful radicals are, consequently, casting about for some sufficiently drastic means of social conservation. They both recognize the danger of social dissolution as a result of the inability of society to control the centrifugal forces which are being unloosed in its midst. They both are protesting against the stupidity of not rallying to meet the existing crisis. They both are demanding the adoption of measures which will strengthen the forces of social cohesion, and they both realize that social cohesion cannot be made effective without some measure of social compulsion. But whatever importance they may attach to compulsion, they both propose to supplement it with an attempt to strengthen by educational means the spiritual foundation of society. The increasing clarification and emphasis of this purpose is the salutary and promising aspect of the existing situation. Once it can be clearly understood that whatever else loyal democracy may mean and a more exacting ideal of social fulfilment may demand, and whatever else society must do to preserve and promote its own integrity, the creation of an adequate system of educating men and women for disinterested service is a necessary condition both of social amelioration and social conservation — once this underlying condition is fully and candidly accepted, then a fair chance exists of ultimately uniting disinterested and aspiring people upon a practicable method of accomplishing the purpose.

At present, however, the common use of the phrase "social education" by radicals and conservatives does not bring with it any agreement upon a common meaning or method. While both may agree in attaching the utmost importance to the adoption of effective measures of social and technical discipline, they differ widely in their estimate of the function of moral and physical coercion in social education, and of the conditions under which it can be righteously and fruitfully imposed upon a community of freemen.

That in the past moral and physical coercion has played an enormously important part in the drama of social education is a plain inference from historical facts. The economic organization of society concentrated in the hands of a small minority a very large part of the fruits of economic labor. The class which controlled the land and the property also controlled the government. It was obliged to use physical force to prevent its external enemies or the less fortunate classes among its own people from taking away the property and the power. Any minority which succeeded in keeping possession of very desirable economic and political privileges was obliged to exhibit some ability both to make others obey and to control themselves. During the early history of civilization political and economic power rested frankly on the exercise of force, and disappeared quickly before the impact of a superior force or as a consequence of the loss of the fighting virtues.

Little by little, however, the human race began to accumulate a fund of social virtue as well as a fund of property and power. This fund of civilization consisted in a spiritual heritage, which could be passed on from one generation to another and finally from one society to another. Its existence gave an increasing value and prestige to social continuity and social stability. It enabled many human beings, who were not distinguished by valiancy and strength, to lead more liberal lives, and resulted in the creation of a class whose special business it was to safeguard and, if possible, to increase the spiritual heritage. The class of learned or holy men has always been devoted to the task of strengthening the social bond, because only in a comparatively stable society, which recognized binding social obligations, did they, as men of peace, have any chance to flourish.

During the early phases of civilization these friends of society were almost always placed in the position of standing with their backs to the wall. The anti-social forces within and without the community loomed far more powerful than the saving remnant of social conservators. In order to protect the fund of civilization intrusted to them, they were obliged to use extremely desperate remedies, which usually took the form of attaching a religious or spiritual sanctity to the existing social order. By so doing they were using a powerful but a dangerous weapon. The existing social order, in spite of the protection it afforded to essential civilizing interests, rested partly on arbitrary violence and upon the economic and military domination of a class. It scarcely deserved a consecration which attributed an ultimate religious sanction to very imperfect forms of political and social organization. A large amount

of hypocrisy and pretension invaded the political consciousness of the more civilized people. The prevailing social
order, instead of resting candidly upon its physical strength,
justified the coercive measures necessary to its preservation
by portentous and reverberating moral and religious
oracles. Little by little a tradition of moral coercion was
established, which was used to prevent and repel attacks on
the social order; and this tradition of moral coercion for
the benefit of what were supposed to be the spiritual interests of society was erected into a regular system of social
education. Its inculcation was confided, until the advent
of modern democracy, to the class of professionally religious instructors; and one of the great grievances of many
conservatives against democracy is that it has deprived the
church of the function of social education without providing any substitute.

The device of attributing a religious sanction to a very
defective social order seems to have been necessary. If
unruly men had not been scared and hypnotized into
accepting the prevailing social organization, imperfect as it
was, civilization could hardly have survived. But a moral
coercion, which might have been justified during the weakness of civilization, may lose its justification as soon as the
social order is more firmly established. After the value of
social order had been firmly wrought into the consciousness
of the Christian nations, it became desirable to distinguish
more sharply between devotion to a social ideal and devotion to any existing imperfect specimen of the social
order. Under such conditions the needs and program of

social promoters began to diverge from the traditions of social conservators. Reformers began to demand, as, indeed, they had always demanded within narrower limits, that a social order to which such a sacred quality was attributed should become worthy of its own pretentious sanctity. Instead of continuing to conceal social injustice under the fair exterior of a divine order, the ideal underlying the authentic social order began to modify the methods of exercising social coercion. The consecration of the state has been the excuse for much distasteful hypocrisy; but the attempt to consecrate anything has its formative psychological reaction. In the long run the reënforcement of an imperfect social order with an exalted social ideal has done less to corrupt the ideal of social justice than it has little by little to push organized society up the steep slope towards the goal of its pretensions.

The conviction and habit of moral coercion remains, however, embedded in the minds of social conservators. They are the real socialists, because they want to socialize by force. Both their systems of morality and their method of propagating their moral standards are based upon constraint. They expect to educate the new democracy for social service, as they have educated the powerless masses of other days, merely by inculcating the virtues of self-restraint and devotion to duty. Their program is one which makes discipline assume the proportions of an absolute ideal. One of the most unequivocal recent expressions of it is contained in Senator Root's "Experiments in Government." He says "Religion, the philosophy of morals, the teaching of history, the experience of every human life point to the same conclusion — that in the practical conduct of life the most difficult and necessary virtue is self-restraint."

The morality of repression and restraint occupies a radically different practical standing in a genuine democracy from that which it has occupied under the various class political systems. In the good old days a philosophy of restraint was reënforced by an effective agency of constraint. Moral coercion was backed up with the ominous threat of physical coercion. A man who did not exercise the kind of self-restraint which contributed to the security of the social establishment was soon beheaded or hanged or sent to the galleys. But in the present emergency the social conservators cannot support the philosophy of self-restraint by the old formidable and unanswerable arguments. The democracy itself is threatening to become unruly; and in the democracy is lodged at least the technical power of physical coercion. Hence those who propose to save society by the inculcation of self-restraint are placed at a grave disadvantage. Their chief agency of conversion is words and exhortations; and when their words are uttered, they sound hollow and almost ridiculously unavailing. If the causes of the prevailing social unrest are really such as to threaten the social order, can the crisis be sufficiently confronted, as one eminent conservator pretends, by a "serious appeal to the conscience of the nation to believe in discipline and self-control"?

If mere discipline and self-control are the moral qualities

which are supremely necessary for the conservation of the social order, discipline and self-control will eventually be secured, because the social order must be preserved. But if so, they will be secured, we may predict with confidence, at the expense of democracy and of the generous social aspirations associated with democracy. In a democracy the people may and will necessarily be asked to submit to discipline, but not to discipline for its own sake. The mass of the people will need to have the discipline made interesting to them. They will rightly demand the same motive for submitting to discipline that their conquerors have had. A man can reasonably be asked to impose self-restraint upon himself, whenever self-restraint is necessary as a part of a positive and desirable individual or social activity; but he cannot fairly be asked to accept a life of which self-restraint is the preponderant character. That, in substance, is what the social conservators are asking the democracy to accept. The democracy is not listening to them and is quite right in its inattention. Social order has in the past required the sacrifice of the many to the few and of the present to the future. Be it admitted that this cruel method of making the great mass of living men and women pay with their lives for the larger opportunities of a small minority may have been necessary. They were being sacrificed not merely to their conquerors, but to the hope that their frustrated lives might quicken those of their children and children's children. Be it admitted, also, that if the sacrifice of the living has been necessitated in the past, a measure of the same necessity may still exist.

But if so, it should exist as a recognized evil, whose presence is barely tolerated until proper preparations can be made for its banishment. In any event the sacrifices now demanded must hold a larger promise of immediate or proximate compensation. The old sacrifices were demanded and offered in obedience to the general ideas that they were assuring the creation of a consummate community in this world and earning the reward of personal happiness in the next. Such ideas are losing their authority. The consummate community is not a fact to which the good citizen must bow down, or a prophecy which can exercise constraint on events. It is an ideal which fascinates the attention and binds the will to its service. If it is to exist in a larger measure, it must be partly realized in the aspirations and opportunities of living men and women. It must have an immediate and a positive moral value for the democracy of to-day. It must bring with it a new and frank assertion of humanism.

Unless democracy is a hypocritical delusion, it seeks not human repression, but human expansion. As long as effective authority, political, ecclesiastical, economic or social, was concentrated in a few hands, the rulers could successfully and cheerfully arrange for the sacrifice of the enormous majority of their fellows in obedience to some divine law; but just in proportion as the actual power becomes more widely disseminated, the new rulers will not, in the long run, prove to be willing victims. The tradition of subordination may keep them subdued for a few generations, but sooner or later they will challenge the divine law in the interest of their own liberation. Democracy has been made possible as a consequence of the accumulating surplus of human welfare, which has been created by the increasingly fruitful control of man over nature. It will be made actual in so far as this surplus of human welfare can be converted into cash value for the lives of men and women. Progressive democracy cannot consent to have this surplus appropriated by a minority and to be paid for popular impoverishment by worship of an idol of self-restraint.

As the democracy becomes alert, experienced, critical and self-confident, its attention becomes fastened on its own immediate needs and purposes. It will refuse to be distracted by the ghosts which its pious instructors pluck from the grave in order to terrify it withal. It will refuse to be chilled by the cold and dense fogs which frequently drift in from the ocean of an unknown future and obscure the brightness and security of the day. It cannot ignore the past or disregard the future, but it must live in the present. If anything is to be accomplished in the matter of individual and social fulfilment, some part of it must be the work and the reward of actual human beings. Theirs is primarily the freedom. Theirs is the opportunity. Theirs the responsibility. Theirs the penalty. They must have faith and deserve faith. They must be trained and hand training down. They must increasingly understand and be understood. They constitute the only possible bridge to the better future. The better future must begin in them. It exists for the present not as a prophecy but as a purpose. No other kind of reality can be attached to it without making humanity the victim of a mere mechanism of civilization. Social improvement, like charity, must begin at home — that is, in the actions, in the aspirations, in the responsibilities and in the compensations of our contemporaries.

Thus the social education appropriate to a democracy must be, above all, a liberal education. It must accomplish for the mass of the people a work of intellectual and moral emancipation similar to that which the traditional system of humane culture has been supposed to accomplish for a minority. This traditional culture never could become really liberating, because of the narrowness and sterility of its human interests. Those who were being liberally educated were the flowers of a plant whose roots derived their strength from the lives of the masses. It was intended to emancipate only a few privileged people; and it was, consequently, associated with limited human sympathies, enfeebled social faith and a merely repressive moral code. The beneficiaries of an indifferently human social system were obliged to reconcile an ideal and technique of humane culture with moral standards which made self-restraint obligatory on all except themselves. They were to enjoy the advantages of immediate moral and intellectual liberation, which would enrich their experience, quicken their imagination, satisfy their curiosity and release the internal springs of instinctive goodness. But the mass of men and women were to be morally appraised, not by virtue of what they succeeded in doing with their lives, but by virtue of what they refrained from doing. The

2 E

method of socially educating the few differed essentially
from the method of socially educating the many; and this
difference added a strain of hypocrisy and illiberality to a
system of education which needed above all to be candid,
inquisitive, thoroughgoing and humane.

The insistence by American conservatives, such as
Senator Root, on a morality of restraint, is a most trustworthy indication of the want of democracy in our traditional legalism. When the conservatives declare that the
traditional American political system depends upon the
character of the American people, what they mean by character is self-control, moderation and circumspection. A
nation whose proudest boast has been that it deprived no
one of liberty or property without due process of law and
due trial of a law-suit — such a nation would be obliged,
at least officially, to attribute the utmost honor to the man
who respected and defended legal rights. No doubt it is
better to do honor to men who are bound to respect and
defend legal rights, even when legal rights can be made
the excuse for exploitation, than it is to do honor to men
who were licensed to override legal rights. Legalism was
an enormous improvement on the official tyranny of a
class or an individual. It introduced into political and
social organization the rule of live-and-let-live and some of
the spirit of that rule. But in practice the rule of live-and-
let-live has never successfully expressed its underlying
spirit of fair play. Its usefulness has been impaired by
an unfair division of labor. Upon the rich have been conferred the opportunity and the obligation of living; upon

the poor, the opportunity and obligation of let-living. The moral code of moderation and self-repression is intended for their benefit. They must show their character by allowing the rich to live, and by refraining themselves from any more generous participation in life than the behavior of the well-to-do permits them to enjoy.

To be sure the moralists of self-repression profess to apply their standards impartially. The rich who do not exercise self-control in the art of living are orally and scripturally visited with the same kind of condemnation as the poor who do not rise to the opportunity of moral enhancement afforded by the art of letting other people live. But have the rich ever paid any attention to their admonitions? Has not "ostentatious waste and conspicuous leisure" been of the very essence of their lives? And is not society in as grave danger now, because of the tendency of the rich to overdo their living, as because of the threat of the poor to underdo their let-living? There has always been this fundamental difference between the two cases. When the rich lived without self-control, they did not incur any official penalty for their excesses, except the condemnation of a few negligible moralists. But when the poor showed any inclination toward self-control in their devotion to the rule of let-living, they usually ran into the arms of a law and they always incurred a furious storm of moral disapprobation. They were held up to general detestation as the enemies of society and the violators of the Divine Order.

It is a Stoic rather than a Christian moral code which

attributes such an exaggerated importance to self-restraint
in the formation of character. Stoicism conceived the
moral world as determined by a rigid moral law, to which
the human will, in so far as it was enlightened, would voluntarily conform. In actual practice the moral law was
embodied in a group of specific rules, obedience to which
was believed to be socially necessary. The whole impulse
and authority of the aspiration for moral and social righteousness was attached to this specific code, because its
social utility had to be hammered into human consciousness. Catholic Christianity, as soon as it became fastened
to the social establishment and responsible for immediate
social safety, adopted this Stoic moral code and sought to
impose obedience to the law on generation after generation
of its brethren. It was a cruel and inhuman discipline;
but as soon as the social necessity of repression became less
urgent, it resulted in a luxuriant revival of humanism, the
benefits of which the western civilized nations are still
trying to gather.

When the Christian Church took over the Stoic moral
code, it was, in point of fact, temporarily departing from the
spirit and the words of Jesus and the exhortations of his
greatest disciple. It is not true, as Senator Root declares,
that either the Christian religion or the experience of every
human life attaches in the hierarchy of virtues a peculiarly
eminent position to the virtue of self-restraint. Where in
all the gospel of Jesus can any such laudation of self-control
be found? It is not the dutiful, the moderate and the
circumspect who will inherit the earth and share in the

radiation of the Divine grace. It is the repentant, the humble, the kindly and those who love the Father. St. Paul is even more explicit. He declares the peculiarly Christian virtues to be Faith, Hope and Love; and of these which was the greatest? The emancipation of humanity from constrained obedience to a law or a code is of the very essence of Christianity and is accountable for its power to regenerate individual Christian lives so many centuries after the death of its founder.

Modern psychology, like Christianity, affords no sufficient excuse for a morality of repression. It conceives both individual and social life as fundamentally active, and it is able to translate both emotion and thought into the results or forms of activity. Since life consists essentially in activity, a wise system of educational discipline, either individual or social, should seek primarily to release and develop rather than to dam up the instinctive sources of action in human nature. Indeed the attempt to dam them up is fruitless, and results merely in the substitution of pathological for natural forms of expression. More and more are social psychologists seeking to discover social outlets for the expression of human instincts. A social outlet for an instinctive human activity will frequently bring with it the modification of its own source. Human nature was furnished with its equipment of instincts under the pressure of material and social conditions radically different from those which now prevail; and they might easily instigate unsocial behavior, unless their expression were subjected to social discipline and moulded by social ideals. But modification does not mean repression. It still allows an outlet for wholesome and generous activity; and it is such an outlet which a sincere democracy must furnish to the mass of its citizens. It must manage to provide for them the same interest in being active and alive that the minority of the well-to-do have always had.

A democratic nation cannot provide the mass of the people with the needed opportunity of activity and life merely by distributing among them the wealth owned by the minority. Any such distribution would scatter among the poor the germs not of social activity, but of social lethargy. The masses need, of course, a larger share of material welfare, but they need most of all an increased opportunity of wholesome and stimulating social labor. Their work must be made interesting to them not merely because of its compensation, but because its performance calls for the development of more eager and more responsible human beings. In so far as social labor is necessarily irksome and tedious, it should not be forced upon any special group of citizens, but should be socialized by being distributed. The sting and the offence will be taken away from disagreeable and monotonous work only if and when all our fellow-countrymen participate in the burden. Work of this kind, when pursued for a short time and shared by the whole community, might be a useful social discipline; but when fastened on one man throughout the whole of his life, it cannot but result in stupefaction and impoverishment. The distribution of stimulating and concentrating work among those whose labor is stupefying, involves necessarily a distribution of grinding and monotonous toil among those whose work, in so far as they work at all, has every chance of being peculiarly interesting.

The important point, however, is this: If progressive democracy can arrange for a socially educative distribution of work, the socially desirable distribution of wealth will take care of itself. The opportunity of expansion, which will convert the wage-earner into a better man and a better citizen, is fundamentally an opportunity of participating on equal terms with his fellow-citizens in responsible and internally remunerative social labor. No doubt the wage-earner is frequently claiming a very different kind of opportunity. No doubt labor agitators seem frequently to be aiming at the forcible dispossession of the well-to-do, apparently for the purpose of providing for the masses a humbler version of the irresponsible and enervating privilege of possession. But a society which socializes labor, both in its internal burdens and its internal rewards, need not fear revolutionary agitation in favor of dispossession. A socializing system of labor constitutes an infallible and indispensable means of social education. It converts a worker into a good citizen, not by demanding of him the prostration of his own life before the idol of self-repression, but by encouraging him to renew his life through exhilarating activity for his own benefit and that of his fellow-citizens.

The wisest of modern educators has declared that "the only way to prepare for social life is to engage in social life." The rule applies to society conceived as a school no less than to the school conceived as a society. Men and women will become better citizens by participating in those political and social activities which liberate and intensify the human will.   An industrial and political system which offers the opportunity of participation to them places them on their best behavior.   It challenges them to make good.   The moralists of repression must claim that the majority of them will not respond to the challenge.   A democratic moralist must trust that a substantial majority will respond to the challenge — a majority large enough to dominate social behavior.   The democratic moralist has no way of proving that he is right; but neither has his opponent any means of proving that he is wrong.   History and psychology can pronounce no final verdict on the matter, but they afford grounds for encouragement.   Neither is the verdict of traditional ethics and religion unequivocal, although eventually the more equivocal aspects of the moral and religious tradition must be discarded.   Progressive democracy lives upon the conviction that the challenge will be accepted.

Thus we must fall back once again upon the creative power of the will, which insists, even though its brother, the reason, cannot ascertain.   Admitting that human nature is in some measure socially rebellious, admitting that the ambitions of different classes and communities are dangerously conflicting, admitting and proclaiming the inability of society to attain cohesion by obedience to any natural law or moral and social code, democracy has still no reason for discouragement.   What the situation calls for is faith.   Faith is the primary virtue demanded by the social education of a democracy — the virtue which will prove to be salutary — in case human nature is capable of salvation. Only by faith can be established the invincible interdependence between individual and social fulfilment, upon the increasing realization of which the future of democracy depends. It consecrates the will to the recognition of the most fundamental and exacting of personal and collective responsibilities. It constitutes the spiritual version of the indomitable instinct which has kept the human race on the road during all the discouragements and the burdens of its past, and which must not be the less indomitable because it becomes the more conscious.

A socially educative faith cannot be imposed upon reluctant democracies. It is not a dogma to which the good citizens must conform or a rule which the good citizen must obey. It is the introduction to a life in which the good citizen must share. If it is not freely accepted, it is powerless and meaningless. Its source exists in every human being in the will to live. In those who have faith the instinctive will to live is translated into the will to live with others in a community. The will to live with others has required for its realization an ever more abundant and complex machinery of socialization — such as tools, governments, codes, languages, creeds, sciences and programs— without which the faith would be devoid of any means of expression. The acceptance of this machinery can be temporarily imposed on particular groups of men under particular conditions; but such coercion is permissible only because the law or code which people are forced to accept has no final authority. It is imposed merely as a matter of convenience and is, consequently, disagreeable but innocuous. A constraint which is justified by expediency is far more tolerable than a constraint which is justified by supposed necessity. The former is tolerable because it is temporary, and can and will be changed for sound reasons. The latter is intolerable because it is not to be relaxed or escaped. Temporary constraint may help an individual to live with others by leading him in the path of enlightening social experience. But an authoritative law divides society against itself just as it divides the individual against himself. It risks the whole social authority upon the adequacy of a particular social contrivance, and the particular contrivance is never adequate. Faith in individual and social fulfilment, having no axe to grind, does not need the coöperation of a source of physical power with which to turn the stone. Its influence is binding, because it is at once invincible, inclusive and flexible.

If the prevailing legalism and a repressive moral code are associated with the rule of live-and-let-live, the progressive democratic faith finds its consummation rather in the rule of live-and-help-live.[1] The underlying assumption of live-and-let-live is an ultimate individualism, which limits the power of one human being to help another, and which binds different human beings together by allegiance to an external authority. The underlying assumption of live-and-help-live is an ultimate collectivism, which conceives different human

---

[1] I owe the phrasing of this distinction to the book of Professsor Albion Small, entitled "Between Two Eras."

beings as part of the same striving conscious material, and which makes individual fulfilment depend upon the fulfilment of other lives and upon that of society as a whole. The obligation of mutual assistance is fundamental. The opportunities of mutual assistance are inexhaustible. Wherever the lives of other people are frustrated, we are responsible for the frustration just in so far as we have failed to do what we could for their liberation; and we can always do something on behalf of liberty. Every victorious selfish impulse, every perverse and cowardly thought, every petty action, every irresponsibility and infirmity of the will helps to impoverish the lives of other people as well as our own lives. We cannot liberate ourselves without seeking to liberate them; and their bondage is merely an evidence of the often unconscious but all the more maleficent bars which restrict our own freedom of movement. Thus the progressive democratic faith, like the faith of St. Paul, finds its consummation in a love which is partly expressed in sympathetic feeling, but which is at bottom a spiritual expression of the mystical unity of human nature.

In our efforts to give reality to the rule of live-and-help-live, we are not confined to ordinary methods of social service, such as philanthropic work, social reform or a public career. Philanthropy is manifestly only a means of temporary alleviation, which brings with it the serious danger of fastening on individuals responsibilities which should be recognized as collective. The amount of permanent good which can be accomplished merely by giving is pathetically small, and affords perhaps the most conclusive illustration of the meagre social value of great individual possessions. In the same way the practical work of social amelioration is an immediately necessary, but an essentially inferior, way of living-and-help-living. The western nations are just at present excessively preoccupied with the economic mechanism, but the preoccupation is caused not by its intrinsic importance, but by its wretched maladjustment to human needs. Perhaps the greatest benefit which civilization will derive from an improved economic organization is that of enabling good citizens more frequently to forget the economic aspect of life. Of course, it can never be actually forgotten. A large part of the day will necessarily be given up to the labor of the journey; and a large part of the labor of the journey will always be devoted to improvement of the machinery of travel. The discipline and the experience of the road are indispensable to the making of good democrats, but they are not sufficient to the making of good democrats. The most fruitful opportunities of living-and-help-living are to be found in another region.

The way in which people spend their leisure after the day's journey is over — the way in which they play — offers them the best chance of contributing to the enhancement of one another's lives. If the time ever comes when poverty is comparatively negligible and when human impoverishment can no longer be charged up to gross economic maladjustments, — if such a time ever comes, as it well may, the rule of live-and-help-live will assume a better meaning than it has at present and will challenge the development of a better quality of human nature. Only then, when the end of the day's journey leaves the travellers comparatively lively, will the brethren and the sisters be so situated that they can make life very interesting and remunerative for one another. They will enjoy many ways of contributing to the enhancement of the individual and social life; but the different ways will all be reducible to an ardent and intelligent cultivation of the essential art of living. Culture of this kind implies an indomitable socializing will, which the critical intelligence takes for granted. It implies the individual dignity, and the common insight into human relations and destiny, which comes to those who take their share of the necessary social labor. But the social culture itself will partake rather of the nature of play. It will be the bloom of social achievement rather than the servant of a social purpose. It will live in an atmosphere of restless and relentless curiosity the object of which will be the knowledge of others and of one's self. Men and women will be stimulated to a much clearer understanding of one another's motives and actions and of the resulting comedies and tragedies. The courting of a woman by a man might mix high comedy with a liberal education — if only sexual attraction were made the excuse for candid, mutual curiosity rather than reciprocal illusion. It might make every woman into something of a novelist and every man into something of a playwright. The power of utterance would count for much. People would have every stimulus to perfect their means of expression; but a cheap man could not conceal himself behind a pretty

screen of words and figures. The arts most intimately
associated with public life would be particularly enfran-
chised. The drama might win the same kind of attention
in such a society that it did in classic Greece, and pageantry
as in Venice of the renaissance. But vehicles of individual expression would be popular no less than vehicles
of social expression. Each and all could say what they had
to say in any appropriate medium, and could count upon
an audience which would bear some relation to the value
and the beauty of the utterance. Neither would they who
had little to say but much to do suffer in social esteem,
provided they did not take too much credit for being in-
articulate. A society of this kind could put up with almost
anything but shirking and shamming. It would be bathed
in eager, good-humored and tireless criticism, and the bath
would purify as well as cleanse.

INDEX

A

Absolutism of European monarchies, influence of, on American conception of sovereignty, 220–223.

⌐Adams, Henry, quoted on early popular suspicion of power, 33–34.

Administrative commissions and courts, 363–369.

Administrative department of government, weakening of, by Jacksonian ⌐Democracy, 65–74; increased authority and efficiency in, demanded by ⌐⌐progressive democracy, 347; a degree of improvement in, under Roosevelt, Taft and Wilson, 347–348; dependence of old party system upon adherence to traditional methods in, 348; consideration of proper function of, 349 ff.; annihilation of independence of, aimed at by the old democracy, 350; increasing aggrandizement of, at expense of legislature and courts, 350–351; source of popular repugnance to government by officials of the, 351–353; sharp distinction to be drawn between executive and, 354–355; tenure of office desirable for
⌐ officials of, 355–357; functions of, under new social program, 358 ff.; officials of, to become custodians of a part of the accepted social program, and to a degree promoters and propagandists, 360–362; growing dependence of success of social legislation upon good faith and competence of representatives of, 362; question of ability of expert administrators successfully to accomplish work imposed upon them, 369–370; a general staff provided for progressive democratic state by, 370–371; ability of, to obtain and keep popular confidence, 371–372; error of applying the recall to, 372–373; proper methods for keeping articulate with the democ-

racy, 373; suggestions for reorganization of our inherited system, to fit the needs of a progressive democratic state, 374 ff.; desirability of more widespread higher education for popularizing expert, scientific work of, 376–377.

Agricultural interests, alliance of industrial interests and, in Middle Period, 85 ff. *See* Farmers.

Agricultural land, recent increase in value of, and consequent benefits to descendants of pioneer democracy, 110–111.

Amendment of Constitution, difficulty of, 130–131, 230–231; need for a more easily operated machinery of, 231–232, 237, 243; as an aid in nationalizing the American democracy, 243–244.

American system, question of origin of, 29.

Amidon, Judge, quoted on success achieved by Federal Constitution, 129.

Associations, rise of voluntary, to act as formative elements in American public opinion, 316–318.

B

Ballot, arguments in favor of a shorter, 289; principle of the short, in the Oregon plan, 293–294.

Barnes, William, Jr., 3.

Beard, Charles, researches by, 48.

Bergson, an illustration from, 166.

Bill of rights, effect of insertion of, in Federal Constitution, 55; mistake made by American people in regarding as a radiant sun of political knowledge instead of a mere guiding torch, 217–219.

Bills of rights, American democratic, as formulated in state constitutions, 35–36.

Bipartisanism. *See* Two-party system.

Boss, the political, 254.

431

justifiable suspicion with which American public opinion has regarded work of, 236–237; history of process of imposing limitations on powers of, by local democracies, 248 ff.; not really representative agencies, 274–275; in the Oregon plan, 298–300; under new program, 319–320.

Lloyd, Henry D., 9.

Lowell, A. Lawrence, on the success of the Federal Constitution, 129; on the reliance of the power of the courts upon the good-will of the people, 152.

M

Majority rule, public opinion and, 303 ff.; developed and consolidated by a progressive democracy, 304–305; initiative and referendum not the instruments of, 306; the two-party system an effective method for the organization of, 311; under leadership of the executive, 312 ff.; effect of direct primaries on, 342–343.

Massachusetts, theories upon which state constitution was formed, 31–39.

Mazzini, expression of progressive democratic faith uttered by, 202.

Middle Period, position of political parties in the, 78–80.

Miller, Chief Justice, quoted, 21.

Minority rule, initiative and referendum as instruments of, 306 ff.

Monarchy of the Word, the Law in the shape of the Constitution called, 44.

Moral fibre, relaxation of the American, 207.

Muck-raking, era of, 5.

Mugwumps, characteristics of, 9–10.

Municipalities, success in operation of commission form of government for, 286–287.

N

National Bank, reëstablished by national Republicans after War of 1812, 63; abolition of, by Jacksonian Democracy, 75.

Nationalization of American democracy, what is implied by, 241 ff.; revision of amending clause of Constitution a step in process of, 243–244.

Nationalizing influence of partisan organization during Middle Period, 79, 81.

National Republican party, causes leading to formation of, 63; principles and aims of, 63–64.

New England, early assertion of popular political responsibility in, 31–32.

"New Freedom," Wilson's, 16–18, 19; object of, as a political program, 338.

O

Officialism, Anglo-Saxon repugnance for professional, 351–352.

Oregon, operation of direct government methods in, 284–286; plan of state political reorganization prepared for, by People's Power League, 292–302; majority rule and public opinion under program proposed for, 303 ff.

P

Partisan government, originated by Jacksonian Democrats, 67, 74–75; use put to, when appropriated by new Republican party, 90–91; change in character and purpose of, with growth of power, 99; effect of direct primaries on, 342–343; will persist for a time, but will become increasingly less effective, 343–344.

Partisan politics, analysis of reasons for despotism and corruptness of, 158, 160.

Patten, Simon N., quoted, 111.

People's Power League of Oregon, 292–302.

Political parties, strong organization of, achieved during the Middle Period, 63–80; nationalizing influence of, 79.

Political power, an object of suspicion to people of the American provinces, 33–34; made subservient to law by the early state constitutions, 35–41.

Politicians, part taken by, in old economic nationalism, 94–95.

Popular government, achievement of, by introduction of direct government, 258–260.

Popular sovereignty, advent of, after

the Declaration of Independence, 29–30; an examination of, 220 ff.; influence on, of old conception of royal sovereignty, 222–223; made a political bogie by American constitutional conservatism, 223; difference between that of France and that of America, 223–224; in America is submissive to rules of orderly procedure, 225; seat of, not in the electorate, but in public opinion, 228–229; distribution of power necessary in the practical exercise of, 229–230.

Populism, stigma of, 3; causes leading to movement, 105.

Pound, Roscoe, quoted, 180–181; on subordination of administration to the law, in the states, 251–252.

Privilege, remedies for evil of, under modern programs, 107–108; recognition of, implied by the new policy, 111–112.

Program, necessity of a, for realizing an ideal of social righteousness, 215–217.

Progressive party, formation and present position of, 335–336; future of, 336.

Progressivism, advent of, 1–2; evidences of power of, 2; disintegration of political traditions and classifications by, 2–4; difference between old reform methods and, 8–9; Roosevelt's leadership of forces of, 11; disruption in ranks of, after termination of Roosevelt's official leadership, 12; new lines of attraction and repulsion in, 13 ff.; President Wilson's attitude toward, 15 ff., 337; fundamental issue of, obscured by Wilson's vague and equivocal version, 18–19; necessity for clear understanding of relation between conservatism and, 19–20; Insurgent phase of, 105–107; economic and social policy of, a development of the Republican system, 123–124; method advocated by, for building up popular political character, 163 ff.; faith necessary to fulfilment of, ideal of, 168–183; faith needful for, effective through agency of social ideal rather than individual ideals, 200; the ideal and the program of, 201 ff.; insistence of, that

the national will has not been enfeebled, 208; mutually dependent and mutually supplementary relation between political and social democracy signified by, 211–212; distinction to be preserved by, between its social program and its ideal of social righteousness, 217; association of, with Democracy or Republicanism, 331; question of relations to be preserved with the old parties, 333 ff.; adoption of, by President Wilson, for use of Democratic party, 337–339; possible effects on, of President Wilson's attempt to keep it within the confines of the old party system, 339; impossibility of permanently reconciling, with Democracy, 346.

Protectionism, policy of, in program of national Republicans, 63, 64; reduction of, by Democratic party, 75.

Public opinion, majority rule and, 303 ff.; voluntary associations which act as formative elements in, 316–318; the recall as a means of keeping an administration in touch with, 326.

R

Railroad rates cases, attitude of Supreme Court in decisions regarding, 235.

Railroads, land grants to, 86, 87.

Recall, objection of lawyers to the, 255–256; view taken of, by partisans of direct government, 269; application of the, to commissions for governing municipalities, 286–287; value of, as an instrument of genuinely democratic government, 325–327; mischievous effects of applying to administrators under new social program, 372–373.

Referendum, the, 256, 269, 273; working of, in Oregon, 284–286; in Wisconsin, 290; an instrument of minority rule, 306 ff.

Reform, old methods of, contrasted with modern progressivism, 8 ff.

Rent, connection between increased burden of, and high prices, 11, 118.

Representation, necessity of setting aside present method of, 273; conditions of effective, 274.

Representative government, relations